# ARTHUR C CLARKE'S

# WORLD
## OF
# STRANGE
# POWERS

## John Fairley & Simon Welfare

GUILD PUBLISHING
LONDON

This edition published 1985
by Book Club Associates
by arrangement with William Collins Sons & Co. Ltd

Set in Linotron Ehrhardt by
Rowland Phototypesetting Ltd
Bury St Edmunds, Suffolk

Made and printed in Great Britain by
William Collins Sons & Co. Ltd, Glasgow

# Contents

# Foreword
## ARTHUR C CLARKE

AT A GENEROUS ASSESSMENT, approximately half this book is nonsense. Unfortunately, I don't know *which* half; and neither, despite all claims to the contrary, does anyone else.

Before you demand the return of your money (or at least 50% of it) let me hasten to qualify that opening sentence.

In the first place, the nonsense in this book is of the very highest quality – some of the best that has ever been produced by the minds of men (and, dare I say it, perhaps even more frequently by the minds of women – who seem to provide the majority of guides to the Spirit World). Anyone studying it can hardly fail to be entertained, amused, sometimes saddened, and always instructed. It teaches a great deal about human psychology and the motives controlling the behaviour of even the most intelligent and rational members of that peculiar species, *H. Sapiens*.

This fact alone would justify studying the 'Strange Powers' described in the following pages, but in addition there are good practical reasons. There is no doubt that *some* of the phenomena discussed, though often astonishing, really do occur, even though our present theories cannot explain them. Full understanding could lead to results of great value in, for example, medicine and psychiatry. At the very least, it would throw new light upon that ancient and most fundamental of mysteries, the relationship between Mind and Body. And, perhaps even more important, between Mind and Mind.

From the beginning of time, the human race has been fascinated – as well as awed and terrified – by the range of phenomena which we now usually describe as Paranormal. The once popular adjective 'supernatural' can be objected to on logical grounds (after all, if it *really* happens, it must be natural!), and also because of its religious associations. Paranormal (meaning 'beyond the normal') sounds a little more scientific – but don't let that fool you. Giving something an impressive name is no proof that it exists,

and is often merely an attempt to conceal ignorance – or, worse still, to claim spurious knowledge.

Science is full of such examples, now forgotten except by specialists. Before it was understood that combustion is a chemical process in which oxygen combines with other elements (usually carbon and hydrogen) to produce energy, fire was 'explained' by the release of a mysterious entity christened 'Phlogiston'. That sounded more scientific than 'essence of fire', which was what it meant in plain English, and Phlogiston encumbered chemistry for decades before it was finally exorcised.

Similarly, when it was discovered that light consists of waves, nineteenth-century physicists invented the Ether as a medium to carry them – on the not-unreasonable assumption that where there's a wave, *something* must be undulating. However, when Einstein showed that Nature wasn't always reasonable, the Ether was abandoned, and the word will not even be found in a modern textbook of physics.

Perhaps the same fate may one day befall such terms as Psychokinesis, Poltergeist, Parapsychology and so forth. If the phenomena they attempt to label turn out to be non-existent, they will be forgotten. On the other hand, if they are real, their names will be replaced by precisely defined terms in the vocabulary of some new science – exactly as happened when electricity and magnetism emerged from magic, to transform our world.

Will this happen again? More than thirty years ago, in the novel *Childhood's End*, I put these words into the mouth of the alien Overlord Karellen, when he spoke to the human race for the last time:

In the centuries before our coming, your scientists uncovered the secrets of the physical world and led you from the energy of steam to the energy of the atom. You had put superstition behind you: Science was the only real religion of mankind . . . there were no forces which did not come within its scope, no events for which it could not ultimately account . . .

Yet your mystics, though they were lost in their own delusions, had seen part of the truth. There are powers of the mind, and powers beyond the mind, which your science could never have brought within its framework without shattering it entirely. All down the ages there have been countless reports of strange phenomena – poltergeists, telepathy, precognition – which you had named but never explained. At first science ignored them, even denied their existence, despite the testimony of five thousand years. But they exist, and if it is to be complete, any theory of the universe must account for them.

During the first half of the twentieth century, a few of your scientists began to investigate these matters. They did not know it, but they were tampering with the lock of Pandora's box. The forces they might have unleashed transcended any perils the atom could have brought. For the physicists could only have ruined the earth; the paraphysicists could have spread havoc to the stars.

*Childhood's End* is of course fiction, and I was careful to preface it with the now rather notorious disclaimer 'The opinions expressed in this book are not those of the author.' Then what, you may well ask, about the opinions in *this* book, and the television series on which it is based? Stay tuned . . . As far as possible Simon Welfare, John Fairley and myself have tried to present the evidence without passing it through the filter of our own preconceptions, so that you can judge for yourself. However, a great deal of selection was inevitable, because of programme balancing and the availability of material. For example, one can write whole volumes about poltergeists, but few have conveniently presented themselves to the television camera (and even if they did oblige, I doubt if they could put on as good a show as Steven Spielberg).

It is also possible that our personal biases may have caused us to exclude material which seemed fraudulent, but was not. This is an area when scepticism must be balanced against credulity, because either can be taken too far. A classic example, often quoted by researchers on the borders of the unknown, is the attitude of scientists towards meteorites.[1]

From the earliest times, men believed lumps of rock and metal fell from the sky, and frequently worshipped such objects as gifts from the gods. The intellectuals of the eighteenth century laughed at such primitive superstitions, and refused to accept even the most well-authenticated reports of meteorites. When such a claim reached Thomas Jefferson (probably the most brilliant and cultured man ever to occupy the White House) he dismissed it thus: 'I would sooner believe that two Yankee professors lied, than that stones fell from the sky.'

Jefferson's attitude was very reasonable – but his conclusion was completely wrong. The Yankee professors weren't lying (this time, anyway) and Jefferson lived to see the study of meteorites become a respectable and accepted scientific discipline.

This story could be matched many times in the history of science, and we can draw a lesson from it which is highly – perhaps devastatingly – relevant to the study of 'parascience'. Every startling new discovery or revolutionary theory may expect violent opposition from those whose ideas it challenges because, contrary to general belief, scientists are just as emotional as anyone else, and are liable to become quite unhappy when they see a lifetime's work destroyed. Yet all *genuine* scientists welcome the truth, however uncomfortable or surprising it may be, and as a result it is very unusual for major disagreements to last for more than a decade or so. That is normally long enough for new discoveries and theories to be either confirmed or refuted, after which the shouting and arm-waving rapidly die away. Sometimes there may be one or two conservatives who stubbornly refuse to accept the New Order, but they are regarded as embarrassing fossils by their colleagues, who breathe a sigh of relief when *Nature* prints their tactful obituaries.

Our century has seen several such revolutions – all vigorously disputed, all swiftly accepted. The Quantum Theory, the Theory of Relativity, Heisenberg's Uncertainty Principle are the classic examples, and within

---

[1] Not to be confused with *meteors* – the streaks of light in the sky caused by objects entering the earth's atmosphere. Most of these are so small that they are completely burned up; only the rare ones that reach the surface qualify as meteorites.

the last generation we have seen Geology converted from stamp-collecting to science by the discovery of plate tectonics.[2]

Though it is risky to generalize, it might be fair to say that the whole cycle, from first announcement, through controversy and checking, to universal acceptance (or refutation) takes a minimum of ten years and a maximum of fifty. Sometimes, of course, an element of luck is involved, especially where the events concerned are beyond human control or experimental investigation.

This is exactly what happened in the case of meteorites. Towards the end of the eighteenth century a commission of the French Academy of Science formally endorsed the Jeffersonian viewpoint that stones couldn't possibly fall from the sky. Unfortunately for the distinguished members of the commission, the matter was settled rather decisively when many *thousand* descended at the town of L'Aigle, not far from Paris itself. In this case, the interval between authoritative denial and embarrassed recantation was about thirty years. Where laboratory checking is possible it is usually much shorter – seldom as long as a decade.

Yet nothing like this has happened in the study of the paranormal. Generations – *centuries* – have passed, and we are still arguing about the validity of the evidence itself. It may well be, as some surveys have indicated, that a substantial proportion of scientists (perhaps as many as two-thirds in both the United States and the UK) considers that telepathy, extra-sensory perception and so forth are either an established fact or a likely possibility.

But this is simply not good enough. Surely, if there was *any* truth at all in these matters, the percentage of scientists who took them seriously would by now be 99.999 per cent – and a good many of those would be busily searching for a comprehensive theory. Today we not only lack a Newton or Einstein of the paranormal; we still await its Aristotle, despite so much effort by whole armies of investigators.

Perhaps this is a good point at which to ask: what evidence would be necessary to convince a complete sceptic – and, conversely, what evidence would disillusion a confirmed believer? It's much easier to answer the second part of the question than the first; the sad history of paranormal research provides many examples, some of which would be hilarious if they were not so pathetic.

To be on the safe side, let's go back into the past and look at the Strange Case of Sir Arthur Conan Doyle – creator of the second most famous character in the whole of fiction.[3] In middle age, Doyle became a fanatical

---

[2] The idea that all the continents once fitted together, like pieces of a jigsaw puzzle. The chief advocate of this theory was the German scientist, Alfred Wegener (1880–1930), but his hypothesis of 'Continental Drift' was bitterly disputed for half a century, until the modern techniques of deep-ocean surveying established it beyond doubt. One distinguished geologist has recorded that the only time he ever saw a man literally foaming at the mouth was when he mentioned Wegener to a colleague. So much, once again, for unemotional scientists . . . It is also worth mentioning that Wegener was not a geologist, but a *meteorologist*. The 'Not Invented Here' attitude can be encountered in any field of human affairs.

---

[3] The first? Tarzan, of course. How many of Asia's and Africa's billions have ever heard of Baker Street?

convert to spiritualism, and devoted much of his vast energy and considerable wealth to spreading the faith (he even wrote a now forgotten novel on the subject, *The Land of Mist*, featuring the characters he had earlier created in his superb adventure *The Lost World*). So powerful was Doyle's will-to-believe that even when his favourite mediums were exposed as cheats, his faith never wavered (even if they were faking it *this* time, he argued, the earlier manifestations were perfectly genuine . . .)

It was in vain that the great magician Harry Houdini tried to educate the stubborn knight, by demonstrating the (often ridiculously simple) techniques that had been used to fool him. Doyle would have none of it; indeed, he eventually tried to convince the frustrated Houdini that he was unaware of his own supernormal powers!

Houdini's spiritual (if he will excuse the word) successor, James Randi, whom you will encounter later in this book, has been enraged by exactly the same phenomenon. I have seen Randi – in my own office, and with no opportunity of making preparations in advance – perform feats which left me completely baffled, and would certainly have convinced any true believer that he was in the presence of the paranormal. But I am prepared to take Randi's word for it that he was using only the tricks of the magician's trade, and I quite understand his determination not to reveal professional secrets. Yet Randi has run into people who flatly refuse to believe that he *is* a stage magician, making his living by honest deception, and have tried to convince him that he is a genuine psychic. Since poor Randi can't explain how he does his tricks without being drummed out of the union, he has to grin and bear as best he can the unwanted testimonials of the besotted believers.

It is clear that those afflicted by the Conan Doyle Syndrome could never be deprogrammed without total brainwashing, because it is a matter of Faith, not Reason.[4] One might as well hope to convert an Ayatollah to Christianity as to persuade a true devotee of the paranormal that there are *fewer* things in Heaven and Earth than are dreamed of in his philosophy. Extreme credulity has its precise counterpart – one might say its mirror image – in pig-headed scepticism. A recent total eclipse of the sun, witnessed in North Africa, provided a beautiful example of this – and a somewhat unusual one, because in *this* case the scepticism was itself based on firm religious beliefs.

When the visiting astronomers started setting up their equipment in preparation for the eclipse, the local Mullahs could hardly conceal their amusement. 'Only Allah,' they proclaimed, 'knows how the sun will behave. How ridiculous for these infidels to boast that they can predict His actions!' Naturally, when the eclipse began and ended exactly on schedule, the reverend gentlemen were asked if they had any second thoughts. Not at all; they were completely unabashed. But it was, they admitted, quite a remarkable coincidence . . .

That the teaching of astronomy in some Muslim countries is now almost

---

[4] The death of his son in the First World War must have been a major factor in Doyle's conversion to spiritualism, which claimed to provide direct evidence for belief in an afterlife. Countless others, faced with similar bereavements, have let their hearts rule their heads; and who can blame them? One even hesitates to condemn those fraudulent mediums who provided genuine solace which, on occasion, they undoubtedly did.

as backward as the teaching of biology in Tennessee or Alabama is certainly one of history's little ironies. We should never forget that it was the scholars of the Arab world (such as the mathematician Omar Khayyam, when he was not dabbling in poetry on the side) who preserved and extended the knowledge of the Greeks while Europe was in the Dark Ages. One would like to know just how many eclipses it would take to convince the Mullahs that infidels really do know something about astronomy. At the same time, this prompts another thought. How many demonstrations of *genuine* paranormal phenomena would be needed to convert a total sceptic – for example, one of those reputed to have said 'I won't believe it even if I see it?'

Confession is supposed to be good for the soul, and I must admit that in the past I have wavered between the two extremes (and will probably do so again – see the Epilogue). In the 1930s, under the influence of J. B. Rhine's famous books (such as *The Reach of the Mind*) I felt reasonably sure that telepathy and precognition occurred, and was even prepared to admit that the mind could exert a direct influence over matter (anyone who thinks that this idea is necessarily ridiculous should try to answer the question: 'Exactly what happens when I decide to move my little finger?').

Over the years, lack of any progress in this field made me more and more sceptical but still open-minded enough to remain interested in the subject. So when Uri Geller burst upon the scene in 1973, I welcomed the opportunity of meeting him.

The encounter, at Birkbeck College on 22 June 1974, was typically chaotic, and not at all a controlled scientific experiment (but then it wasn't supposed to be). Among those present were Dr David Bohm, the well-known theoretical physicist; Arthur Koestler (who bequeathed half a million pounds to set up a chair of parapsychology at a British university); physicists Arthur Ellison, John Hasted, Ted Bastin, Jack Sarfatti; and my friend the late Val Cleaver (Chief Engineer, Rolls-Royce Rocket Division).

To quote from Uri's own account:

> The scientists were all very attentive, but I couldn't tell what they were feeling. I sensed that I really wasn't getting through to Arthur C. Clarke, however.
>
> I thought that maybe, if I interrupted my talking and bent his house key for him, Clarke would feel differently. I asked him to hold his key out in his own hand and watch very carefully so that he would know that I wasn't substituting another key, or taking it away from his hand, or putting pressure on it.
>
> Within moments, his key began bending. And he said: 'My God, my eyes are seeing it. It's bending!'

After performing further marvels (setting a Geiger counter clicking furiously, deflecting a magnetometer, dematerializing a crystal . . .) Uri was pleased to note:

> By that time, Arthur Clarke seemed to have lost all his scepticism. He said something like, 'My God! It's all coming true! This is what I wrote about in *Childhood's End*. I can't believe it!'

Clarke was not there just to scoff. He had wanted things to happen.

He just wanted to be completely convinced that everything was legitimate.

Since it is, of course, utterly inconceivable that Uri could tell an untruth, I am quite prepared to accept his account of my behaviour; most naive observers react to his performance in exactly this way. But his memory is at fault in one important respect; he *did* take the door-key out of my hand, and he placed it on a *firm metal surface while stroking it*. Interesting, to say the least . . .

I should also add that two of the most enthusiastic endorsers of Uri's London demonstrations, Dr Jack Sarfatti and Dr John Taylor (Professor of Mathematics, King's College) later made a complete *volte-face* and decided that no paranormal phenomena were involved. And Arthur Koestler, in a note I received from him a year or two later, was also having second thoughts.

If, after all this, you ask me whether I believe that Uri is a total fraud, I'll refuse to give a straight answer – but will urge you to study the books of his implacable though as yet only partly successful nemesis, the Amazing Randi. Make up your *own* mind – after you've read *Flim-Flam* and *The Truth About Uri Geller*. For my own part, I freely admit that I like the scamp, and we exchange friendly notes from time to time. He provided the world with much harmless entertainment during a gloomy period of history, and made some distinguished people look very foolish – always a most enjoyable spectacle from the sidelines. For a superb example of such a group, preserved like flies in amber, see *The Geller Papers*, edited by Charles Panati. Many of the authors of this astounding farrago must now wish that the entire edition had dematerialized.

My copy is inscribed: To Arthur. I wish you Health! Peace! Love! Happiness! from Uri Geller.

And the same from me, Uri . . .

In the Epilogue, I have attempted to give my reactions to some of the phenomena described in this book, and have added a few favourites of my own. I have also suggested possible explanations – or at least promising lines of research – that might lead to greater understanding of them. However, on the whole I have tried to follow Wittgenstein's wise advice: 'Whereof one cannot speak, thereof one must be silent.'

Once again, it is a pleasure to acknowledge the assistance of my colleagues Simon Welfare and John Fairley, who suggested both the book and the television series and did the research that made them possible, as well as that of our editor Robin Baird-Smith.

I hope that Yorkshire Television's new production will be as successful as its precursor, *Arthur C. Clarke's Mysterious World* – which, after its third run in the United Kingdom, inspired the ultimate compliment of a parody from that team of television clowns, the Goodies. May they also in due course produce a sequel to 'Man or Myth?' – their badly organized and totally unsuccessful quest for the 'legendary and elusive' . . .

Arthur C Clarke

# 1

# Maledictions

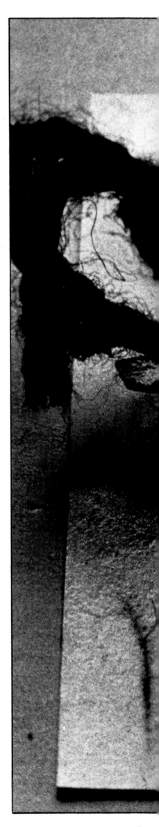

EVEN TODAY MEN AND WOMEN are hexed to death – killed by fear and spells – not only in Dahomey and Haiti, the lands of voodoo, but in London and New York, Montreal and Oklahoma City.

The symbols and instruments of death are freely on sale. Call in at the Cracker Jack Store, 435 South Rampart Street, New Orleans, or down the road at 521 St Philip Street, and the black candles of death are only three dollars each. The system is to buy seven candles and burn them for seven minutes on seven days. Underneath must be a picture of the victim – or merely the name, on a scrap of paper. If the candles are turned upside down each day, the hexing is allegedly even swifter and more efficacious.

In the Harlem market in New York City, the stalls offer bats' blood and graveyard dust. In Brazzaville, in the Congo, there is a thriving export market in the potions and implements of killing, displayed in rows of competing stalls beside the butchers and the yam sellers. A severed gorilla's hand is 1000 francs, the heads of tropical birds a mere 300 francs, the dried corpses of bats available by the kilo. Much of this is for domestic use, but agents send regular supplies to Paris and to Notting Hill in London.

Europeans have testified to the effectiveness of hexing ever since the age of exploration began and they came into contact with more primitive, or at least less rationalist, peoples. In 1587 Soares de Souza saw men from the Tupinambas Indians collapse and die when sentenced by the priests of the tribe. In New Zealand, one of the early settlers reported that a Maori woman died within the day when she was told she had eaten 'forbidden fruit' taken from a tabooed place. Another New Zealander reported in 1890: 'I have seen a strong young man die the same day he was tapued; the victims die under it, as though their strength ran out as water.'

In Australia, Dr Herbert Basedow saw a man 'boned' – a bone pointed at him as a sign of death. 'He stands aghast, with his eyes staring at the treacherous pointer, and with his hands lifted as though to warn off the fatal

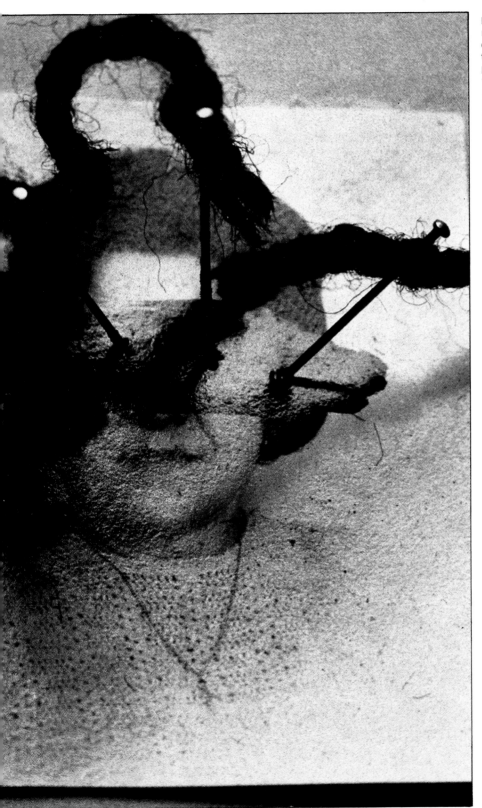

**Hexing and voodoo are not by any means confined to Haiti and the West Indies: this photograph of a woman with eyes and ears struck with the intended 'malice' was published in Italy's** La Stampa.

**South Carolina: The Charleston Cut Rate Drug Store displays the pre-packed ingredients of good and evil spells.** *Far right:* **Malign formula – grey root bag with recipe for evil; Long John Conqueror root; graveyard dust; hair and nail clippings purloined from the intended victim; a swallow's heart; and a fragment of under-clothing pierced with a pin to signify pain.**

medium, which he imagines is pouring into his body. His cheeks blanch and his eyes become glassy, and the expression of his face becomes horribly distorted. He attempts to shriek but usually the sound chokes in his throat, and all that one might see is froth at his mouth. His body begins to tremble and the muscles twist involuntarily. He sways backwards and falls, and after a short time appears to be in a swoon, but soon after he writhes as if in mortal agony and, covering his face with his hands, begins to moan.

'After a while he becomes very composed and crawls to his wurley. From this time on he sickens and frets, refusing to eat and keeping aloof from the daily affairs of the tribe.'

Death quickly follows.

The only escape seems to be to persuade the person who inflicted the 'boning' to withdraw its power. Dr S. M. Lambert of the Rockefeller Foundation was called to deal with Rob, a missionary's assistant in Queensland. He had been boned by Nebo, a famous aboriginal witch doctor. Dr Lambert could find no physical symptoms of fever or disease, yet it was plain that Rob was seriously ill. Dr Lambert went with the missionary to Nebo and threatened that he and his people would have all their food supplies cut off if the boning were not lifted. Nebo went with them to see Rob, merely leant over his bed and told him the boning was a mistake and, according to Dr Lambert, the very same evening Rob was restored to full physical strength and back at work.

The psychiatrist, Dr John C. Barker, most diligent and indefatigable of researchers into 'voodoo death' in our own time, recorded an episode in Kenya. The head dresser at a medical centre discovered that one of his staff at an outlying station was delivering only half of every prescribed injection

At Bassin Saint Jacques in Plaine-du-Nord, Haiti, followers of voodoo believe ritual bathing will ward off evil spirits.

and selling the rest off privately. The man was disciplined but, soon after, the head dresser found himself bewitched.

He told the doctor that his strength was ebbing away. 'I did not feel there was much I could do at the time,' the doctor reported. 'Then one day the head dresser came to me with a little bundle of sticks and leaves. This he informed me was the witch doctor's spell and he said that if it were opened there would be found in it some object that at some time had been part of his body: hair, nail clippings or even a tooth extracted years before. The little bundle had been found over the entrance of his hut. Every time he passed under it the spell would exert its baneful influence.'

The doctor was a decisive man. He immediately summoned all the dressers from the outlying stations. Despite threats and cajolements he could make no impression. Sterner measures were required. 'I went to my dispensary and prepared a most revolting concoction of drugs, which had an evil appearance and smell, but was quite harmless. The assembled company were then told they must take the medicine; the innocent would not be harmed but the guilty one would be immediately struck dead. Only one man refused. I then told him I was going to make him take the medicine by force and that it would undoubtedly kill him. Thereupon he confessed. I gave him twenty-four hours to arrange for the witch doctor he had employed to remove the spell. He carried out my orders without delay. Thereupon the head dresser, who had manifestly grown weaker day by day, began to recover immediately and, as far as I know, is still alive to this day.'

Equally decisive was brain-washing expert Professor William Sargent. He had seen hexings, so when a woman came into St Thomas's Hospital in London, turned her face to the wall and announced she had been hexed, Sargent gave her two massive electric shocks. When she came to, he told

Dr James Mathis, who investigated what he believed to be a fatal case of hexing in Oklahoma in 1960.

her the shocks had conquered the hex. She believed him, and recovered. In recent times, though, it has become apparent that the Western medical sophistication which saved Rob in North Queensland and the head dresser in Kenya, can often fail when confronted by the powers of death in Europe and America. For fear, threats and hexing claim victims still, in the face of all the efforts of modern medicine.

One day in January 1960 a man was brought into the Veterans Administration Hospital in Oklahoma City, Oklahoma. He was 53 years old and a successful businessman. Before the year was out he was dead, killed, doctors believed, by a curse laid upon him by his own mother.

The Veterans Hospital in Oklahoma City is one of the best equipped in the whole of the United States, with a distinguished medical staff. At first they were perfectly convinced that they could cope with their patient. Mr X, as the official records describe him, (thus protecting themselves from accusing a named person of causing a death) was brought in, semi-conscious, suffering from asthma. After two weeks he had recovered sufficiently to be allowed home.

It was six months before the Veterans' doctors saw their patient again – later research has revealed him to be Finis P. Ernest, a nightclub proprietor – but in that time it appeared that he had been in and out of private hospitals six times. Though he was by now having fits and convulsions, they could find nothing organically wrong. Cardiac readings showed no sign of heart trouble. Again, after rest, he recovered and went, as it transpired, directly to his mother's home.

As the case report recounts: 'In a few hours he was wheezing again and in less than 48 hours he was re-admitted by ambulance in a near-terminal condition. Medical management aborted the attack, but the patient became extremely depressed and voiced feelings of utter futility and hopelessness.' Another recovery followed, then a further relapse after he had been allowed out to visit his mother. By now, the psychiatric doctors had tumbled to the connection and allowed him out only on condition that he did not visit his mother. He progressed well until the fateful evening of 23 August. At 5 p.m. that day he had a long and cheerful interview with a doctor. Sometime around 6 p.m. he telephoned his mother. At 6.35 p.m. he was found gasping for breath and semi-conscious. By 6.55 p.m. he was dead.

Distressed and perplexed at his patient's death, one of the Oklahoma doctors, James L. Mathis, determined to investigate further. He discovered that Ernest's father had died when the boy was in his early teens, leaving him effectively the 'man of the house', responsible also for four other brothers and sisters as well as the mother. Twice before the age of 30 he married against the wishes of his mother; twice there was a quick divorce. Then, at the age of 31, in partnership with his mother, he opened a night club which proved to be very successful. At 38, he at last met a woman of whom his mother approved, a schoolteacher some years younger than himself, and Finis and Josephine were married. All went well for 15 years until he received a handsome offer to sell the business and, with Josephine's support, decided to accept.

The wrath of his mother was immediate and overwhelming. 'Do this,' she pronounced 'and something dire will happen to you.' Though he had

The victim, the late Finis P. Ernest, and his mother.

had excellent health for at least ten years, this man of 53 was, within two days, stricken with difficulties in breathing. He went ahead with the sale and in a final outburst his mother shouted repeatedly, 'Something will strike you, something will strike you.'

Dr Mathis reports: 'Numerous hospitalizations, asthmatic attacks three to four times per week, three convulsions and the apparent inability of the medical profession to help him, dovetailed into Mr X's growing idea that mother was right again. The depression for which psychiatric consultation was sought was marked by his frequent protestations of the hopelessness of his condition. A hopeful sign appeared when he was able consciously to see some connection between the asthmatic attacks and contact with his mother. However he did not forget that mother had previously proved infallible; in fact he reminded me of this on the afternoon of his death.'

Dr Mathis then went on to investigate the circumstances of the final phone call. After talking with her mother-in-law, Josephine was able to give him the gist of it. Her husband had plucked up the nerve to tell his mother that he proposed to re-invest the money from the night club in a new venture in which she would have no part. Dr Mathis's account ends: 'His mother made no attempt to dissuade him but ended the conversation with a statement to the effect that regardless of how he or the doctors felt, he should remember her warning and be prepared for her prediction of "dire results". Give or take a few minutes, Mr X was dead within the hour.'

Dr Mathis was left with no alternative but to label it, as he put it, a 'sophisticated version of voodoo death'.

If the sinister mother of Oklahoma City loomed like a character from the Brothers Grimm, not long afterwards some doctors from Johns Hopkins

University in Baltimore felt they were facing another fearful fairy tale, ending before their very eyes in the City Hospital. This time it was the wicked fairy attending a baby girl's birth, but without a good fairy to transmute death into gentle sleep.

The Baltimore patient was a black woman of 22. She was overweight, breathless, clearly anxious, but otherwise, as far as every available test could show, perfectly healthy. Yet the medical staff had seen her go into a steady decline. Three days before her 23rd birthday, the woman told her doctor the story of the day of her birth.

She came from a remote area of the Okefenokee Swamp in Georgia. There was only one midwife. On that day – a Friday the 13th – she had delivered three baby girls. The midwife told the mothers that the babies were hexed: the first would die before her 16th birthday, the second before her 21st and the last before her 23rd. The first girl duly died in an accident the day before her 16th birthday. The second, fearful of the hex, was filled with relief when her 21st birthday arrived, and insisted on going out to celebrate. As she walked into a saloon, a stray bullet hit and killed her.

It was the third girl who now lay, in that August of 1966, convinced she was doomed, in front of Dr Gottlieb Friesinger and his colleagues. She developed a galloping pulse and heart irregularities. They tried an operation to ligate the veins, but the improvement was only temporary. The day before her 23rd birthday, she started to sweat profusely; her breathing became wild. By nightfall she was dead. At the post mortem no natural cause could be found. Only the hex.

**Sorcerers' dolls from Basongo, Africa.**

A Dutch nursing home matron was confronted with another bizarre case reported that same year. Two women arrived at the front door of the home with their mother one Friday afternoon, and insisted in the most vehement terms that the old woman should be admitted at once, as she was going to die the following Thursday. The mother was apparently in the best of health and merely stood there silently while her daughters argued. Finally, the matron gave way and let the mother stay. For the next few days she pottered about the home doing odd jobs and occasionally discussing her imminent demise. The nursing home doctor pronounced her to be fully fit and, on the Thursday, she got up and took breakfast as usual. But then, in mid-morning, the matron was staggered to see the old woman's entire family – half a dozen in all – appear at the door, all in their Sunday best. They had taken a day off from work – one daughter from a launderette, the son against the specific threat from his boss that he would be fired.

The mother, who was about 70 years old, went to lie down. By half past one she had gone into a coma and the family gathered round her bedside singing psalms. The nursing home doctor, by now thoroughly alarmed, never left her patient's side. But by half past three she was dead. The death certificate read: 'Heart failure'.

The reasons for hex death are obscure, despite recorded medical evidence. Some victims weaken themselves by refusing food and drink. Also, extreme anxiety does seem to influence the so-called sympathetic nervous system; the blood pressure falls, plasma escapes from the blood cells, and a state of shock ensues. The heart beats faster and faster, finally collapsing into a state of constant contraction. On the other hand some believe that the familiar image – 'he was rigid with shock' – may continue into a state of prolonged rigidity or catalepsy when the lungs are paralyzed with fear and simply fail to supply the necessary oxygen. Again, the evidence about the Australian aborigines would seem to suggest that, in their hopelessness, it is the parasympathetic nervous system of the victims which comes into play, slowing down breathing and heart rate until life expires, leaving for the post-mortem knife only a heart distended with blood – and no other clues.

The reactions which play upon the victim in these cases are complex. First and foremost appears to be the absolute certainty of the power and immutability of the death prediction. And it is a certainty which seems to be able to reach out across many years.

In 1965 three doctors from Labrador in Canada wrote to *The British Medical Journal* about a case of a mother of five children who had suddenly died after an apparently successful minor operation. She was one week short of her 43rd birthday. Only afterwards did the doctors discover that, 38 years previously, when she was five years old, a fortune teller had informed her she would die before the age of 43.

The woman had come through the operation, for an incontinence problem, at the North West River Hospital in Labrador, perfectly normally: she regained consciousness and seemed fine. Then suddenly, an hour later, she collapsed with all the symptoms of shock, including low blood pressure. Oxygen, cortisone, the full array of indicated treatment, had no effect and she died the next day at five in the morning. On the morning of the operation she had told a nurse she was sure she was going to die.

Unknowing, the doctors went ahead with the operation. At the post-mortem they found bleeding round the adrenal glands and elsewhere, but nothing to indicate why a perfectly healthy woman had succumbed, as she had prophesied. Only then did it emerge that she had told her sister, who knew of the prophecy, that she did not expect to emerge from the anaesthetic, and that for years she had told her daughter that she would die by the age of 43.

Once the prophecy, the hex, the threat of death is known to a victim and the conviction of its power has lodged in the mind, it seems it can achieve its end in different ways – sometimes by a submissive and deadly abandonment of hope, sometimes by naked terror. For fear itself can kill.

Early in 1975 the people of Britain were for many weeks agog with speculation over the fate of a 17-year-old girl from Bridgnorth in the English Midlands. She had been kidnapped and a ransom demanded. Only when she was found, more than seven weeks later, was it realized that she had undergone perhaps the most horrific experience of unremitting terror known in modern times.

Lesley Whittle was the daughter of a wealthy man who had made his money in the road transport business. From time to time his name, tales of his expansive gestures, pictures of his family, had appeared in the local newspapers. When he died, his substantial will received a lot of publicity. This attracted the attention of Donald Neilson, an ex-soldier who, quite coldly, was looking for a victim for a big kidnap coup. He selected Lesley. For many weeks beforehand Neilson carefully scouted the area around Bridgnorth. It was an elaborate undertaking, for Neilson was a loner and there would be no assistants to give him away – or to share the takings.

Everything had, therefore, to be planned most carefully – the kidnapping itself, the getaway, the victim's hiding place, a means of securing her while he returned to normal life with his wife and daughter in a terraced house a hundred miles away, the delivery of the ransom demand, its collection, and his own safe escape. But by 14 January 1975, everything was ready.

Neilson watched from his car as Lesley's mother went out to a dinner party. Lesley was alone in the house. She went to bed early. Shortly before midnight, she was awoken by a light shining in her face and a hand over her mouth. The man wore a navy blue woollen hood over his face. In his other hand was a sawn-off shotgun. It was a cold night and she was wearing a light nightdress. Neilson grabbed her and hurriedly took her out to his car. Lesley was dumped in the back seat, apparently with her hands, eyes and mouth taped. Neilson, the gun beside him, set off on the 65-mile drive to his destination – a large area of heath and parkland at Kidsgrove in Staffordshire. He pulled Lesley out of the car and carried her across the heath to a small hillock. There, he dumped her on the ground beside a manhole which led into a new system of underground drains and flood-works, completed only two years before. He pulled back the cover and carried Lesley into the frightful catacomb that was to be her prison.

The shaft dropped straight down 30 feet to a roaring torrent full of winter flood waters running away to the Brindley Canal. A fixed metal inspection ladder ran down the side with, about 12 feet from the surface, a small working platform. Neilson had already made his preparations. There was a wire noose attached to the ladder at exactly the right height. Neilson padlocked it round Lesley's neck. Then he told the girl her fate. If the ransom were not paid, she would be despatched into the raging tunnel of water below. If she moved, slipped, fainted and fell from the platform she would be hanged by the wire noose.

Neilson climbed back up the ladder and closed the manhole. By five o'clock that morning, he was back home and in bed in Grangefield Avenue, Bradford, Yorkshire. Over the next days Neilson, using tape recordings planted in telephone boxes, attempted to extract a £50,000 ransom from Lesley's brother Ronald. Desperately Ronald tried to meet the conditions of the kidnapper, but Neilson was never satisfied there wasn't a police trap. At least twice in that time he went back to the dark manhole where the girl still stood, inside a sleeping bag, in the dark and cold, the noose around her neck, the floodwater still tumbling past in the blackness 20 feet below.

It is not known how long she lived. But at some time – probably when Neilson returned one night – the unutterable terror finally overcame her. Though it was many weeks before the body was found, the post-mortem doctors were quite clear. Lesley had died, not of violence or exposure, but of 'vagal inhibition'.

Vagal inhibition is familiar to doctors who have seen 'voodoo death'. At first, the victims show all the symptoms of panic – adrenalin is pumped out, the heart rate accelerates, there are wild movements and sweating. But then, as the realization of the hopelessness of their situation takes over, there is a reverse reaction – what is known as a parasympathetic reaction – the heart slows, the breathing slows, there is a steady drop in blood pressure. Sometimes death comes quite quickly.

A research team at Johns Hopkins Medical School was able, during some other experiments, to produce a similar effect in rats. Taking the fierce, wild Norway rat which usually shows the utmost aggression and determination in escaping from difficult situations, they put it first in a tight grip from which it could not struggle loose and then released it into a glass jar full of warm water.

The team, under Curt P. Richter, discovered that the wild rats seemed almost instantly to give up hope when they could see no possible means of escape. They died within minutes from the same 'vagal' death. But if they were once released from the grip or plucked from the water and returned, then they seemed to be immune to this particular kind of death: they knew that there was hope of rescue and no longer became susceptible to what the team call 'death from fear'.

Lesley Whittle and her kidnapper, Donald Neilson.

The curse of the witch doctor, voodoo's dramatic ritual, strikes an immediate terror. But it seems the fatal stroke can be laid on men and women by slower and more insidious means.

The Rev. Donald Omand, the well known Anglican 'Chaplain to the Circus', was handed a letter by an old lady, 'a true fairground queen, the head of five generations, ruling her children, grandchildren, great-grandchildren and great-great-grandchildren with what might be described as a velvet hand within an iron glove.' She asked Omand to keep the letter unopened till her death. Assuming it to be her will, he locked it away.

Some seven years later she died, and Omand was asked to conduct the funeral service. Afterwards the envelope was opened in the presence of the family. But it was not a will. Inside was a piece of paper folded seven times. On it was simply scrawled the day, the month and the year of her death.

This was not the first time the Rev. Omand had encountered such a phenomenon. He had been sent for by the family of a circus owner who had died of a heart attack. They were in great distress because only a week before the man had summoned his sons and told them he had just a week to live. They had brought in a doctor who assured the man that his heart, blood pressure, all his vital functions were in perfect order. Yet he had died on the predicted day.

Omand was then shown a curious bundle of envelopes – 13 in all – which had been found among the man's effects. Posted from different cities in Europe, but all in the same handwriting, they had arrived once a year on the same date. In each was an ordinary printed birthday card. But, on every card the word 'birthday' was crossed out and the word 'deathday' written in. Then just a date and a man's signature. The date was always the same – the date on which the circus owner eventually died. It transpired that the man who had pursued his victim with such a patient vendetta had been a performer dismissed for drunkenness in the same year that the first deathcard was sent.

Some victims seem almost gladly to embrace their fate. In Norway in 1934 a prediction and death resulted in a celebrated murder trial. The accused was an attractive Oslo woman called Mrs Ingeborg Köbler. She was alleged to have drowned her father, an eminent judge, while they were swimming in the Oslo fjord at Hanko. Mrs Köbler had predicted the time, place, and manner of her father's death while supposedly in a sleeping trance. As he was worth 60,000 kroner in accident insurance, sceptics felt this was too neat to be true and took out a bill of indictment.

Ingeborg Köbler, daughter of Judge Dahl, had started producing phenomena after her brother Ludvig drowned, followed five years later by another death – her brother Ragnar. She would begin with a sleeping trance, progressing to a waking trance. There were various 'wonders' performed: messages coming from Ludvig via a suspended pencil and planchette; Ludvig reading lines from Wordsworth's poetical works and

Judge Dahl and his daughter, Ingeborg. Could she have 'suggested' his death by drowning?

other books selected by guests at the séances; Ingeborg writing letters from various dead people in their own handwriting – once indeed two different letters at the same time, one with the right hand and the other with the left. But the fatal communication came via a number code the Dahls had been using: each letter of the alphabet was given a number, apparently unknown to Ingeborg.

Then, in her sleeping trance state, she would produce a string of numbers which, when decoded, gave a message from someone 'on the other side'. One day in 1934, Judge Dahl and his family took down the numbers which spelled out what was to be the manner of the Judge's death. All the evidence is that the Judge had become a passionate believer in his daughter's powers. Indeed, so much of the family's money and the Judge's time had been spent on supporting Ingeborg's work that the family had run into debt and the mother had gone so far as to purloin funds from her work as local community treasurer in Fredriksstad. As she wrote in a later suicide note: 'My husband, the judge, felt it was his life work to bring this message to mankind. In doing so he took a great and unselfish task on his shoulders. But he was quite innocent of the great demands of daily living and did not realize that our family economy was threatened.'

From the evidence of two years' examination by the Norwegian police and judicial authorities it seems indisputable that the judge, calmly and with total certainty, accepted his daughter's message about his death. Ingeborg had been in a supposed sleeping trance and the family never subsequently mentioned the subject.

On 8 August 1934 Judge Dahl and Ingeborg went for a walk along the beach at Hanko. Four months had passed since the prediction séance. The judge decided he would swim. Ingeborg declined. He took off his clothes, plunged into the sea, and stayed swimming for a long time before suddenly being attacked by cramp. There were no witnesses, but Ingeborg said she then rushed into the sea, and succeeded in getting the drowning man back to the shore. She tried to revive him, failed, went for help; but, by the time she got back with others, he was dead.

It was only when the President of the Norwegian Society for Psychic Research, Professor Thorstein Wereide, revealed the story of the prediction at what he thought was a closed meeting, that the newspapers got hold of the tale and started the rumpus which resulted in Ingeborg's arrest. She was held in prison for five months while the investigation proceeded. Finally, she was released on the grounds that she could not have known in her sleeping trance the content of the message about her father, nor had she been told later.

Whatever the truth about Ingeborg, it seems clear that Judge Dahl was a firm believer. Quite deliberately and calmly, under no immediate duress, on that warm summer's day at Hanko, he went out to meet what he believed to be his fate.

In the last decade or so, scattered reports of doctors have begun to confirm such powers of death, whether self-inflicted or through some outside agency like a fortune teller. Dr Francis Ellis, of Cheshire in England, described a pregnant woman with signs of heart disease who was in hospital and well-controlled as her time was approaching. Unfortunately during a

*Opposite:* **Voodoo frenzy in Haiti.**

bedside discussion the words 'heart failure' were mentioned. 'Although it was discounted at once by our tutor,' recalls Dr Ellis, 'I could see the look of terror remain on the patient's face for several seconds.' The same day, she collapsed and died.

A London doctor, Peter Young, said he had seen a number of cases. One concerned a man of 37 who was terrified of having an operation for varicose veins – worse, it was twice postponed. On the day when it was actually to take place he collapsed and died. A post mortem revealed no cause of the fatal heart attack. Another of Dr Young's patients was a market gardener who suffered a heart attack. 'He told me that after a full and satisfying life he now expected to die,' recounts Dr Young, 'and that he had left his will and a letter to his solicitor on the table at home. He was told that after a few weeks' rest he should be able to go home, but he contradicted this with a smile. His condition improved rapidly, but he never doubted his end was near. Three weeks after admission, he suddenly collapsed and died.' The man was a bachelor and deeply religious. Perhaps the prospects after death seemed more attractive than living on, deprived of the work he loved.

In the Western world there seems little doubt that fortune tellers are responsible for directing many people to their appointments in Samarra. Today they flourish as never before.

The St Leger horse race meeting at Doncaster in Yorkshire is traditionally accompanied by one of the best fairs in England. The fastest hurdy gurdies, the most ferocious dodgems, the latest rides, are invariably gathered in September on the Town Moor. And each year there seem to be more fortune tellers in ever more luxurious *vardos* and wagons – in 1983 more than a dozen Genuine Gypsy Rose Lees 'as seen on television', their doorways papered with testimonials to their powers from the great and the famous. Standing affably at the top of their caravan steps, or peeking from behind gaily coloured curtains, they rarely lack for custom. They claim never to speak of death, even when it makes its ubiquitous appearance in the cards, the tea leaves, the palms or the crystal ball.

But there is no doubt some fortune tellers do call the design of death. Dr William Nixon of University College Hospital, London, had a patient of 35, obviously under dreadful terror as the birth of her first child approached. 'I asked why she was so fearful,' said Dr Nixon. 'All her pent-up emotions exploded when she recounted that at the age of ten when walking on the South Downs between Worthing and Brighton she had met a gypsy who predicted that either she or her baby would die in childbirth.' On this occasion, both mother and baby survived, but Dr Nixon had already seen death ensue from such a warning. While he was working at the Tsan Yuk maternity hospital in Hong Kong, one of his patients, aged 21, had a perfectly normal delivery but refused to suckle the baby or even speak. Eventually, on the sixth day, she spoke and said she was going to die. On her way into hospital she had gone into one of the fortune tellers' booths which cluster round Tsan Yuk and had been told that on the sixth day after the birth, she would die. It happened as predicted, and, at the autopsy, nothing could be found to account for her death.

Dr John Barker bravely submitted himself, along with a gallant assistant whom he calls Mrs Noble, to a series of contemporary English fortune

tellers, in order to discover what they did actually tell their customers.

They applied to a dozen varied practitioners, specializing in everything from tarot cards and psychometry to clairvoyance and astrology, and operating mainly from London and the English south coast. Both Barker and 'Mrs Noble' were singularly impressed by some – though by no means all – of the fortune tellers. They both paid five guineas for a 30-minute session with a gypsy-clairvoyant with a booth on a south coast pier.

Barker wrote: 'She was remarkably and uncannily accurate. I gave her no information whatsoever. After practising psychiatry for eleven years I could not possibly have told her a fraction about herself to compare with her quite amazing knowledge about myself and my past life.' The gypsy used a crystal ball, holding Barker's hands wrapped around it. She got his occupation right, his literary work, and salient features of his past life.

Mrs Noble emerged from another session with the gypsy and noted: 'Her accuracy was fantastic. She showed remarkable insight into my personal conditions, giving the date of my marriage correctly and the number and sex of my children.' In this instance, the gypsy predicted bereavement and not death. Indeed she predicted, alas wrongly, a long life for Dr Barker. But many of the other fortune tellers in Barker's survey did predict death.

Another gypsy, described by Barker as 'a brusque elderly woman' immediately opened the session by telling him that he would die suddenly of a stroke when aged just over 70. This was given added force for 'She claimed I nearly died three and 13 years ago, which was substantially correct since I had severe illnesses at both these times.'

Two others forecast that Barker would live a long life, and some flatly refused to predict a time of death. Both he and Mrs Noble were told that they would soon suffer bereavements. They were very impressed by how convincing some of the fortune tellers could be – a feeling reinforced by meeting other clients in the waiting rooms who had travelled the breadth of England for a consultation 'because we have heard she is so good'. Barker had personally treated two women who had been terrorized by the threats of gypsy palm readers – one after refusing at first to pay to have her hand read, and the other because her short and broken life-line had been pointed out.

An Indian palm-reader told John Snell of Poole in England that he would die on his 45th birthday. For 20 years he ignored the warning; he became a Guinness drinker and long-distance lorry driver. But in his 44th year he began to worry. He gave up drinking altogether. On his birthday in October 1982 he refused to leave the house. Two days later the local newspaper reported the death of John Snell of Poole on his 45th birthday. But the palm reader was wrong. There were two John Snells, living 100 yards apart – and the one whose palm was read is still alive.

'"Scared to death" is not an idle saying,' as Dr Ansel Fry wrote. 'A feeling of "I am afraid I am going to die" may actually result in death.' The extent of lethal voodoo, particularly in the United States, seems to be growing. The Haitian refugees who have congregated in Brooklyn and Miami seem to be responsible for some of the more lurid cases – a man's body found on a

New York lot in 1980 burned, mutilated and surrounded by chicken feet, feathers and candles; a head found in a bag in Miami, together with wax, and chicken and turkey bones. But voodoo seems also to have an extensive hold all across the old South.

Professor Kenneth M. Golden of Little Rock, Arkansas, made an initial report on voodoo death in *The American Journal of Psychiatry* in 1977 and thus alerted his colleagues in Little Rock and also at St Louis, where he is visiting professor at Webster College. By 1982 he was able not only to report more than a dozen cases of hexing which had been brought to his attention – but also to suggest treatment for the hexed patients.

A black man had come to the University Hospital, bent double and in great pain, but showing no symptoms to normal examination including a brain scan. It emerged that the man's wife practised black magic; she suspected him of infidelity and had probably placed a hex on him. Furthermore the woman's two previous husbands had both died for no apparent medical reason.

Of another patient involved in an eternal triangle Golden says: 'He was confused, agitated and almost delirious on the ward, necessitating bed restraint and large doses of chlorpromazine. All neurological findings, including a brain scan, proved normal. The patient died two weeks later of cardiac arrest. The autopsy provided no basis for the failure.' The man was only thirty-three years old. According to his wife, it was the 'other woman' who had hexed him: she was known to cast spells and heal people.

Golden's reports include a woman hexed and suffering uncontrollable spasms of her arms and legs after rejecting lesbian advances from a voodoo woman. A man of 36 became 'emaciated, dehydrated, disoriented, apprehensive, unshaven, his hair long and matted', after his wife had 'throwed at him' when he left her for another woman. This man was cured by being given a placebo – no drugs in it whatsoever – and being assured by the doctor in the strongest possible terms that it would work. Indeed, the treatment Dr Golden recommends to his fellow physicians is to all intents and purposes white counter-magic:

> Use placebos and emphasize their potency as positively as you can.
> Do not belittle local healers and spiritualists; offer hospital treatment as an alternative not a substitute.
> Try hypnosis.
> Do not disdain getting the patient to healers whom they think can counter spells, especially if they are unwilling to go on seeing a local doctor when they go home.

Golden himself had had great trouble with the lady suffering from the lesbian hex. He tried all his usual methods and succeeded in reducing the spasms in her arms and legs but, as the time came for her to be sent home, her fears reappeared. 'She still felt a powerful hex was upon her house,' says Golden, 'and that harm would befall her. I suggested she knit a small square that would protect her. She did so readily and was much relieved. She told me she would put it in her top dresser drawer with her panties as soon as she arrived in her house.'

At the time of writing, this most bizarre of prescriptions was still successfully working its wonders.

# 2

# The Noisy Spirits

IN THE WINTER OF 1967 chaos descended upon a respectable lawyer's office in the town of Rosenheim in southern Germany.

The first sign that something odd was happening had come in the summer when the practice's telephones began to play up. Sometimes they would all ring at once, although no one turned out to be on the line, and conversations were frequently disrupted by irritating clicking sounds. The office manager complained to the telephone company; some engineers were sent to put things right. It should have been a simple task, but they were totally unable to pinpoint any fault. Indeed, their investigations convinced them that the mechanism was in perfect working order.

After weeks of meticulous tests the men from the telephone company gave up in bewilderment and, since the trouble seemed to be growing worse, a team of experts from the Post Office moved in. They installed a meter to monitor every call; it did nothing to sort out the problem, in fact the mystery deepened, for the meter showed that dozens of calls were being registered from telephones which the office staff swore on oath were not being used at the times shown on the print-out. Some numbers were being dialled with astonishing speed and frequency, and on one particular day the meter showed that 0119, the number of the Speaking Clock, had been rung 46 times in 15 minutes. As usual, none of the office staff had been spotted making any of the calls. In any case, there was no need for them to ring the Speaking Clock – they all had watches and there were two churches nearby with clocks which could be relied upon to chime loudly.

As tempers and telephone charges mounted, other office equipment began to behave strangely. Fluorescent tubes repeatedly twisted themselves out of their sockets, light bulbs exploded, drawers shot out of desks, pictures rotated on the walls and developing fluid gushed from the photocopiers. The electricity supply fluctuated alarmingly. The place was in uproar. Yet the experts – telephone engineers, electricians and a team of

Rosenheim solicitor Sigmund Adam (*left*) with the bill which revealed the strange behaviour of his office telephone. Dr Hans Bender (*right*), doyen of German parapsychologists, suggested a poltergeist might be the cause of the trouble.

eminent physicists – were forced to admit defeat after intensive investigations. They could find no reason whatsoever for the extraordinary events, which by now had been witnessed by 40 trustworthy people. The baffled physicists concluded unhappily that the havoc was being caused by 'intelligently controlled forces with a tendency to evade investigation'.

Finally, Germany's most respected parapsychologist and psychical researcher, Dr Hans Bender, was summoned to the beleaguered office. Unlike the other experts, Bender and his colleagues were immediately able to diagnose the cause of the trouble. They had come across cases like this one many times before. A poltergeist was at work in the Rosenheim law practice.

As only those who have been the victim of one can truly know, the word poltergeist (from the German, meaning 'noisy spirit') does not begin to describe one of the most grotesque phenomena in the psychical investigator's casebook. It is very much more than a mere noisy spirit: far more sinister, far more destructive and baffling. After studying cases 'in all lands and in all ages', the celebrated British researcher Harry Price concluded in 1945 that 'The Poltergeist is mischievous, destructive, noisy, cruel, erratic, thievish, demonstrative, purposeless, cunning, unhelpful, malicious, audacious, teasing, ill-disposed, spiteful, ruthless, resourceful and vampiric. A ghost *haunts*; a Poltergeist *infests*.'

Price's contemporary, Dr Nandor Fodor, amplified this difference between ghosts and poltergeists in his *Encyclopaedia of Psychic Science*. He defined poltergeists as 'noisy spirits, causing periodic psychic disturbances of a malicious character in certain places in the presence of a certain, mostly unsuspecting, sensitive person. The appearance is as if, parallel to haunted houses, there existed haunted men.'

At Rosenheim Hans Bender picked out the haunted person with little difficulty, for he noticed that the phenomena seemed to flourish in the presence of a 19-year-old clerk called Annemarie Schneider. Every time she was away from the office there was peace; but when she was there, the strange events began again. For example, lamps would swing as she walked beneath them; pictures on the wall rotated like propellers, to the amazement of the lawyer's clients; and cigarette money flew out of the cashbox in which it was kept. The case was finally closed when Annemarie left the office staff; the lawyer's practice returned to the peaceful routine that the girl's arrival had so violently disrupted.

Many (though by no means all) poltergeist cases do seem to centre on one young person – the poltergeist 'focus' or 'agent'. Most of them are unhappy and frustrated at the time, as Annemarie undoubtedly was; but such observations merely pinpoint some of the most striking characteristics of the poltergeist – they do not explain the cause of the phenomenon.

In the search for truth about poltergeists there is, at least, plenty of raw material to work on. Michael Goss, a British writer and bibliographer, has compiled a list of eyewitness reports, books and articles in the English language alone. It fills a 350-page volume with more than 1000 entries detailing outbreaks in countries throughout the world: from Africa, where a family of Sikhs in Kampala was 'troubled by objects thrown and upset' in 1966, to Yugoslavia, where a mysterious stonethrowing poltergeist had hit the headlines in 1885. A survey conducted in 1982 by the Institute of Psychophysical Research at Oxford brought responses from all over Britain and, according to the *Sunday Telegraph*, examples included a heavy ashtray which dented a wooden table, a musical box which wound itself up in the middle of the night and played a tune, shattered crockery and self-spilling oil, and a car was said to have moved undriven in a house driveway . . .

A closer look at cases reveals not only that the poltergeist comes in many guises but its reasons for choosing victims appear capricious and obscure.

The residents of five houses in Thornton Road, a quiet suburban street in Birmingham, have spent several distressing and expensive years desperately trying to figure out why they, of all the people in Britain's 'second city', should have been singled out for a devastating and almost nightly bombardment of large stones, which seem to come from nowhere. Windows and rooftiles have been repeatedly broken, and, as a result, the householders have had to take expensive protective measures.

From the front there is nothing about the appearance of the houses to suggest they are under siege; but the scene at the back is very different: windows have been boarded up and screens of chicken wire shield the fabric of the buildings from the impact of the stones.

Soon after the stonethrowing began, and when the householders realized that there were no obvious culprits such as gangs of mischievous children, the people of Thornton Road called in the police. To Birmingham's skilled constabulary it seemed a simple matter at first but, after months of careful investigation had failed to crack the case, it was put in the capable hands of a senior officer, Chief Inspector Len Turley. Turley brought to Thornton Road a team of experienced officers, kitted out with the latest in crime-breaking equipment. Some of the men spent entire nights in the gardens, huddled in sleeping bags in the depths of one of Britain's coldest-ever winters, 1981–2. P.C. Danny McMahon recalls the bitter night when all he had to keep him warm was a flask of hot soup. By the time he opened it, the soup had frozen solid. Occasionally, the sound of a stone clattering against the buildings broke the silence and tedium of the vigil, but there was never a clue as to who or what had thrown them, or how.

Night-sights, image intensifiers and automatic cameras yielded no results. The only signs of life or movement on the infra-red video came from scampering rats or mice; rabbits trotted past, and a wary fox. Inside the houses, the increasingly edgy occupants tried to sleep, wondering when to expect the next stone.

By the end of 1982 Chief Inspector Turley and his team had spent more than 3500 man-hours in fruitless investigation. In that time, the same police division had solved five murder cases, but the file on Thornton Road was still, frustratingly, open. 'We are completely baffled. We have tried everything we know without being able to find out who is doing this,' Turley told a reporter. Two years later, the police could report no progress.

Such clues as there are merely compound the mystery: the stones which fly are of the same type as those to be found in all the Thornton Road gardens, but the ones which have hit the houses have neither fingerprints nor any other marks on them. Indeed, they are clean of soil and forensic experts say they look as though they have been washed. Meanwhile the householders wonder whether their insurance will pay for the damage – so far £700 for broken glass at one address, £300 at another. And they still have to live in an atmosphere of menace. Going out into the garden at dusk is an ordeal, to be faced only if really necessary, and then with trepidation.

Even in the early days of the siege, things reached such a pitch that one young man, Christopher Malcolm from No. 30, used to stay out in the garden for hours after dark in the hope of solving the case. For protection against the stones he wore the wartime tin hat that had belonged to his father, or a hard riding hat. More recently, one housewife remembers taking a pair of trousers from her washing-line. It was just getting dark, and an overpowering sensation that she was being watched from the shadows swept over her. No sooner had she hurried into the kitchen, a mere dozen steps from the washing-line, than a stone thumped against the wall.

Whatever the outcome of the Thornton Road case, many of the hallmarks of classic poltergeist assaults are present. Indeed, stonethrowings have occurred so frequently over the centuries that Dr Nandor Fodor devoted a whole section to them in his *Encyclopaedia of Psychic Science*, starting with a case dating from 858 AD when, in the small town of Bingen on the Rhine, 'Stones were thrown about by a malignant spirit, or so it was thought, and they struck the walls of simple dwellings as if with a hammer.'

In 1849, the French police were called in to investigate a case of stonethrowing very similar to the one faced by their Birmingham counterparts 130 years later. Every night for three weeks a house and a woodyard were showered with stones. The police, who were nonplussed by the case, took refuge in urgent, if rather quaint rhetoric: 'Whence came these projectiles, which are paving stones, fragments of the demolished walls near, and ashlar stones entire, which from their weight, and the distance they are hurled, are clearly from no mortal hand?' asked the writer of the official report in *La Gazette des Tribunaux*.

In Sumatra, Indonesia, Mr W. G. Grottendieck awoke one night in 1903 to find stones raining down on him from his bedroom ceiling, and no less an eyewitness than Bishop Weston of Zanzibar intrigued readers of the *Daily Express* in 1923 with his account of a visit to a clay hut in which he saw 'large pieces of earth violently plucked from the walls and thrown into the air'.

More recently, America's *National Enquirer* of 28 September 1982 told how a poltergeist plagued a family from Belize, Central America:

'The sleepy, quiet life of Reginaldo Salam, 63, his wife Felicita, who is also 63, and their 13-year-old granddaughter Maria was shattered one day late last year. As Felicita and Maria walked to the nearby village of San Antonio, suddenly a continuous hail of small stones pelted them out of thin air. "It was horrible!" Felicita recalled with a shiver. "It was as though we were being stoned by a group of people – but there was nobody around! We were frightened!" So much so, that after being bombarded as they sat eating dinner one night in a closed room, they fled to stay with relatives in Belize City. According to *The National Enquirer*, the uncanny scenes were witnessed by an American priest: 'While the family was in our church, the rocks seemed to come right through the two-foot-thick walls! One flew right at me, but when it hit, it had no more impact than a feather!" '

Oddly, few victims of stonethrowing poltergeists seem to suffer serious injury – in Thornton Road the only person hurt in any way was grazed on the cheek when a stone winged its way right into his living-room. Usually, for some unexplained reason, the stones seem to land very gently.

But other, rather different, poltergeists have inflicted more serious casualties. Harry Price, the English psychical investigator, undertook a series of probes into the case of a young Rumanian teenager called Eleonore Zugun, the protegée of the exotically-named Countess Zoë Wassilko-Serecki of Vienna. From her infancy, Eleonore's presence seemed to trigger poltergeist events, but what most interested Price were the inflamed marks that appeared frequently on her body, produced, according to some

The houses in Thornton Road, sedately suburban by day, but at night the target of an elusive stone-thrower. The stones have yielded no clues to Birmingham's investigating police officers, headed by Chief Inspector Len Turley (*top*), who continue to collect the evidence of mysterious missiles.

of the experts who examined her, by a poltergeist that bit and scratched.

In the spring of 1926 Price travelled to Vienna to meet Eleonore and noted later with a rather curious mixture of distaste and satisfaction:

'At Vienna during the first few minutes of my preliminary observational period, Eleonore gave a short, sharp cry of pain and Countess Wassilko at once pulled up the left sleeve of the child's bodice, and on the fleshy part of the forearm, some distance above the wrist, were the deep indentations of teeth-marks, six above and five below, forming together an elliptical figure. If the reader will bite the fleshy part of his own arm, he will get an exact representation of what we saw.'

To stave off any doubts about the genuineness of the phenomenon (and, no doubt, to prevent an epidemic of self-inflicted arm-wounds amongst his readers), Price quoted the testimony of observers like Colonel W. W. Hardwick, who wrote after meeting Eleonore in London: 'At 5.40 p.m. after tea, Eleonore was tying up a box, when she gave a gasp and moved her right hand towards her left wrist – distinct teeth-marks appeared on her wrist, then scores like scratches appeared on her right forearm, cheeks and forehead. Shortly after, a series of marks like some form of letters appeared on her left forearm, all rising to distinct white inflammatory swellings within three or four minutes, fading slowly. The girl was under close observation, and could not have produced these herself by any normal means.'

In modern times the newspapers assiduously report the plight of people who have apparently been driven from their homes by poltergeists. In August 1981, the Burden family of Abbott Road in the select English holiday resort of Bournemouth fled their home, resolving never to return, after the house was apparently ransacked by a poltergeist. The pictures splashed over the newspapers showed broken crockery and food strewn all over the kitchen floor, and the accompanying articles told of furniture which suddenly took to the air before crashing to the ground.

Just over a year earlier, a young couple with a baby left their council house in Penhill, Wiltshire after only three days. According to one newspaper: 'Lights went on and off, a poker flew across a room and a

The Rumanian girl, Eleonore Zugun, claimed she was the victim of a poltergeist which bit and scratched. Strange marks and swelling regularly appeared on her face and hands.

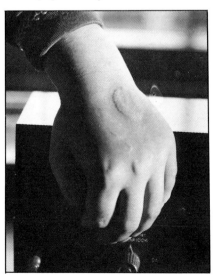
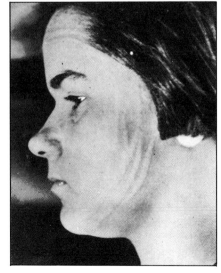

cassette recorder was apparently flung at the sleeping baby.' The local council was sympathetic; a spokesman was quoted: 'The couple are not telling lies about this house and we are going to rehouse them right away.'

A family in the English Midlands was also rehoused after pints of water seeped through the floorboards, although there was no leak in the plumbing system; there was also an incident in which a kettle of scalding water was apparently wrenched from a girl's hand by an unseen entity. In addition, this poltergeist produced inexplicable raps and loud thumps, a phenomenon which has become a hallmark of classic cases. In Thun, Switzerland, in 1967, three women were unable to sleep for the raps and bangings that plagued them at night. The sounds persisted long enough for them to be captured on tape, as they were in a case at Sauchie, Scotland, in 1960, when the local priest was able to feel the vibrations of sounds coming through the top of a child's bed.

Another common feature of poltergeist outbreaks is the inexplicable movement of household objects; sometimes, witnesses say, they see things flying slowly from one place to another and landing gently with no resulting damage. The *Sheffield Morning Telegraph* achieved a remarkable photographic scoop in 1965 when it published a picture of a walking stick dancing above the head of 14-year-old Michael Collindridge as he lay flat on his back in bed under close observation. At a nursing-home in Malvern, in 1942, a poker flew some 12 feet from its place on the wall in the presence of seven witnesses.

Harry Price took the obvious precaution when he investigated a poltergeist outbreak in the bedroom of 12-year-old Alan Rhodes in 1945. He tied the boy's arms to the end of his bed but this did not prevent a clock and a box which had been out of his reach at the side from appearing on the bed itself.

In 1979 Larry Mead was hit by a fireplace-tile during an all-night vigil at a poltergeist-ridden gift-shop in the resort of Rio Grande, in southern New Jersey, and an electrician reported that a set of tools had scattered across the floor while he was working overtime in the building, quite alone. This

Visitors to the bedroom of Michael Collindridge above the Cranberry Arms pub in Barnsley, Yorkshire, were amazed by the antics of a walking stick which appeared to dance about the room of its own accord. When he revisited the room almost 20 years later, Michael (*right*) recalled how the stick used to tap out tunes requested by friends.

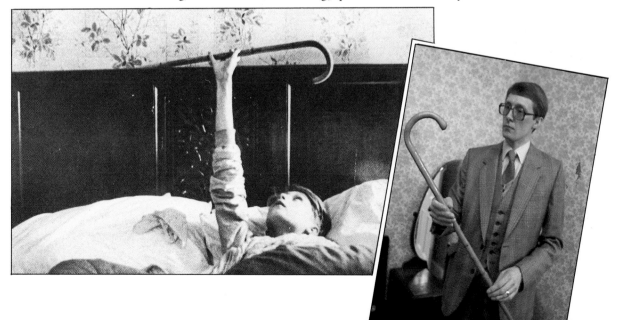

Derek and Brenda Newman, with their son Lee, outside their flat in School Street, Sheffield. 'Strange banging noises' woke them one night in January 1982; the place was on fire but thanks to the eerie warning system the family escaped unharmed.

particular poltergeist, incidentally, seemed to be of a technological bent, for the shop's music system turned itself on and off when no one was apparently near it, an unattended sewing machine started up and began to sew, an adding machine, six feet away from the nearest person, suddenly began to print out zeros, and the security company's chief electrician said he went nearly crazy when the burglar alarm repeatedly sounded false alarms, despite having been entirely replaced three times.

Uncanny as such events appear to be, a few cases achieve even greater heights of weirdness; none more so than that of the Rev. Dr Eliakim Phelps of Stratford, Connecticut, whose home and peace-of-mind were disrupted by a particularly inventive poltergeist in 1850. There were the usual raps and breakages, but the most unnerving sign that unseen forces were at work appeared on a Sunday when the family had been out at church for a short while. They returned to find that many of their possessions had been mysteriously moved and, in a hitherto locked and empty room, they discovered an elaborate tableau of stuffed dummies, made from the family's clothes. According to a description published by the local *New Haven Journal and Courier*, the 11 figures were all: 'graciously and imposingly arranged, so as to have the appearance of life. They were all female figures but one, and most of them in attitudes of devotion, with Bibles before them, and pointing to different passages with the apparent design of making the Scriptures sanction and confirm the strange things that were going on . . . Some of the figures were kneeling beside the beds, and some bending their faces to the floor in attitudes of deep humility. In the centre of the group was a dwarf, most grotesquely arrayed; and above was a figure so suspended as to seem flying through the air.'

In comparison with this and other tableaux that appeared from time to time, the other manifestations of the phenomenon – levitations of furniture, the flight of cutlery and other household objects and the ripping of children's clothes – seemed rather small beer, although there was considerable relief when the disturbances ceased altogether some eight months after they had begun.

Although poltergeists deservedly get a bad press in most cases, their victims very occasionally find themselves ironically grateful that they have been chosen as a target. In January 1982, the Newman family of Sheffield in Yorkshire awoke in the middle of the night to the familiar sounds of a poltergeist which had been plaguing them for more than a year, throwing ornaments and household objects around and making loud banging sounds. That night the noises spurred Derek Newman into action. He told a reporter: 'It was like someone running round the lounge with a hammer. It was a tremendous clamour. I picked up a hammer and opened the bedroom door and dense smoke just poured in.'

Newman believes the poltergeist saved his life and those of his wife and three children, for the flat was on fire and full of smoke. Had they not been roused by the rappings, they would probably not even have been able to reach the balcony from which they were rescued by firemen. On the other hand, at least one family has found their encounter with a poltergeist far preferable to the events that followed publicity given to it, as the *Daily Telegraph* of 17 September 1962 gleefully reported: 'It was not the poltergeist that drove the Daughtreys from their farmhouse in Portsmouth, Virginia. It was the curiosity-minded thousands who turned up to see what was going on. Police estimated there were 20,000 visitors in two weeks following reports of vases dashing round corners, mattresses flying off beds and a young member of the family being lifted from a chair. "I ain't scared of anything in that house," said Mrs Daughtrey, 78, "but the people terrorize me."'

Recording the effects of a poltergeist, taking eyewitness reports and visiting the location are the stock-in-trade of the psychical researcher, but finding an explanation for these extraordinary outbreaks is quite another matter. A major problem is that few investigators have ever managed to see many of the principal signs of poltergeist activity for themselves, still less record it on film or videotape – poltergeists have a disconcerting habit of quietening down whenever an objective observer is present. In the title of a book published in 1964, Dr George Owen, who was directly involved in the examination of the Sauchie case, posed a question asked since the early days of psychical research: *Can We Explain The Poltergeist?* While many cases do remain baffling, the answer in some instances is: 'Yes, we can.'

The most obvious possibility is that people who are involved in poltergeist cases are the perpetrators or unwitting victims of fraud. Certainly, the literature of psychical research is embarrassingly full of hoaxes played upon parapsychologists by ordinary people. Early in 1982, for example, the citizens of Lower Bavaria were fascinated by a story which, as one British commentator put it, 'grabbed the Gothic-reaches of their imagination'.

A dentist in the small town of Neutraubling claimed that his surgery was being harangued by a rough, staccato voice which spoke from the ceiling, the power points, his medical equipment and even from the plughole of the washbasin and the bowl of the lavatory. The police were called in and a Post Office team renewed the entire telephone system before leaving nonplussed. 'You'll never find me,' said the voice, in a thick Bavarian accent; but it proved an idle boast. Eventually the source of the mysterious voice was revealed to be the dentist himself and his pretty young assistant. It had

In 1981 Charlie Burden and his family moved from their home in Abbott Road, Bournemouth after the house was apparently ransacked by a poltergeist.

all started as a game which went too far. The dentist and his wife were fined a total of 12,400 marks (about £3,200) for staging the hoax by a court in Regensburg, which ruled that the dentist had been seeking publicity. The case was closed, and so was the dental practice.

One of the best-documented, and most comic, cases of poltergeist fraud occurred in the town of Windsor, Nova Scotia in 1906. A probate judge, known as 'Mr X' in the report later published in the *Proceedings of the American Society for Psychical Research*, wrote to James H. Hyslop, one of America's foremost early psychical researchers, with a very remarkable tale. It all started when he saw what appeared to be the headless figure of a man. Later the same 'spirit' materialized in a bag and in a box being carried across the street. The box got heavier and heavier, but when Mr X had summoned help and opened it, the 'body' had unaccountably disappeared. Even more mysteriously, a hogshead barrel began to zoom around the town. Soon afterwards, coins began to fall when Mr X went into shops, knockings were heard in the cellar of a grocery shop, things were thrown about a restaurant, and electric lamps were ejected, by some unknown force, from the barber's shop. Hyslop despatched Hereward Carrington to the town at Mr X's insistence.

Carrington was an exceptionally experienced investigator, and Mr X's story did not detain him in Windsor for long. He rapidly confirmed what any reader of the judge's letters would have suspected all the time – that many of the inhabitants of Windsor had ganged together to have fun at the expense of the credulous judge. In one factory, some of the workers had rigged up strings to make empty chairs seem to rock of their own accord, and had run speaking-tubes from one floor to another to broadcast mysterious voices. Other townsfolk had perfected the art of throwing things without anyone being able to detect their arm-movements. There was a sleight-of-hand expert in the barber's shop who made foreign coins materialize, a mischievous eight-year-old in another store who could make objects appear to fly spontaneously, and schoolboys who pretended to go into trances and threw objects which they had earlier hidden in their pockets. The terror all this inspired in Mr X made it impossible for him to investigate these apparently paranormal events with objectivity or thoroughness. Carrington found it had all started as a joke at a factory and that soon almost the entire population of the town was engaged in the conspiracy in the hope of enlivening what might have otherwise been a dull winter. To Mr X's chagrin, Carrington concluded 'that fraud and trickery is the complete explanation of all the phenomena witnessed or recorded in this case . . .'

The increasing use of cameras in modern times is likely to aid detection of fraud. Already Dr Hans Bender has videotaped a little girl, supposedly the 'focus' of a poltergeist like Annemarie at Rosenheim, in the act of cheating. At first, the tape shows the child tucked up in bed, hidden beneath blankets and a duvet. But as soon as the coast is clear, she leaps out, disappears to the other side of the room and re-emerges right in front of the lens with an ornament. She throws it and, as a loud crash rings out, hops back into bed and calls for her mother in a suitably surprised and anguished tone. Later, after reassurance from her mother, she settles down under the bedclothes and all is still – for a few minutes. Then, she gets up and the pattern of events is repeated. Unfortunately for her, the camera kept running.

Incidents like this, particularly those which involve small children, have convinced some researchers that poltergeists are always the result of fraud, whether conscious or unconscious. Among the first to put forward this view was Frank Podmore, an influential figure of the early days of psychical research. He advanced what became known as 'the naughty little child' theory because he believed that many supposed poltergeist effects are in fact created by young pranksters. Certainly, sceptical investigators have often felt justified in accusing people of trickery, although the allegations have been vigorously denied. A celebrated instance of this concerned a German doctor, Hans Rosenbusch, who accused Eleonore Zugun and her protector, Countess Wassilko-Serecki, of producing the scratches: allegations that caused a furore at the time and were never proved.

In many cases a mixture of mischief and bad observation seems to have resulted in the impression that a poltergeist is at work. This may explain the strange events that cruelly disrupted the lives of the Rev. Samuel Wesley and his family in December and January 1716–17. They lived at Epworth Rectory in Lincolnshire's beautiful Isle of Axholme. For weeks, the house echoed to strange noises – groans, knockings and the thud of heavy footsteps. The family's prayers were drowned by frenzied knockings and the dog cowered in fear.

But the British researcher, Dr Trevor Hall, believes that the 'poltergeist' was not the work of the devil, as the Wesleys thought. His re-examination of the case reveals that the family was unpopular in the parish; the local people disliked not only Samuel Wesley's theological outlook but also his

**Epworth Rectory, Lincolnshire, the scene of a famous 18th-century poltergeist case. The Rev. Samuel Wesley (*right*) denounced the terrifying events as the work of the devil, but modern researchers suggest they were caused by parishioners with a grudge against the Wesleys.**

tendency to run up debts. The frightening events at the Rectory may have been an attempt to drive him out of the parish, masterminded by the family's manservant, Robert Brown. Brown, according to Trevor Hall, had plenty of opportunity to create most of the effects himself and, rather suspiciously, was sole witness to some of them.

After so many years, definitive proof of fraud or genuineness is impossible to establish, but in at least one case from long ago, a sceptical attitude and an eagle eye proved decisive. In 1738, an elderly tailor called Flower and his wife, of Portishead near Bristol, suffered painful indignities:

'This old man and his old wife have severely felt the effect of it, for at every instant one or other had a bang on the head, or some other part of the body, with large stones, spoons, knives, etc., and divers people who visited the house for their satisfaction and truth of the matter, met with the same reception, and saw the windows broke, but knew not by what means . . .' An obvious poltergeist; but further investigation by a 'gentlewoman' who put 'no faith in such chimeras' unmasked a heartless young prankster.

According to *The Political State of Great Britain, February 1738*, she

The case of the Isle of Man's 'talking mongoose' was investigated by R. S. Lambert, editor of The Listener, seen (*right*) with Voirrey and Jim Irving who claimed 'Gef' lived in their farmhouse. When casts of 'Gef's' pawprints were debunked by an expert from London's Natural History Museum, few people continued to take the story seriously, but it inspired cartoons throughout the 1930s and today, 50 years on, it is commemorated by a local beermat.

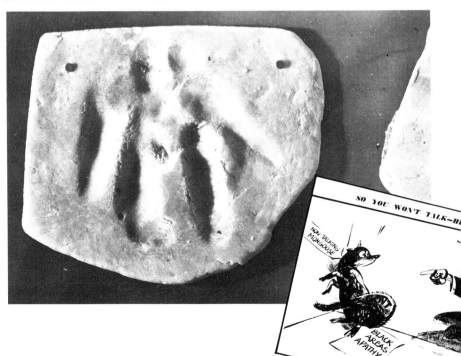

'began to look with a suspicious eye upon a little girl of about twelve years old, grand-daughter to the old people who, she always perceived, placed herself in a window behind whatever persons came into the room, and she receiving a blow on the arm with a spoon, conjectured it must come from the girl, and therefore immediately searched her, and to her surprise found two large pockets full of large pebble stones, etc., under her petticoats, which she artfully flung at convenient opportunities, and carried on this subtilty so far as to occasion much wonder that a little witch so young could manage her scheme so well to deceive a whole parish; for beside this she had a knack in changing her voice to several tones.'

Perhaps the most striking warning that good observation may yield dividends, in spite of all the trappings of paranormality, comes in a letter preserved in the voluminous correspondence files of the Harry Price Library at the University of London.

One of the most outrageous cases that Price was called upon to investigate concerned a talking mongoose called 'Gef', which a family named Irving claimed shared their lonely farmhouse in the Isle of Man. Although Gef was seldom seen (Price never so much as caught a glimpse of him on his visit to the farm) the mongoose was, reportedly, a loquacious little fellow, and also had quite a repertoire of popular songs.

The story was a 'natural' for the newspapers during the early 1930s, and reporters climbed the 700-foot hill to Gef's residence in trilbied droves. Harry Price was fascinated and amused by the tale, and enlisted the help of a team of investigators and scientists. By the time they had finished their work, the evidence for the existence of Gef was meagre indeed: a few blurry photographs of something in the fields outside the farmhouse, and some hairs, said to have been plucked from the mongoose but which, under the microscope, bore an uncanny resemblance to the fur of the Irving's dog, Mona. Price was inclined to think that Gef was a fantasy which provided entertainment and interest for the isolated family.

Like most of the rest of the population of the British Isles, a Unitarian Minister, the Rev. Rosamond H. Barker, and her mother and brother had enjoyed the story of the talking mongoose, but their reaction to it was coloured by the memory of a strange series of events that had occurred in their own house. Accordingly, she wrote to Harry Price from her home in Malton, Yorkshire, and urged him to consider all the possibilities, especially that one of the Irving family might have invented Gef and been responsible for his weird utterances. She told Price:

'For three years a middle-aged woman, who gave every appearance of being perfectly normal and trustworthy, played a somewhat similar trick on us: my father being dead, we three lived together; this woman – whom I will call X – acting in the capacity of working-housekeeper. She did everything possible to terrify us – created loud thumps in the middle of the night – whistled – ourselves thinking that the whistling came from outside, sometimes even from the surrounding hills although, at the time, X could not possibly have been more than a stone's throw from the house and must, indeed, very often, have been indoors, in bed. In judging of the whistling, I suppose one must, of course, allow for the fact that in our over-strung state, we may not have "located" it very correctly!

'When we came into a new house, we believe that X also simulated the crying of rats, so as to distress us with the fear that, on top of everything else, our new house, about the spotlessness of which we had been very particular, was infested . . .

'We lived in two places during this trying three years . . . In the first place – only a village – the police were unsuccessful in finding the culprit, but after we moved to the second district, a town, the police quickly discovered her. X had also, at this stage, become more daring and less circumspect. Looking back, the amazing fact is that we none of us, nor our relatives and visitors, suspected X . . .'

The Barkers were quite unable to establish any motive for this distressing behaviour; as Rosamond Barker told Price: 'We always treated X with the greatest kindness. Our only supposition is that, in some strange way, she was jealous of our social position and means and wished to ruin us.'

Some 'poltergeist' effects turn out to have explanations as natural as the functions of their human observers. In January 1979, for example, the residents of the Mount Pleasant Estate in Wisbech, Cambridgeshire, were alarmed by a menacing rumbling noise, rather like distant thunder, which recurred every half-hour or so during the evening. Sometimes houses vibrated so violently that ornaments flew from their places on shelves. One householder described a set of brass ornaments cascading to the floor.

Tension mounted on the estate. The strange vibrations seemed to grow in intensity. The police were called. After a few days of painstaking investigation they came up with an answer. The noises and shakings were being caused not by a poltergeist, but by something distinctly unparanormal: the failure of air-relief valves in the rising main of the local sewage system. Even the uncanny regularity of the outbreaks could be explained. This was due, one reporter of the story suggested, 'to the well-known phenomenon of the rise in water consumption coinciding with the "commercial breaks" of Independent Television transmissions'. In other words, when the advertisements came on there was a general rush for the lavatory, and the surge of water was too much for the plumbing system.

There have been many other events ascribed to poltergeists which have a more down-to-earth explanation. Literally so, for they have been caused by peculiar geographical or geological circumstances, usually involving the movement of underground water. Indeed, one British psychical researcher, G. W. Lambert, believes that physical events may be responsible for all poltergeist cases. 'The fact that no ordinary physical cause suggests itself,' he writes, 'does not mean that the cause must be a psychic one.'

Lambert put forward his arguments in 1955, and they form the basis of what is known as the Geophysical Theory of poltergeists. What he did was to look for a common factor in a number of well-documented poltergeist cases. What he found was that nearly half the cases under scrutiny had occurred in areas within three miles or so of tidal water. This fulfilled his hope, expressed at the outset, of pinpointing 'a force that is able to tilt a house enough to spill crockery off the kitchen dresser, to make sofas and chairs slide about in the drawing room, to tilt beds so that the people in them think they are being pushed out of them, to distort windows so that panes are broken (supposedly by stones) and wrench door-frames so that locked doors fly open, and, generally, to strain the timbers of the house in a way that causes them to groan and creak at almost every joint. The force, moreover, must be more often available in winter than in summer and, comparing one area with another, more likely to show itself near the coast than inland.'

To Lambert, the conclusion was obvious: 'So far as I am aware, the *only* force which answers to that specification is flood water, and as the water has never been actually seen 'at work', it must be moving in an unsuspected subterranean stream underneath the building that is affected.'

Since many poltergeist cases happened near the coast, the behaviour of tides must also play an important role. Lambert argued that the theory seemed to fit the facts in some famous poltergeist cases and, for example, attributed the attacks suffered by Esther Cox in 1878 and 1879 in a case in Nova Scotia known as the Great Amherst Mystery, to phenomena initiated by conditions in the nearby Bay of Fundy 'where the tides run higher than anywhere else in the world'.

A further refinement, based upon an examination of Scottish cases, was that earth tremors may play a key role. A surprising number of these have been recorded, indeed there have been enough to fill quite a substantial learned volume called *A History of British Earthquakes*. Lambert suggests that earth tremors can divert underground rivers from their normal channels and cause the water to surface in places which may be a long way from the epicentre of the geological disturbances.

Soon after Lambert had propounded his theory, a case occurred in north Yorkshire which offered some neat support for his arguments. It was solved by Dr Trevor Hall, thanks to his skills both as a professional surveyor and as an experienced psychical investigator.

In 1956, Hall was contacted by a doctor with a practice in a small market town: strange sounds had been heard in a house used by him and his partner as a surgery. The sounds varied, Hall says, and were described as 'explosions, rumblings and noises like the slamming of an enormous book', and they occurred at odd times – on some days they could be heard for an hour, on others the place was silent. The gas, water and electricity systems were checked by experts and found to be normal. The sounds seemed to ring out only when a young maid was in the house, and the medical men knew that poltergeists seem to thrive in the vicinity of young people.

The trouble had started in mid-November. Dr Hall arrived to investigate on 1 February, a day notable both for the violence of the sounds – one witness said it was like 'someone with an enormous hammer and chisel trying to break through the wall' – and for the sudden departure of the maid to nurse her sick mother. From the moment the girl left, there were no more noises.

At that stage, a poltergeist seemed the only explanation, but although there had been raps and bangs aplenty, and even the occasional bottle rolling from its appointed place, Hall was sceptical. For one thing, the maid appeared cheerful and well-adjusted, and very different from the arche-

Bath Road in Wisbech. The key to the 'poltergeist' outbreak lay in the drains beneath the street: the vibrations that terrified householders were caused by the failure of an air-relief valve.

typal poltergeist 'focus', who, according to the literature, tended to be tense and riddled with neuroses.

An inspection of the fabric of the house set Dr Hall off on quite a different trail. There were signs of extensive subsidence: the roof was in a sorry state with a sagging ridge and buckled slates; windows and doors were out of true. Life in Yorkshire, where subsidence caused by mining is a common feature, furnished the next vital piece of the jigsaw, for in the past Hall had come across reports of loud noises to be heard in a house which stood on subsiding foundations.

But why should there have been subsidence near the doctors' surgery? More puzzling still, why did the noises occur only when the maid was there and never when she had gone to visit her aunt and boyfriend in Hull?

This is where Trevor Hall's professional experience came in. He remembered examining some buildings which had been extensively damaged by the underground pumping of brine. He knew that if there were water under the surgery it might have caused damage related to the obvious subsidence. He guessed that surging water might still be damaging the house, and that the 'poltergeist' noises might be caused by its subsiding fabric. If this were correct, then he could explain the abrupt cessation of the poltergeist effects; for 1 February 1956, the last time they were heard, was the coldest day of the century in London. In Yorkshire, 20 degrees of frost were recorded, and the sea froze at Bridlington. If the underground water were frozen, then naturally the house would have stopped moving.

But how could water have got to the house and where had it come from? The doctors' long memories furnished part of the answer. Many years before, workmen digging at both the front and back of the house had discovered an ancient sewer which ran under the building. The investigators did not have to look far for a source of water. The town is dominated by two features: its fine church and the tidal River Ouse. So Hall, and a colleague, Dr Eric Dingwall, formed their theory. They wondered whether the exceptionally dry summer and autumn of that year had affected the foundations of the house and the soil beneath, causing them to be unusually sensitive to surges of subterranean water. Perhaps water from the river was being forced up the sewer at high tide. The resulting pressure in the new conditions might well be the cause not only of the damage to the house, but also of the knockings. Hall and Dingwall went straight to the tide tables. Without exception, the 'poltergeist' noises had all happened not only at the time of high tide but also on the days of the maximum tides. The true cause of the strange noises was established beyond any reasonable doubt.

Even so, there remained some questions. In particular, what was the role of the maid in all this? Why had the noises happened only when she was in the house? The only explanation, the investigators decided, was coincidence: during the weekends when she was away it just happened that the tides never reached the same heights as when the noises had been heard.

While the geophysical theory has interested psychical researchers, many of them have found it difficult to attribute some of the more subtle manifestations of the poltergeist to the shaking of buildings by subterranean tremors or water, or to believe that people inside would be unaware that the shaking was going on.

In the summer of 1961, the Cambridge researcher and authority on poltergeists, Tony Cornell, decided to test Lambert's theory. He persuaded the city's Borough Surveyor to lend him a small terraced house. Although it was due to be demolished, it was structurally sound and free from damp. With the help of a specially-constructed vibrating machine, the house was thoroughly shaken and, in addition, a metal weight of just over 60 pounds was used to pummel the end of the building. Inside, 13 objects were positioned in places where they might be affected by vibrations.

It was a thorough – even heroic – experiment. Although vibrations could be felt clearly, and sometimes painfully when the machine was first run, not one of the objects moved. Five thunderous swings by the 60-pound weight damaged the cement rendering and sent fragments of plaster showering from the ceiling, but the objects stayed exactly where they had been placed. Success of a kind came in the next series of swings with the weight. The third massive jolt moved a tripod leg about three-quarters of an inch from its position by the fireplace, and the fourth finally knocked it to the ground. But there was no movement from a marble which was on the floor and might have been expected to roll away, nor from a matchstick which was precariously balanced on the mantelpiece.

Finally, the intrepid experimenters turned up the machine to its top speed. Tony Cornell and Dr Alan Gauld bravely elected to stay inside and observe the effect of the vibrations. The house shook so violently that clouds of dust rose, plaster cascaded down, and a crack gaped over a window lintel. It was, they thought, 'quite our most terrifying experience in pursuit of the poltergeist'. But it was also one of the most conclusive, for only a few of the objects moved at all, despite the fact that the house was virtually being shaken to bits: a plastic beaker on the edge of the upstairs mantelpiece tumbled off a couple of times, a cup and saucer also fell off and a plaster ornament travelled three-quarters of an inch from the wall.

Enough was enough. They had seen nothing resembling the effects of a typical poltergeist. The geophysical theory as an explanation for all poltergeists lay in ruins, and Gauld and Cornell decided to end the experiment

Tony Cornell contemplates the problems of reproducing poltergeist effects. When the vibrating machine was up to speed, tremors could easily be felt in the walls of the house, but few objects inside moved at all.

before a similar fate overtook the house with them inside. A further test conducted by Tony Cornell in 1983 yielded similar results and did nothing to alter his earlier conclusions.

The results of the Cambridge investigations are a reminder that clear-cut explanations for apparent poltergeist phenomena are the exception rather than the rule. Certainly, there is no obvious solution to the macabre case of the moving coffins of Barbados.

The tale, set in a shadowy tomb on one of the most beautiful of all the Caribbean islands, with its overtones of voodoo, grave-robbery and sinister skullduggery, has caught the imagination of many psychical investigators.

The tomb is known as the Chase Family Vault and it lies in the graveyard of Christ Church, serving the settlement of Oistins in the south-west of Barbados. The churchyard is small and unkempt, and the Chase vault itself is architecturally unimpressive, with only its arched stone roof above the ground. A short flight of steps leads down to the entrance, now barred by a wrought-iron gate. Beyond, the chamber is dark and bare.

The curious events which made this unassuming grave famous throughout Barbados and, later, throughout the world, began many years after the grave was first hewn out of the Barbados limestone to be the final resting-place of a local worthy called the Honourable James Elliott who, according to the tombstone:

> was Snatched away from us
> the 14th day of May Anno Dom 1724
> in the 34th year of his age:
> and died Lamented by all who knew him.

No one knows whether the Hon. James was ever buried in the vault or, if he was, what became of his body; for in 1807, when Mrs Thomasina Goddard was interred there, the place was empty. A few months later, a tiny lead coffin containing the remains of Mary Ann Chase, the infant daughter of a local landowner, the Hon. Thomas Chase, was borne sadly into the shadows of the chamber and placed near Mrs Goddard. On 6 July 1812, the vault was re-opened for the funeral of one of Mary Ann's sisters, Dorcas.

Everything appeared to be in order but, the following month, when Thomas Chase himself died and the vault was prepared to receive his body, the lead coffins of his children were found to have moved. In particular, the tiny one holding the infant Mary Ann appeared to have been thrown from one side of the tomb to the other, and was leaning head down in the corner, almost upright. Perplexed, the funeral party straightened out the mess and sealed the tomb carefully.

Another infant, Samuel Brewster Ames, was next for burial. Again, when the tomb was opened, the other coffins were strewn around higgledy-piggledy. A similarly chaotic scene was discovered a few weeks later when Samuel Brewster, who had been murdered by slaves, was interred.

By the time Miss Thomasina Clarke came to be buried, on 7 July 1819, the parishioners of Christ Church knew all too well what to expect. Sure enough, when the heavy sealed door of the vault swung open, the lead caskets were in total disarray, and the wooden coffin containing the remains of Mrs Goddard had also been smashed, so that it had to be tied in a bundle before being put back in the vault next to Miss Clarke's coffin.

Large crowds had assembled at the churchyard, out of curiosity rather than grief, and the Governor of Barbados, Lord Combermere, had also turned up to witness the scene for himself. Rumour and suspicion were rife. The plantation owners suspected the negroes had staged the grisly tableaux. The local people themselves muttered that it was surely the work of 'jumbies' or 'duppies', the local daemons everyone feared.

As a result Combermere personally supervised security precautions. After an exhaustive but fruitless search for hidden tunnels or concealed entrances into the tomb, the coffins were carefully arranged in orderly fashion, the slab that sealed the vault was cemented into position, and the Governor made a series of 'secret marks' designed to alert him to any future tampering. The islanders were on tenterhooks to see what might happen next and, on 18 April 1820, some ten months after the vault had last been opened, the final act in the strange drama of the moving coffins began.

Lord Combermere and some friends decided to visit the graveyard. One of them, the Hon. Nathan Lucas, grandfather of the writer Charles Kingsley, wrote an account of what happened:

'We took eight or ten of the men directly with us to the Church Yard to open the Vault and sent off for the Rector, the Rev. Dr Thomas H. Orderson, who very soon arrived. His Lordship, myself, Robert Boucher Clarke and Rowland Cotton Esqrs: were present during the whole time.

'On our arrival at the Vault every outward appearance was perfect; not a blade of grass or stone touched . . .' Inside, of course, it was quite a different story, and to his narrative Nathan Lucas attached two drawings, made by the Hon. Major Finck who had joined the party at the vault. As Lucas rightly concluded, the pictures speak for themselves. The first shows the coffins as they were left on 7 July 1819, after the funeral of Thomasina Clarke. On the left-hand side lay the coffin of Dorcas Chase next to those of her father, Thomas Chase, and of Samuel Brewster. The tiny coffin of the infant Samuel Brewster Ames had been placed on top of Dorcas's, while the caskets containing the remains of Mary Ann Chase and Thomasina Clarke reposed on the lids of the neighbouring coffins.

In the picture showing the scene in 1820, the arrangement has been rudely disturbed: Dorcas Chase's coffin has skewed round and is lying at right-angles to those of Samuel Brewster and Thomasina Clarke, which appear to be in their original positions; while Thomas Chase, S. B. Ames and Mary Ann Chase are at the back of the vault. Oddly, the bundled-up remains of the coffin of Mrs Goddard lay where they had been placed ten months before, and are not shown in the pictures.

Lucas was eager to make it clear that the scene could not have been stage-managed especially for their visit: 'Indeed collusion or deception was impossible; for neither ourselves nor the negroes knew anything of the matter; for the subject was hardly started in conversation before we set out for inspection and the Church Yard cannot exceed half a mile from Eldridge's.' And the Rev. Orderson affirmed that, in any case, the vault would have been virtually inaccessible to would-be mischief-makers, for

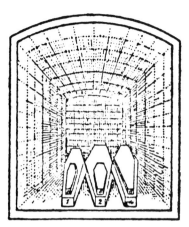

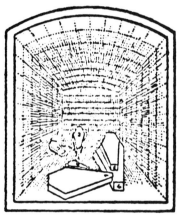

The entrance to the Chase Family Vault at Christ Church, Barbados where coffins seemed to move of their own accord. After a funeral in 1819, a sketch was made to record the coffins' exact positions; when the vault was re-opened the following year, they were in disarray, as the second sketch shows. The Governor of Barbados, Lord Combermere, could find no explanation for the macabre mystery.

'the descent into it is covered with a large block of blue Devonshire Marble which will take some hours to be removed and replaced again in its proper situation. It will take at least four able men to remove the stone.'

By now, understandably, the Chase family had had enough, and the coffins were removed from their unquiet tomb and buried in a grave, there to rest in the peace which had hitherto been denied them.

Although this is the most famous case of moving coffins, it is not the only one. In 1871, Dale Owen, in a book with the evocative title *Footfalls on the Boundary of Another World*, told a story he had heard from an acquaintance, Baron de Guldenstubbé. The tale, which is shot through with the gothick gloom of Baltic Europe, concerns a public cemetery on the Island of Oesel.

For some time, ghastly noises had been heard emanating from the cemetery chapel, and the horses of the local people were prone to break out into fits of sweating which, for a few unfortunate nags, resulted in a lingering death. At a funeral for a member of a local noble family, the matter came to a head.

'During the reading in the chapel of the service for the dead, what seemed groans and other strange noises were heard from beneath, to the great terror of some of the assistants, the servants especially.'

When a few brave souls descended to the vault beneath the chapel they found, 'to their infinite surprise, that, of the numerous coffins which had been deposited there in due order side by side, almost all had been displaced and lay in a confused pile'.

After this had happened for the second time, a commission of inquiry was appointed. Its members locked and doubly sealed the vault, strewd the floor with ashes to show up tell-tale footprints, and posted relays of guards outside. After three days and nights, the commissioners returned:

'Both doors were found securely locked and the seals inviolate. They entered. The coating of ashes still presented a smooth, unbroken surface. Neither in the chapel nor on the stairway leading to the vault was there the trace of a footstep, of man or animal. The vault was sufficiently lighted from the chapel to make every object distinctly visible. They descended. With beating hearts, they gazed on the spectacle before them. Not only was every coffin, with the same three exceptions as before, displaced, and the whole scattered in confusion over the place; but many of them, weighty as they were, had been set on end, so that the head of the corpse was downward. Nor was even this all. The lid of one coffin had been partially forced open, and there projected the shrivelled right arm of the corpse it contained, showing beyond the elbow; the lower arm being turned up toward the ceiling of the vault!'

Barbados has boasted (if that is the right word) at least two other stories of moving coffins. All these macabre movements have, at various times, been attributed to the work of poltergeists, for the precautions taken in many cases against the possibility of hoaxes or human interference make the events hard to explain in normal terms. This is no doubt why, over the years, some desperately fanciful theories have been advanced as solutions. One of them is that the gases from the decomposing bodies somehow propelled the coffins around the vault, although why so few unfortunate corpses should have suffered from this odd post-mortem condition is not explained.

Then again, a letter, quoted by the broadcaster Valentine Dyall and said to have been written by a relative of Samuel Brewster Ames, one of the children buried in the Chase Vault, puts forward a different, but equally extraordinary theory. The writer suggests that the coffins may have been moved by giant fungi:

'We know that the force responsible for the "happening" is one capable of lifting great weights and yet subject to some geographical limitations: for not all the remains were disturbed. Vegetative growth of a fungoid character fulfils all these requirements. The explanation, therefore, is physical.

'Men of science have recorded that giant spherical fungi, similar to our native puffball but having a circumference of over twenty feet, grow in caverns in Honduras. Though anchored in crevices by a thread-like stem, these fungi will lift great rocks. When ripe the spheres explode noisily, disintegrating into fine powder. Favourable winds could carry spore to Barbados.'

Undoubtedly the most popular theory is that the coffins were moved by flood water which, by the time the tomb was opened on each occasion, had dried up. Nathan Lucas, though, was pretty doubtful that this was the explanation: 'Why were the coffins of wood in situ? And why was the bundle of Mrs Goddard's decayed coffin found where it had been left? Wood certainly would first float. There was no vestige of water to be discovered in the vault: no mark where it had been; and the vault is in a level Church Yard, by no means in a fall, much less in a run of water.' Furthermore, the churchyard is on top of a hill.

More recent investigations have cast up different theories. In the 1970s Iris M. Owen of the New Horizons Research Foundation in Toronto took the opportunity offered by a holiday in Barbados to visit the Chase Family Vault. A detailed examination of the site revealed two possibilities. The first was a rusty iron pipe which she found running along the back wall of the vault and which seemed to be part of the original construction. If the pipe had been in place at the beginning of the 19th century, it could easily have leaked or funnelled water into the vault during hurricane storms.

The second thing Mrs Owen noticed was that the vault is very near the churchyard wall. 'It could have been a comparatively easy matter to remove bricks from the churchyard wall, dig out a few inches of earth, and then break into the rough rubble at the back of the vault. It is reported that the Hon. Chase was a cruel and unfeeling man. He may have been a hard taskmaster to his slaves . . . The churchyard is off the main road even today, and at night time it must be very quiet and one could work undisturbed. At the time of the happenings it would have been quiet and dark indeed. It could have been an act of revenge, in an effort to frighten away a cruel and unfeeling master . . .'

As long as the story is still told, people will advance new theories – another recent one is that the whole saga is an elaborate Masonic myth. What is clear is that this is one of the many cases where the evidence for the phenomena having been caused by a poltergeist is outweighed by more prosaic possibilities, in this instance, floodwater, resentful slaves, or even faulty plumbing.

There are still many poltergeist cases which cannot easily be explained away. Physical phenomena do not seem to provide all the answers, and complex theories involving electromagnetic forces and other weird effects have also received short shrift. Few experts today have gone to the opposite extreme and suggested that the events are caused by some kind of malicious spirit. The general consensus is that the answer lies somewhere in the human psyche and, possibly, in the medical conditions that affect it. Only the supporters of the fraud hypothesis contemplate the problem with any degree of certainty, and they have by no means managed to produce conclusive evidence in many cases.

One lead, which has been hotly pursued, concerns the poltergeist 'agent' or 'focus'. This stems from the fact that a child is often at the centre of an outbreak and that the strange and unpredictable events usually take place when he or she is nearby. This would be a reasonable assumption if children were involved in all or most poltergeist cases, but, inconveniently, it is not so. Another piece of conventional wisdom is that the poltergeist is the product of unhappiness, guilt or sexual frustration, particularly in adolescent children, a release of emotion converted into a playful force which can move objects or disrupt households. No one, however, has suggested a mechanism by which this might come about.

A different possibility is that someone in the vicinity of a poltergeist outbreak is unconsciously using psychokinetic powers, an idea given such wide currency in recent years that many researchers now refer to the phenomenon as RSPK – Recurrent Spontaneous Psychokinesis.

Recent work has revived an old theory – that poltergeists are symptoms of conventional, though unusual, medical conditions; interesting similarities have been shown between the phenomena produced by poltergeist 'agents' and malfunctions of the central nervous system, such as Tourette's Syndrome and Psychomotor Epilepsy. This may, indeed, be the cause of some cases, but as a general solution it is unconvincing.

Little has changed, in fact, since Harry Price asked *Can we explain the poltergeist?* back in 1945, and gave as his answer: 'No! We know nothing whatsoever about *why* Poltergeists should infest a place, what they are, how to get rid of them, or how to attract them ... We cannot explain the mechanism of Poltergeist movements, displacements, 'voices', how they transport things, or how they produce fire or water, or the many varieties and varying intensities of sounds and noises. We do not know where they obtain the energy with which to move objects – sometimes heavy objects – or how they can hallucinate some people into believing they see or hear certain things or sounds, while other persons in the immediate vicinity see and hear nothing. And where do all the 'apports' [things that spontaneously 'appear' during an infestation] come from? Who loses them? And where do they go to when, as often happens, they disappear?'

We still do not know.

# 3

# Inside Information

ONE SATURDAY MORNING in the summer of 1974 Mrs Lesley Brennan lay on the sofa at home watching an old movie, *The Nevadan*, on television. Suddenly the film, she says, was interrupted by a newsflash announcing that there had been a serious explosion in the large chemical plant at Flixborough, in Lincolnshire. Many people had been killed and injured.

Irritated though she was at the interruption to the adventures of the Nevadan, Mrs Brennan registered the story particularly, because it was local. The Flixborough Nypro plant which produced caprolactam, a basic material of nylon, covered a 60-acre site 20 miles inland from Mrs Brennan's home at Cleethorpes, near Grimsby, on the east coast of England. Shortly afterwards, around noon, two friends, Janice and Peter East, came in from work and Mrs Brennan told them the news. They then forgot about the incident until they were watching the early evening television news.

Mrs Brennan says: 'We sat laughing, because they said it had happened at teatime. We sat there saying: "Silly reporters. Got it wrong again. It was midday, dinner time, not teatime, it happened." Anyway, next morning we got the paper, *The Sunday People*. It said the accident happened at five o'clock in the afternoon.

'I went ever so cold. I really went funny. We went out and got another paper and that said teatime too. My friends said, "You told us at dinner – twelve o'clock." In fact the Nypro plant had blown up at 4.53 p.m. in the afternoon of Saturday, 1 June 1974, killing 28 people and damaging nearly 2000 factories and shops. By chance, though the site was remote, a Yorkshire Television camera team happened to be in the area, and filmed some graphic scenes within minutes. The event took place about five hours after Mrs Brennan had claimed to have heard about it from the newsflash. The two friends confirmed the story immediately afterwards to Mr Robin Furman, who then wrote an account for the *Grimsby Evening Telegraph*.

Mrs Lesley Brennan (*inset*) at Flixborough, scene of the 1974 disaster in which 28 people were killed and news of which she 'saw' on television hours before it happened.

*Right:* **Rescuers help survivors of the sunken submarine HMS Artemis at Gosport.** *Above:* **Sandra MacDonald, who made a nightmare prediction of the accident.**

Grimsby, as it happens, already held a place in the history of precognition. It was a Grimsby woman, Sandra MacDonald, who claimed to have foreseen the dramatic sinking of the Royal Navy submarine HMS *Artemis* in 1971. Then 17 years old, Sandra had gone out with a number of the sailors from *Artemis* when the boat had paid a 'courtesy' visit to Grimsby. At the Mecca Dance Hall the submariners made an exotic addition to the squad of lads from the local fishing fleet. They made a big impression on the girls of Grimsby, and then, as sailors do, they moved on.

Three days later, Sandra MacDonald came running downstairs after a terrible nightmare in which she had seen the submarine sinking in a port or dockyard. 'I saw it disappearing under the water. There were people running all over. Then for some reason there were three men that were in this compartment, and I knew they were trapped. It was Doug and Taffy

and another man I didn't know. In my dream one of them died.' Sandra told the story to her mother, and also to a number of friends. 'Well then, a week later, I came home from Tiffany's and my Mum said, "I've got bad news for you. The submarine's gone down. And there's three trapped." I just broke down and sobbed.'

*Artemis* had in fact sunk at her moorings at Gosport in Hampshire because she had been wrongly ballasted. It was ten and a half hours before the three trapped men were rescued from the watertight compartment to which they had retreated. But, contrary to Sandra MacDonald's dream, they all survived, including the two she had dreamt of. There seems little doubt from the array of testimony collected by Dr Keith Hearne that Sandra had indeed reported her dream in quite precise detail to a number of friends as well as her mother in the days before the sinking took place.

Across the Atlantic in the summer of 1976 the Teton Dam in eastern Idaho failed on 5 June, killing 11 people and causing damage on a massive scale. Dr Lucille Wood-Trost, who lived in the area, took the opportunity to ask through local radio and newspapers whether there had been any precognition of the disaster. She had 18 replies. One woman, the wife of a man who had worked on the dam, had had a persistent dream that her neighbour's goats were being washed away in a flood and drowned. The dream recurred at least three times, despite the fact that in real life the goats were never normally near the water. But the day before the flood, the neighbour moved them to pasture on an island in the middle of the Snake River. They were all lost. Another woman, who had not lived in Idaho for 19 years, dreamed the night before of going back to visit her relatives. As they crossed the Snake River Bridge, 'Huge waves began to come over it. They finally snapped the bridge in half.' The bridge did indeed break in the real flood the following day. Both dreams were confirmed by the women's husbands.

**Dr Lucille Wood-Trost, who investigated claims of premonition about the Teton Dam disaster, Idaho, 1976.** *Below:* **Flood waters force a breach.**

Sensations of premonition and clairvoyance – seeing across time and space – are probably the most universal of the mind's 'strange powers'. Even among the upmarket readership of *The Times*, more than half of the respondents to a questionnaire admitted to at least one personal experience of precognition – having 'an impression, hunch or vision concerning events you did not know about or expect, but which turned out to be true'.

It is important in assessing such experiences to try to separate them from the mind's extraordinary powers of visual imagination. Everyone dreams at night, many have a fantasy life more vivid than their mundane reality. The mind will absorb clues to the future. Frequently perceptions of imminent death can be ascribed to a friend or spouse unconsciously noticing some tell-tale signs of sickness or decline. The hidden logic of the mind draws its fatal conclusions.

Professional clairvoyants, the Genuine Gypsy Rose Lees, the suburban practitioners operating through the small ad columns of newspapers, rely more consciously on small signs and give-aways among their clients. Professional magicians use the same techniques on stage in mind-reading and clairvoyance acts. If necessary, and if the effort is worth it for professional or even criminal intent, the clairvoyant may, like the medium, indulge in some prior research. It has been a lucrative field for at least a hundred years on both sides of the Atlantic. But when the clutter of avarice and fraud has been cleared away and all cases with a known rational explanation disposed of, there still remains an extraordinary body of challenging testimony to consider.

War has inevitably produced the most intense premonitions of imminent death. Wing Commander George Potter from Bushey in Hertfordshire developed a terrifying facility for foreseeing deaths among his comrades during the relentless RAF campaigns against Rommel's German troops in the Western Desert in 1942. Once he saw the commanding officer of a torpedo aircraft squadron drinking in the officers' mess. 'Gradually I saw his head and shoulders moving in a bottomless depth of blue-blackness. He had eye sockets but no eyes, the flesh of his face was dully blotched in greenish purplish shadows, with shreds peeling off near his left ear.'

The CO died within two days, shot down off Benghazi – the 'blue-blackness' of the Mediterranean had claimed him. Wing Commander Potter had other premonitions too, but with thirty or forty million casualties in the Second World War and the universal tensions and stresses of those six years of conflict, it is inevitable that nightmares and hallucinations, anxieties and apprehensions, should have, on statistical grounds alone, produced what seemed like premonitions fulfilled.

However, the war was over when one of the most striking of such incidents occurred to Air Marshal Sir Victor Goddard of the Royal New Zealand Air Force. In January 1946 he was in Shanghai. Goddard's friend George Alwyne Ogden, the new British consul, decided to give a cocktail party on the night before he was due to fly home. It was a crowded occasion. Suddenly, through the hubbub, the Air Marshal heard a voice behind him say, 'Too bad about Goddard. Terrible crash.'

The speaker was an English naval officer, Gerald Gladstone – later

*Right:* **Air Marshal Sir Victor Goddard before the flight home to New Zealand.** *Below:* **From wireless operator James Bryant's wartime photo album, the Dakota, call-sign Sister Ann, after it had crash-landed.** *Far right:* **Sir Victor with his scrapbook of the strange – and exactly predicted – events.**

FORCED LANDING OF "SISTER ANN" ON BEACH, TAKACHI, SADO ISLAND, JAPAN, 14-1-46 PASSENGERS : A/M. GODDARD — HB. Ms CONSUL GEN SHANGHAI, MR G.H. OGDEN — W/CDR. TAYLOR — S/LDR ALLAN — MISS BRAKESPEARE

Admiral Sir Gerald Gladstone. The two men knew each other. Goddard turned. And Gladstone froze. 'I'm terribly sorry . . . I mean, I'm terribly glad.' Then he began to entreat Goddard not to fly, saying he had had the most vivid, involuntary vision of Goddard in a Dakota plane in a snowstorm. It had come over mountains in a storm and then crashed in the evening on a 'rocky shingly shore'. There had been two civilian Englishmen and a girl on board as well as the crew.

Goddard relaxed, for although he was indeed due to fly on to Japan in a Dakota – Lord Mountbatten's personal plane – he was taking only his military crew, certainly no passengers. Only a few minutes elapsed, however, before a messenger came in to the party with a radio signal for the consul: Ogden was asked to go to Tokyo at once for an urgent meeting. He asked Goddard to take him along. Then an English reporter, Seymour Berry of the *Daily Telegraph*, begged a ride. Reluctantly, Goddard agreed. Just as the party was ending came another message. A secretary was needed in Tokyo. Could Ogden bring one with him? The girl chosen was Dorita Breakspear.

The party in the Dakota, call-sign *Sister Ann*, took off for Tokyo the following morning. It was a long flight. The radio went down. By three in the afternoon there was snow. Goddard registered that time was beginning to tick off Gladstone's premonition – a Dakota, two men and one girl civilian passengers, failing light, and snow. Then, as they came over the Japanese coast in ten-tenths cloud – mountains. It was clear they were off course. Fuel was low. What were they to do?

They decided to look for an emergency landing. Below the clouds, as they came down, was a howling snowstorm. The first thing they could make out was a small fishing village and the only flat area in sight a stretch of 'rocky, shingly shore'. Out at sea the waves were mountainous. There was no alternative to an emergency landing on the beach. Goddard, by now certain that fate had caught up with him, watched as the pilot tried three times to land. The plan was to come in with the wheels down, then retract the undercarriage to stop *Sister Ann* sticking in the shingle and cartwheeling. On the third pass the Dakota hit the ground. There was no time for any action on the undercarriage. The plane slewed across the beach to the sound of tearing metal. Ogden was thrown out of his seat. Then silence. After a few moments Goddard realized he was still alive. So was Ogden. So was the girl, Dorita Breakspear, and Seymour Berry and, indeed, the whole crew. Villagers ran down to help them out of the wreckage, all unscathed. The premonition had been fulfilled in every respect. Except the last.

The frisson that follows violent, random, sadistic death despatches its vibrations rapidly through any community. In the damp autumn of 1979 the people of England's largest county, Yorkshire, were experiencing perhaps more acutely than any peaceful community in modern times, the tremors from a series of frightful killings. Already 12 women were dead and four others had barely escaped with their lives. The last murder, with knife, hammer and screwdriver, had been as horrific as the previous 11, though the public had not yet been told the dreadful details. Still, enough was known to make every woman in the county careful about going out after dark. Firms organized special cars to take their staff home at night;

university clubs and societies cancelled meetings unless they could provide coaches or escorts to take girls back to their homes; the night life of Bradford, Leeds and Huddersfield was at its lowest ebb. In the charged atmosphere, naked fear was dominant as the police seemed no nearer to capturing a murderer armoured by what seemed supernatural impunity.

It is not surprising, either, that there were presentiments and premonitions, clairvoyants who 'saw' the time and place of the next killing, dreamers who described the features of the 'Ripper', women who were certain that if they went out that night they would be the next victim. They all telephoned the police. And the police, already overwhelmed with reports from a frantic public, took note – and took such precautions as they could. The press and television dutifully and sceptically investigated the tips and visions that came the way of their news desks.

So it was in no great mood of expectation that a girl from the London office of the *Yorkshire Post*, Shirley Davenport, made her way to an address in south London one day in October 1979. She had been sent to interview Mrs Nella Jones who was claiming to have had a clairvoyant vision of the Yorkshire killer. Miss Davenport is an experienced reporter. She knew that whatever Mrs Jones said would never get in the paper: it might inspire a 'copy cat' killer; it might merely add further tangles to the jungle of information already smothering the police. Nevertheless, she made careful note of what Mrs Jones had to say, went back to the office and wrote it up. The story was duly 'spiked' and never published. Three months later Mrs

Peter Sutcliffe, the 'Yorkshire Ripper', in the cab of his lorry. Nella Jones, who reported to the Yorkshire Post that she had had a clairvoyant vision of the killer.

Jones came up with more information. Again Shirley Davenport noted it, but without writing it up. At the beginning of November 1980 Mrs Jones reported 'seeing' the next killing. It would be 17 or 27 November, she said.

On the night of 17 November the 13th victim died. Shirley Davenport was shaken. She went back through her notes, but still the paper refrained from publishing anything. The New Year of 1981 came, and then, at last, by a combination of luck and 'normal police work' the Yorkshire killer was caught. Ignoring the usual restraints, the networks fed the nation with every detail they could find about Peter Sutcliffe, killer of 13 women. Shirley Davenport, sitting in front of a television set 200 miles away in London, watched with growing astonishment.

Peter Sutcliffe was a lorry driver working for a firm called Clark Transport. Miss Davenport remembered that in the very first interview, a year and four months earlier, Mrs Nella Jones had said the 'Ripper' was a lorry driver called Peter and that she could see a name beginning with C on the side of his cab. Miss Davenport went for her notebooks. The January 1980 report was quite specific. The killer, said Mrs Jones, lived in a big house in Bradford, No. 6 in its street. It was elevated above the street behind wrought-iron gates, with steps leading up to the front door. In amazement Miss Davenport watched as the first pictures of Sutcliffe's home came up on the screen. It was No. 6 Garden Lane, Bradford. As the police and press milled about in the road, the house itself loomed above them in the dark. There were indeed wrought-iron gates. There were indeed steps up to the front door.

It has to be said that Nella Jones made a stream of predictions about the 'Ripper', some utterly wide of the mark, some, in her subsequent accounts, differing from her reported statements at the time. But Shirley Davenport says: 'It was still the most weird experience. It went far beyond anything coincidence or guesswork could possibly have provided. And you have to remember that for the previous two years all the public signs had been that the police were looking for a man who came from the north-east of England, a hundred miles away and who worked in an engineering plant.'

Premonition need not be doom-laden. Throughout the Western world, punters scouring the *Daily Racing Form* or the *Sporting Life* pray fervently every morning that some vision will be vouchsafed to them – preferably at a transparently attractive price, like 33 to 1. And it does happen – Lord Kilbracken, the late English peer, claimed to dream of race horses with a clairvoyance worthy of *The Rocking Horse Winner*.

His successes began when he was an undergraduate at Balliol College, Oxford, in 1946, and still plain John Godley. He dreamed that two horses, Bindal and Juladin, were winning at Plumpton and Wetherby racecourses. When he woke up he checked the paper and the two horses were listed. That afternoon they both won. Within a month Godley dreamed of another double. He told his friends Kenneth Harris and Angelica Bohm. This time he decided to eliminate all scepticism by having the names of the horses, Baroda Squadron and The Brogue, witnessed and time-stamped by the Oxford Post Office. Again, both won.

Godley became Racing Correspondent of the *Daily Mirror* and the gift stayed with him sporadically for more than a decade, including a hefty win on the 1958 Grand National winner, Mr What, an outsider at 18 to 1.

The Grand National had provided another Fleet Street tale more than 30 years before, when the celebrated columnist, Hannen Swaffer, reported in the *Daily Graphic* on the morning of the 1921 race that his friend, Dennis Bradley, had had a dream. All the horses in the race had fallen except three, and the winner was a horse in tartan colours – Shaun Spadah. Though 35 horses started – events turned out precisely as Bradley had dreamed.

Peter Fairley, then Science Correspondent of Britain's Independent Television News, had a series of profitable visions of winners of England's classic races, though the horses' names seemed to come to him more through coincidence rather than dreams. Though not a betting man, he heard the name Blakeney four times on the morning of the 1969 Derby – none of them connected with the horse of that name which, to Peter Fairley's advantage, duly obliged at Epsom that afternoon at 15 to 2. Two years earlier he had backed a filly called Pia in the Oaks at 100 to 7 after receiving a letter from a lady called Pia and then reading a story about Pia Lindstrom, when previously he had never heard of the name. L'Escargot won for him at 33 to 1 after he had found out there was a horse of that name while eating in the eponymous restaurant in London's Soho. The run went on. 'But then, for no apparent reason, I seemed to lose the gift,' said Fairley.

Fairley himself was the recipient of the forecasts of a young Australian George Cranmer, who first dreamed of a horse called Foinavon winning the English Grand National in 1967 – he saw the jockey's colours. In one of the most dramatic and casualty-strewn races ever, Foinavon, the rankest of outsiders, picked his way through the fallen to win at 100 to 1. Then Cranmer reported seeing a horse carrying Ribocco's colours in the winning enclosure at the Derby. Unfortunately it was the wrong Derby: Ribocco came second in the 1967 English Derby at 22 to 1, but went on to win the Irish Derby at 5 to 2.

A building company director from Richmond in Surrey, England, had a bizarre experience when one of his customers came to see him in November 1947. The director, Mr M. B. Campbell of Campbell and Co., afterwards gave an affidavit of the circumstances. 'I certify that during the morning of 10th November 1947, Mr A. S. Jarman [the late Archie Jarman, a businessman and diligent psychical researcher whom we shall meet again in this book] called at this office and told me of a dream he had had the previous night relating to a horse winning a race, and the figures 2020. We looked together through the morning paper to see if these figures could be relevant to the statistical figures of a horse running that day, but could find nothing apt. The following morning Mr Jarman showed me a morning paper which reported that a horse named Twenty Twenty had won the 3.45 race at Leicester the previous day. We had not considered the names of the runners when trying to allocate the figures 2020 the previous day.'

It was certainly odd. Twenty Twenty was by a stallion called Rosewell out of a mare called Thirteen. It had won only one race previously in its career before taking the Stoughton Plate with Gordon Richards riding. Jarman, who lived in the seaside resort of Brighton in England, had, he said, seen himself standing between the sea and a race track. As the racing horses came towards him all except one veered away and disappeared into the sea. The lone horse, ridden by a man in a business suit, kept its course. 'Facing the stands,' he recounts, 'was an enormous long white board supported on posts and on this appeared one after the other the figures 2–0 2–0. The horse and horseman had disappeared but they had evidently won the race and it was a popular victory. I felt a sense of elation and shared in the excited talk among the racegoers. That was the end of the dream.' To his eternal regret Jarman assumed that the figures had to do with the winner's previous form or number on the race card. He and Mr Campbell never thought to look at the horses' names. Jarman never again had a racing dream.

There is one horse-racing coup, however, which has been waiting around to be pulled off for 50 years. And it is still waiting. The famous Hollywood character actor, Wilfrid Hyde White, is convinced that there was revealed to him, in 1935, an entire card of winners at Royal Ascot for some time in the future.

Languid, archetypal Englishman in so many films, Wilfrid Hyde White has a truly British devotion to the Sport of Kings and particularly to racing's most elegant occasion – the Royal Ascot meeting in June. One afternoon in 1935, a week or so before the opening day, Hyde White and a friend decided to stroll over to the Ascot course for an anticipatory peek before the crowds descended on the scene. In his own words: 'We were' approaching the stands when we became aware of a murmur of voices. From the Heath came similar sounds, mingled with hurdy-gurdy music and the raucous tones of tipsters.' Then there was the National Anthem, a burst of cheering and the sounds of an invisible Royal procession making its traditional way

**Wilfrid Hyde White, and Royal Ascot in the 1930s. In 1935 he heard a ghostly commentary of a race – which has not yet taken place.**

down the course, as sovereigns have done since George IV's time. They heard the voice of a small child saying, 'Look, the lady isn't wearing a crown.' Hyde White, by his own admission not averse to believing in apparitions, imagined that perhaps they were experiencing the ghostly return of some Royal Ascot of Queen Victoria's day.

'Then something happened,' he asserts, 'which put things in an entirely different light. A disembodied voice began to announce the runners and riders for the first race. I can't remember when this system was first introduced in Britain but it was unheard of in 1935, and we listened in shocked amazement. More surprising still, the names of the horses were completely unfamiliar to us. I, who find it hard to memorize the lines I have to speak in a play or film, can recall the name of every good horse which has run in England since I was a boy. This lot meant nothing to me.'

Hyde White and his friend wandered down to the rails of the deserted racecourse as the voice announced, 'They're off!' 'We heard the thunder of the hoofs, listened to the comments of those about us, and were told who was first, second, and third.' Gradually, according to Hyde White, they realized that they were hearing the noises of a race meeting of the future. The commentator went right through the card and even announced the daily double – £183 – before a shower of rain sent the two men scurrying back to the stand, and back to the present.

They made a careful note of all the winning horses but, half a century on, the ghostly runners still have not appeared before the Queen – and Wilfrid Hyde White's greatest coup has not come off. This odd tale has none of the evidence which makes other premonitions so convincing, but Hyde White has promised that when he is no longer able to lay an earthly wager, he will leave behind the phantom names in case they at last come along to haunt the bookmakers of England.

Peter Fairley, the man who really did have a winner, was instrumental in launching the two serious attempts to validate precognition – the British Premonitions Bureau in London and the Central Premonitions Registry in New York.

Fairley's London Bureau, set up through the *Evening Standard*, was the first systematic attempt to record premonitions, and to see how well they matched subsequent happenings. One event, the disaster of Aberfan, had precipitated the idea. On the morning of Friday, 21 October 1966, a huge mass of coal waste, loosened by incessant rain, moved down the side of a valley in south Wales and enveloped the Pantglas Junior School, Aberfan. It was one of the worst civil disasters in British history – 116 children died and 28 adults. As television screens were cleared to follow the hopeless task of the rescue teams and the story drove everything else from the front pages of newspapers, it became apparent that many people felt they had had a warning of the tragedy. The most heart-rending of these came from a little nine-year-old girl, Eryl Mai Jones, who lived in the valley. The day before she had woken in the morning and said, 'Mummy, you must listen to my dream. I dreamed I went to school and there was no school there. Something black had come down all over it.' Eryl Mai Jones was one of the Aberfan victims.

Dr John Barker was struck by the number of accounts in the newspapers from people who claimed to have had some hint of the impending disaster. He persuaded Peter Fairley to send out an appeal through the *Evening Standard* for people to report these premonitions. There were 60 replies which Dr Barker felt warranted further investigation. Eventually he decided there were 22 which had, without doubt, been reported to at least one other person before the event.

Some were astonishingly close in detail. Mrs Monica McBean, working in an aircraft factory 200 miles away from the scene, had had a vision of 'a black mountain moving and children buried under it'. The vision was so distressing that she had to go to the ladies' room and sit down. She told one of her fellow workers why she was upset. That was half an hour before the Pantglas school was buried. A London woman, Mrs Sybil Brown, reported a nightmare in which a child was followed by 'a black billowing mass'. She woke her husband and told him, 'Something terrible has happened.' This was still five hours before the mountain of soil moved.

The accounts were vivid but, from a scientific point of view, Fairley and Barker felt it was difficult to make anything of premonitions which were known only after the precognized event had occurred. Thus it was decided to set up the British Bureau and later the American Registry. Peter Fairley decided simply to time and date-stamp reported premonitions, then devise a system for calculating their subsequent accuracy. From the moment the first article appeared in the *Standard*, reports had flowed in – hundreds in the first month. Fairley had struck a vein which, unlike the usual nine-day wonders of Fleet Street, showed no signs of decline. There were upwards of 1000 replies in the first year. Fairley moved to Britain's Independent Television channel, to *TV Times*, and the Bureau went with him. Still the flow went on, by phone and by letter, for almost a decade, when it was taken over by Mrs Jennifer Preston.

'We arrived at a way of assessing these premonitions,' says Fairley. 'We gave up to five points for the unusualness of the event, five points for level of detail – in other words, if you saw a plane crash with a tail fin sticking up with a white or red cross on it, then you could identify the airline – and eventually we gave five points for accuracy of timing – a possible total of 15.

'It began to emerge that there were two people, a rather jolly ballet teacher in North London and a night switchboard operator in the East End, who were undoubtedly scoring above chance. So we had them in for interview. And that is where everything started to go haywire. Immediately these people felt they were good at it, they lost it completely – they began to apply conscious thinking. That, along with other research I've done, has led me to conclude, first, that there *is* something in it and, second, that whatever it is, resides in the non-conscious part of the human mind.

'There seems no doubt to me that premonition is literally a flash of intuition, instantaneous, and very overpowering to people when it happens. They just *know* this event is going to happen. There is not a shadow of doubt in their minds. But I'm afraid that with every single person that looked interesting, the same thing happened – they lost it when they started to think they were good at it.

'Now there's a parallel to this in the alpha rhythms of the brain. Basically an alpha rhythm comes through only when the person being investigated is doing and thinking practically nothing. It disappears the moment they try to

**Peter Fairley and** (*right*) **Robert Nelson, who set up British and American bureaux to investigate predictions.**

do something or to make some mental effort. If there is such a thing as premonition, I reckon it's in some way connected with the alpha rhythm part of the brain.'

Fairley himself felt that he lost his own ability to pick horse race winners for similar reasons. 'In the space of about three weeks one year – and not being normally a betting man – I made about £400. These were outsiders, all sorts of peculiar horses, not odds-on favourites. But I liked to laugh and joke about all this with my colleagues at ITN and they started to come up to me and say, "Got anything for the 3.30?" or whatever. And of course it began to go. The moment I applied any kind of conscious thought to it, the whole thing disappeared out of the window.'

The American Central Premonitions Registry was set up in 1968 in New York by Robert D. Nelson and Stanley Krippner of the Maimonides Dream Laboratory in Brooklyn. They felt they had some immediate 'strikes' with people predicting Robert Kennedy's assassination later that year. But, as with the British Bureau, many of the Registry's successes seemed to vanish like fairy gold when subjected to investigation.

For more than half a century spectacular disasters of the air have provided some of the most vivid stories of premonition – the special horror of spiralling helplessly down from the skies, trapped inside some crippled aircraft, has been one of the staple dramas of 20th century newspapers.

The Chicago DC10 crash of 1979 was a lurid addition to the nightmare. Not only was it the United States' worst air death toll, with 273 people killed, but it was particularly engraved on public imagination by the chilling pictures, snatched by an amateur photographer who happened to be near O'Hare Airport, of the stricken plane plummeting to the ground. But one man, David Booth of Cincinnati, Ohio, believed he had been living with that vision for ten days before the crash actually happened.

He had dreamed quite clearly of a big American Airlines jet, a three-engined plane, apparently trying to land. The engines did not sound right. Then, in his dream, he saw the plane roll over and crash in a mass of flames. 'It was like I was standing there watching the whole thing,' said Booth, 'like

The crash of American Airlines Flight 191 on 25 May, 1979 and (*above*) David Booth, who says he experienced a terrifying premonition of the catastrophe.

watching television.' The next night the dream came back again with equal intensity. 'I did everything to stop sleeping from then on. I'd watch TV until 2 a.m. One night I got drunk.' But for seven consecutive nights the dream recurred. Finally on Tuesday, 22 May, four days before the crash, David Booth decided he had to try to do something. He rang American Airlines. He rang the Federal Aviation Administration. He rang Cincinnati Airport control. And he was taken seriously. 'It didn't sound like a prank,' said Cincinnati Airport official, Ray Pinkerton.

On Thursday, 24 May, Pinkerton's colleague, Paul Williams, talked to Booth for about three-quarters of an hour. 'What he described to me, I thought might be a 727, because I knew that American Airlines flew Boeing 727s. Another possibility was a DC10. He specifically identified it as an American Airlines aircraft with an engine on the tail. He described his vantage point as beside a gravel road running up towards a flat-roofed building. He described the plane at rather a low altitude which I took to be two to four hundred feet. It suddenly turned sharply and dived into the ground. He described in great detail the explosion. He became quite distraught, almost as if he was seeing death occurring.' But no one felt there was anything practical to be done.

On Friday, 25 May, American Airlines Flight 191, a three-engined DC10, crashed on take-off. With the engine breaking away, the plane turned over on its back and crashed in flames. Paul Williams said: 'I heard about the crash on Friday afternoon on my way home from work about 5 p.m. As I was listening to the description of the crash on the radio, it sounded like a replay of what I'd heard the day before from David.' David Booth's nightmares stopped. 'It was uncanny,' said FAA official, Jack Barker. 'He named the airline, he called the right type of plane – three-engined – he said the plane came in inverted, which it did, and of course he reported it to officials just four days before it happened.'

Williams reflects: 'Perhaps the most remarkable coincidence of the whole thing was the similarity of the manoeuvre the plane made. It's a very unusual manoeuvre for a plane to make before crashing. Most of them crash with wings horizontal. They run into some obstruction, or there is a mid-air collision. But the manoeuvre David described was very unusual. As a matter of fact, it's the only one I've ever heard of in a plane that size.'

From the early days of passenger aircraft there have been vivid premonitions reported. A certain Mrs G. H. M. Holms, the wife of an Indian civil servant, had an unsettling dream while on holiday in Yorkshire. In the dream it was a cloudy day. Suddenly out of the clouds came the body of a man, shooting down at a terrific pace. 'He landed on his head a few yards from me, with a sickening thud,' she wrote. 'I heard something crack and said, "There goes his skull." The body rebounded and bumped into a tree. I saw some labourers hurry across the grass. They carried the body past me to a plastered thatched cottage, such as is never seen on the Yorkshire moors, with two or three apple trees round it.' Mrs Holms related the dream to her husband and a Welsh friend, M. Riley.

Four days later, on 21 July 1930, there was a gruesome and unusual accident in Kent in which the occupants of a small plane, including Lord Dufferin and Lady Ednam, were tipped out as the aircraft apparently broke

*Below:* **Lord Dufferin, killed in a bizarre air accident in Kent which was foreseen in Yorkshire.**

*Opposite:* **The airship R101 at Cardington, Bedfordshire, September 1930.** *Below:* **Its wreck, 5 October 1930. Several premonitions of the disaster were recorded.**

up. They landed on their heads in an orchard. Harold Ward, who lived at Leylands Orchard, Meopham, Kent, later told an inquest that he saw the plane turn over. Things that looked like small aeroplanes came from it.

'I did not realize what these objects were until they came lower. Then I saw they were human bodies. I rushed down the garden to the orchard. We searched and found four of the bodies. The other was found later.'

Mrs Holms's story would certainly have taken maximum points under Peter Fairley's grading system for timing, precision and unusualness. Unfortunately her two witnesses, her friend and her husband, were not asked to testify to the story until well after the event.

Three months later, when the celebrated airship R101, on a test flight to India, ploughed into the brow of a hill near Beauvais in France, bursting into flame and killing 46 people, there were some well-attested premonitions. A Liverpool man, J. S. Wright had dreamed of the R101 crashing six months previously. His friend Mr G. Coxon said they had considered reporting it to the War Office. 'Knowing, however, from past experience,' he wrote, 'how futile it has been to attempt to make any impression on a Government Department, we refrained from pressing the matter.'

Mr R. W. Boyd of Enfield, London, two days before the crash, told his fiancée, Miss Catherine Hare, of seeing R101 in difficulties, then crashing into a hilltop. He saw burning bodies falling from the aircraft and soldiers arriving at the scene on horseback. Many of these details – including the mounted soldiers – later appeared in newspaper reports and pictures. The glamour and the dangers of the great hydrogen-filled airships of the 1930s were so high in public consciousness, however, that it would perhaps have been surprising had there not been dreams and reports of a spectacular end for a vessel which had been the object of such immense ballyhoo.

There are many stories of statesmen being struck by premonitions. Abraham Lincoln dreamed he was walking through the White House and saw a flag-draped coffin. 'Who is it?' he asked. 'The President,' was the reply. Within days Lincoln was assassinated in Ford's Theater in Washington. Winston Churchill was repeatedly said to act on hunches or premonitions. On one occasion he ordered the kitchen staff into the shelter minutes before a bomb struck; on another he insisted upon getting into his car on the unaccustomed off-side, thus saving it from rolling over in a bomb blast.

Adolf Hitler was supposed to have scrambled out of a First World War trench, impelled by a dream of being buried, seconds before it was struck by a shell which interred and killed all his comrades. Canadian Prime Minister Mackenzie King acted on information about the future received, he seems to have thought, from dead politicians. Even Franklin Roosevelt consulted Jeane Dixon, the Washington 'seer'.

The loss of the liner *Titanic* provided a plethora of reported forewarnings. Almost a century on, it is still unnerving to read W. T. Stead's 1892 article in the London *Review of Reviews*. Stead, fresh from campaigning against child prostitution by buying a small girl for himself and thus jolting Victorian England into action, had turned his uniquely colourful style on

the inadequacies of safety precautions at sea. He described in awful detail the fate of a great liner which struck an iceberg in the north Atlantic and went down with enormous loss of life. Twenty years later, Stead himself went down with the *Titanic.*

There was an epidemic of visions in that April of 1912. Whether it was the passengers singing 'Eternal Father, strong to save' in the second-class dining room two hours before the ship struck the iceberg; or Mr J. Connon Middleton cancelling his trip after twice seeing a liner floating keel upwards in his dreams; or Mr Colin Macdonald refusing to take the job of second engineer, though it would have meant a promotion. The sea and ships are notorious for jinxes, superstitions, hunches – in fact, all the ills bestowed by the albatross upon the Ancient Mariner. But some of the *Titanic* stories are bizarre. Morgan Robertson's book, published 14 years previously, described a liner called the *Titan,* of almost identical dimensions to the *Titanic,* being struck by an iceberg and sinking in the month of April, in the north Atlantic.

Dr Ian Stevenson, Professor of Psychiatry at the University of Virginia, who has analyzed the *Titanic* cases, quotes an account from a lady in Stoke-on-Trent in England, Mrs Charles Hughes. She was 14 years old in 1912. On the fatal night of 12 April she dreamed she was walking towards Trentham Park in Stoke: 'Suddenly I saw a very large ship a short distance away as if in Trentham Park. I saw figures walking about on it. Then suddenly it lowered at one end and I heard a terrific scream.' She went to sleep again after telling her grandmother what she had dreamed. The dream recurred. The girl's uncle – the grandmother's son – was Fourth

Engineer Leonard Hodgkinson. He died on the *Titanic*. In all, Dr Stevenson has collected 19 *Titanic* cases.

Rational explanations are often available, however. Premonitions may simply have been well-grounded fears: for all the stories of the 'unsinkability' of the *Titanic*, icebergs were the prime terror of the north Atlantic sea passenger, as unpredictable and threatening as electrical storms are to the air passenger. A plane crashes somewhere every day in our modern world and few people who fly are immune from all apprehension. Statistics suggest that someone, somewhere, is having a nightmare about a plane crash every night of the year.

Fakery is not unknown, like Tamara Rand's alleged prediction on television of the attempt on President Reagan's life – the tape was in fact recorded after the event. The human memory is notoriously unreliable. Details accrete like barnacles to the testimony of witnesses as well as dreamers – but after the event. Some of the most celebrated cases disintegrate under cool investigation. Yet a string of intriguing and extraordinary cases remain: the little girl at Aberfan, Admiral Gladstone and the Dakota *Sister Ann*, Peter Fairley and the horse races, David Booth and the Chicago DC10 crash, the Flixborough newsflash – even the ability of British trades union leader Clive Jenkins to envisage the front pages of unpublished editions of *The Times* and describe them to his family. All these would suggest, if ever they are indubitably substantiated, that not only unusual powers of the human mind exist, but also a warp in our ideas of time itself.

April 1912. An artist's impression of the sinking Titanic W. T. Stead, who went down with the doomed ship, predicted a similar disaster 20 years earlier. *Below:* The last message from the Titanic.

# 4

# Mind
# Over Matter

STRANGE STORIES from the East are a newspaper sub-editor's surest standby, an entertaining solution to the insistent problem of a 'thin' news day when sensational headlines are scarce and empty columns wait to be filled. So the Peking correspondent of the London *Daily Telegraph* must have seized eagerly upon a report in his *Peking Evening News*, confident that his version of it would be welcome back in Fleet Street: 'Chinese scientists have found two girls in the South-west province of Yunnan who can make tree branches snap and flower blossoms open using mental telepathy, according to a report in a Peking Newspaper yesterday. The *Peking Evening News* reported that researchers from Yunnan University had conducted tests on the two girls to determine the extent of their telekinetic abilities.'

Just as baffling but no less beguiling to newspaper readers was this story, which was published throughout the world and attributed to a spokesman for 'certain Chinese scientists' who claimed: 'We have discovered over a thousand children who can read with their armpits and peel oranges with their minds. These young people will change the face of the world.'

Although nothing has since been heard of the tree-snappers of Yunnan or of the thousand cerebral orange-peelers, psychical researchers have been investigating cases of mind over matter for many years. Their premise is that some people can use their thoughts alone to alter or to affect their physical surroundings. This phenomenon, known as Psychokinesis, or PK for short, is said to be at the heart of all kinds of strange manifestations, including the dispersal of clouds and the levitation of tables.

Most famous of all these manifestations is psychic metal-bending, a feat popularized by Uri Geller, who came to public attention in 1973 and left behind him a trail of bent spoons, twisted latchkeys and arguing scientists.

Despite the doubts cast upon Geller's powers, his reputation as a 'psychic superstar' still lingers. In the summer of 1982, for example, America's mass-circulation *National Enquirer* announced that Geller

*Opposite:* **A 'paperclip scrunch'. Professor John Hasted** (*inset*) **of London University, has investigated claims that children produced these by mind-power.**

would transmit from the observation deck of New York's World Trade Center 'psychic energy that you can use to fix your broken watches, TVs, radios and other appliances'. The instructions to readers certainly promised to be easier, and cheaper, than calling in the repairman: 'If you have a small item that needs repair, place it on top of Geller's photo on this page of the *Enquirer*. If you have a large broken appliance, then place Geller's photo on top of it.

'"Stroke and talk to the broken item for 10 minutes," Geller advised. "Keep repeating to it, 'Work! Mend! Work! Mend!' Don't be bashful – shout it loudly, believing sincerely that it will be repaired. The results will amaze you."'

And indeed they did, according to a later issue, which announced that 'Hundreds of people all over America received telepathic signals' from the helpful Geller. 'Almost from the day of the experiment,' said the report, 'readers excitedly reported broken items started to work again as they concentrated with Geller.

'In Bowen, Illinois, Lynn Schoenherr's 16-year-old music box that hadn't played in years whirred into action. "Even the key that winds it was frozen in a fixed position," she said. "When the time came, I began stroking it and talking to it, saying 'Work, mend, work, mend,' just like Geller said to do. My family thought I was nuts. But after five minutes, the music box started to play 'Lara's Theme' from *Dr Zhivago* – slowly at first, then faster! I was astounded!"

'Margaret Pauley of Carmel, California, psychically cured the slipping clutch on her 19-year-old Mercedes. "Mechanics had told me it would cost over $300 to fix," she said. "I sat in the car, put Geller's picture under my left foot near the clutch and mentally said, 'Mend, mend,' over and over. Later, when I drove my car, the clutch didn't slip anymore!"'

These were just two of the satisfied customers.

There was a time when Geller's stunts attracted front-page headlines all

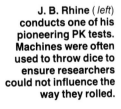

**J. B. Rhine** (*left*) conducts one of his pioneering PK tests. Machines were often used to throw dice to ensure researchers could not influence the way they rolled.

over the world – not just an inside page of *The National Enquirer*. In the decade since he first charmed and amazed his way into the public consciousness, however, the possibility that a few gifted individuals do possess psychokinetic powers has been popularly accepted, and these days only the most bizarre and spectacular manifestations of the PK phenomenon catch the attention of the world-weary sub-editor.

In fact the idea of PK – of mind over matter – is nothing new. After all, spirit mediums long ago discovered that the materialization from nowhere of a bunch of flowers or a keepsake would astound their sitters and provide convincing proof of unearthly powers. Eminent scientists like Charles Darwin had reported that chairs and tables had danced around the room at séances, and in 1871 a remarkable person called Mrs Guppy was said to have managed to transport herself, in the twinkling of an eye, from her home in Highbury, London, right into the middle of a séance being held in Lamb's Conduit Street several miles away – a feat made all the more impressive by the fact that Mrs Guppy was not easily conveyed anywhere by normal means, for she was said to be the fattest woman in London.

In the early days of scientific psychical research there were some fiascos brought about by the investigators' eagerness to believe in the existence of the paranormal and their trusting methods of enquiry. Oddly, the first man to try to put the investigation of PK on a proper scientific footing was not one of the physicists, medical men or psychologists who had dabbled in psychical research, but an American whose training had been in the gentle and quite unrelated discipline of botany. Joseph Banks Rhine set up the world's first university laboratory for the study of parapsychology at Duke University in North Carolina at the beginning of the 1930s. Rhine's inspiration for what became one of the dominant research programmes of his life came from one of the many casual visitors who turned up in his office at Duke University.

The year was 1934, and the publication of Rhine's best-selling account of his early work, *Extra-Sensory Perception* (discussed later in this book), had made him one of the most talked-about people in America. The visitor was a young gambler who told the fascinated parapsychologist that he used willpower to influence the way dice fell at the gaming tables, and that he could affect not only his own throws but also those of his opponents. When the young man had left, Rhine began to experiment with dice and was soon convinced that the gambler (whose name in later years he was quite unable to recall) had spotted something that had gone unnoticed in half a century of organized psychical research. The techniques of the gambling den, Rhine thought, might provide the key to studying the influence of mind over matter in the laboratory.

The experiments that Rhine embarked on at Duke University bore all the hallmarks of the ESP tests that had brought him fame and, in scientific circles, a certain amount of notoriety. Success or failure was measured on a statistical basis: the number of correct predictions of which face would be uppermost after the dice had been thrown was compared with the number that could be expected to occur by chance. In the early days several experiments gave good results, but these were conducted by volunteers in their own homes, unsupervised by scientists. This approach had stimulated stinging academic criticism of Rhine's earlier ESP tests, but he had defended it on the perfectly reasonable grounds that the experimental method was still being developed.

Even so, on the basis of early results Rhine assumed the existence of PK, and his Duke University team embarked upon a research programme which no one, either at the time or since, has been able to castigate for any want of ingenuity. Its purpose was to determine the characteristics of PK and circumstances in which it might flourish. Some researchers threw dice of different sizes, to see whether the mind could move small ones more easily than large (this seemed to be the case). Others rolled dice relentlessly for hour after hour and discovered for their pains that boredom killed PK ability. Some happy souls swigged gin, some sipped Coca Cola: alcohol was no help but the caffeine in the coke seemed to stimulate PK. Divinity students competed with hardened gamblers and both notched up high scores (perhaps because they both had faith, in their different ways); parties were held for children with prizes on offer in PK games. Machines were invented to throw dice and to eliminate unconscious human influence; hypnosis was used to entrance people under test, and character profiles of the participants were drawn up.

When Rhine first published his experimental results during the Second World War, they attracted little public attention: quite properly, matters military took precedence over papers parapsychological. But the criticism, when it came, was every bit as pertinent and hard-hitting as that which had been levelled against the Duke ESP research.

Most telling of all was the failure of other experimenters to replicate Rhine's findings. The early trials were condemned by one critic for being 'largely free-wheeling and off the cuff'. Indeed, he added, 'A well de-signed, rigorously executed test was the exception'. Too often, the subjects had tested themselves without any witness present to verify their findings; the tendency of a dice to fall so that the figure 6 was uppermost – a bias caused by the excavation of the dots in its surface – had seldom been taken into account, especially in tests where subjects specifically wished to make the 6 appear; and there were disturbing indications that people who believed in the phenomenon tended to make errors in favour of PK when recording which way the dice had fallen. 'The Duke experimenters seem to have fallen into pitfalls that an intelligent schoolboy should have avoided,' sniffed one British sceptic, and his reaction was echoed by many others in the orthodox scientific community.

But all this was, for practical purposes, too late; psychokinesis had speedily become an established and flourishing field of study, thanks to the dozens of experiments carried out during the first decade of its scientific 'life'. Above all, the phenomenon had a name and, before long, there were people coming forward with strange tales to tell and even stranger talents to demonstrate.

One of them was Ted Serios. Today he lives in obscurity in a grey clapboard house down a dirt track that cuts through the farmland of the Illinois-Missouri border in the American Midwest. As long as a good supply of beer and cigarettes is at hand, Ted is a happy man, for work has never bothered him unduly: 'If you gotta work and be poor,' he says, 'you might as well not work and be good 'n' poor.' His only regular job, apart from some spells with the US Merchant Marine, was as a bellhop at the Chicago Hilton Hotel. In any case, the weird talent that made Ted Serios an international celebrity was not one that any conventional employer would look for or know how to harness. For a brief but eventful period during the 1960s, Ted was the world's only 'thoughtographer', claiming that he could imprint his thoughts directly on to photographic film. He could apparently point a camera at his face and produce, by sheer thought, pictures of distant subjects such as famous buildings in Europe.

The man who undertook a sustained study of Serios was a respected psychiatrist from Denver, Colorado, Dr Jule Eisenbud. Eisenbud's experiments began in the spring of 1964, after Ted's thoughtographic powers had been brought to his attention by a magazine editor who thought they should be scientifically investigated. The tests took place in all kinds of locations – hotel rooms, lecture theatres, laboratories and television studios. When he decided to investigate his protégé's 'thoughtographic' powers, Dr Eisenbud also had to contend with one of the most wayward subjects ever to have come under the scrutiny of a researcher. Not only was Ted unable to produce his 'thoughtographs' to order, with the result that experiments sorely tried both Eisenbud's patience and his budget, but he would also suddenly leave Denver and go home to Chicago with no warning or date for his return. Added to this, Ted's formidable capacity for drinking those around him under the table meant that Eisenbud had to settle for what proved to be more in the nature of a scientific odyssey than a conventional research programme in controlled conditions. As his initial scepticism turned into conviction, Eisenbud was able to assemble an impressive array of academic witnesses.

Ted operated with a Polaroid camera, which not only produced photographs at the proverbial touch of a button but also eliminated any suspicion that trickery in the darkroom might be involved. He would usually aim the camera at himself or at the room in which he was being tested, but the photographs which emerged were sometimes of locations and scenes a long way from Denver, such as the Piazza San Marco in Venice or London's Westminster Abbey. At best these 'hits' were sporadic, and failures predominated, so that Eisenbud amassed dozens of pictures of his subject grimacing with the effort of trying to project his thoughts. There were also interesting intermediate successes, known as 'whities' and 'blackies'. As the term suggests, 'whities' were blank prints, bleached as though the camera had been pointed into a bright light instead of at Ted's face or a corner of the room. 'Blackies' were also blank but dark; the kind of print which would normally result from light being deliberately cut off from the lens. Needless to say, Ted Serios managed to produce 'blackies' without apparently doing anything to prevent the light from reaching the camera.

In a typical session Ted, Eisenbud and invited eye-witnesses would assemble in the evening. Cameras, preferably provided by the visitors, would be made ready and loaded with film, then sealed and marked against fraud. Meanwhile Ted, invariably with a quart bottle of beer in hand, would wait to become 'hot' enough to think an image on to film. Usually the investigators chose a specific target for him, such as a picture from a book, a well-known landmark, or a postcard, but sometimes the finished photographs showed scenes or objects quite unconnected with the target, though often with an uncanny significance.

As the session wore on Ted would become more and more erratic and domineering as the beer took effect. Eisenbud noted how 'Ted, in various stages of besottedness . . . became the impresario, the field commander, giving everybody orders sharply and authoritatively, as to what they were going to do, where to stand, what to hold, and so forth. As far gone in drink as he sometimes was, he improvised distance experiments with two or more cameras, experiments with cameras out of the room and at queer angles. Sometimes he'd work himself into a frenzy, ordering cameras to be handed to him one after the other – he almost never reached for one himself or handled cameras between trials – even though, as it sometimes turned out, the film in them had run out.'

For some shots one witness might be asked to hold the camera, while another triggered the shutter on a command from Ted. Television news-caster Bob Palmer could hardly believe his eyes and ears when Ted burst into full creative frenzy in his studio: 'During an experiment he is seized with wild desires to innovate: to bounce a picture off the ceiling or through a wall or who knows where; he dances merrily about, shouting orders to any and all in earshot. Occasionally, Ted would bolt out of his chair and charge the television camera. There he would grunt, purr, curse and squint, and with an incantation that would do a dice-roller proud, he'd wind up and let go. On the downhill side of these incidents he'd whirl round and demand, "Did you see anything? Did you see anything?" '

On many occasions no amount of cajoling by Eisenbud or concentration by Ted – 'It knocks the hell out of me' – could stimulate the production of psychic pictures. But at other times Ted registered some astonishing successes which served to deepen the mystery of the exact nature of his weird talent. In May 1965 a whole series of pictures of a store-front appeared in the photographs. On examination this turned out to be a store in Central City, Colorado, and its name, 'The Old Gold Store', could be made out in a couple of the prints. The strange thing was that some years earlier the store's name had been changed to 'The Old Wells Fargo Express Office'; despite a diligent search Eisenbud was unable to unearth any photographs of the place taken when it bore its original name. Even more puzzling was the fact that separate images of the shop seem to have been superimposed, for the sign reads 'The Wld Gold Store' with a 'W' being substituted for the 'O' of 'Old' and the 'W' appearing in exactly the same position as the 'W' of 'Wells Fargo' on the modern store-front sign.

Other pictures presented further enigmas. At one session Ted 'thought-ographed' part of a building later identified as a hangar belonging to the Air Division of the Royal Canadian Mounted Police; curiously, in Ted's version of the photograph, the word 'Canadian' is mis-spelt as 'Cainadain'. Another picture, of Williams' Livery Stable in Central City, Colorado, turned out to differ in striking detail from the actual location: Ted's photograph showed bricked-up windows, and the façade seemed to be made of different material.

In the unconventional circumstances created by Ted's behaviour, Jule Eisenbud did his best to establish the truth about his protégé's paranormal powers. He tested him in steel-walled chambers, looked for signs that

*Top:* **All Ted can produce today is a snapshot of his own face – he has not taken a 'thoughtograph' for years.**

X-rays or magnetic forces might be involved, and had Ted examined by physicians in case there was any peculiarity in his physical make-up from which his talent sprang, but clear answers have always eluded him. The easiest explanation, of course, and one favoured from the start by a number of people Eisenbud consulted or invited to test sessions, was that Ted was cheating, producing pictures not paranormally but by sleight-of-hand. This, indeed, had been Eisenbud's own view before seeing Ted in action, but he later became sensitive to any suggestion that Ted might be cheating.

According to the sceptics, the finger of suspicion pointed to a curious little device Ted insisted upon using as part of his picture-producing ritual. Known as a 'gismo', it was an apparently empty tube, often made of the paper that had come with the Polaroid film, which Ted would usually hold close to the camera when a picture was being taken. He claimed it was only there to prevent him spoiling things by waving his fingers in front of the lens.

Charles Reynolds of *Popular Photography*, and his colleague David B. Eisendrath Jr., also a noted photographer and conjurer, came away from 'an amazing weekend with the amazing Ted Serios' deeply suspicious of the 'gismo'. At the two 'thoughtography' sessions they had attended, several different 'gismos' were used, including several fashioned from black paper, from United Airlines napkin rings, from the yellow plastic core of a roll of cine film, and even from the cardboard tube from a toilet roll. Although the two investigators realized at an early stage that 'One of the results of Ted's style is that it is very difficult to keep your eye on him,' they monitored Ted's handling of the 'gismo' as carefully as they could.

A vital clue to what was really happening came, they believed, when they saw a television film of Ted in action: 'The image looked as if it were being produced by a small optical device pinched in one half of the paper "gismo".' Despite Eisenbud's willingness to allow the 'gismo' to be examined at any time, Ted's reaction on being asked to hand it over after taking a shot was hostile on at least one occasion: ' "Why?" was Ted's response, as he concealed it in his closed fist and took a defensive step backwards. At this point the tensions of the previous two days exploded. Dr Eisenbud first reprimanded us for disturbing Ted and then Ted for acting suspiciously. By that time the "gismo" had gone to Ted's pocket – a rather unscientific handling of this prop which we had noticed several times the previous day but had not called him on because nothing spectacular was being produced. The optical "gimmick" in the "gismo" (if, indeed, there *was* an optical "gimmick" in the "gismo") had been neatly ditched.'

A 'gimmick' is a device which a conjurer conceals from his audience and uses to carry out a trick: in this case, a tiny lens on which a transparency could be mounted. Making a 'gimmick', Reynolds pointed out, would have been a comparatively easy task for Ted, especially if he had adapted a cheap and simple device already on the market: 'A good possibility would be one of the small plastic telescopes, usually containing a girlie picture, and available at many novelty shops for about 25¢.'

To reinforce their point, the *Popular Photography* team later constructed several different 'gimmicks', and a sleight-of-hand expert demonstrated how the lens could be transferred from his pocket to the 'gismo' without anyone noticing. Reynolds and Eisendrath were careful to point out merely that in the rather lax experimental conditions, deception was possible: 'One of the things that we *cannot* say,' wrote Reynolds, 'is that Serios is definitely a charlatan. He was never caught red-handed and, in fact, when under our close observation, did not even produce a definite picture. One of the things we *can* say is that the testing procedures we observed seemed to be highly unscientific, leaving plenty of room for Ted to resort to clever trickery should he have wanted to do so.'

When Eisenbud's book *The World of Ted Serios* was published, other sceptics, intrigued by the story, offered their own explanations. Colin Brookes-Smith, a distinguished British instrumentation engineer and psychical researcher with a keen interest in PK, pointed out that it was not impossible to tamper with Polaroid film, and Professor W. A. H. Rushton, later President of the Society for Psychical Research, made a tiny 'rice grain' optical device which, when positioned with a microfilm photograph in the 'gismo', produced a passable imitation of a 'thoughtograph'.

But there are many objections to these theories and Eisenbud, who was the first to raise many of them in his initial, sceptical dealings with Ted Serios, has devoted much time and effort to answering them. Ted's critics, for example, never once established that he was using sleight-of-hand, although Eisenbud did, on one occasion, catch him trying to sneak a photograph when the witnesses were not looking – it might, presumably, have been produced as a 'thoughtograph' later. However, Eisenbud also points out, crucially, that many pictures were taken when Ted was handling neither 'gismo' nor camera.

Furthermore, the problems of producing tiny microfilms would have been considerable, especially in cases where, after careful checking, researchers concluded that no ordinary source for the picture, in the way of postcards or book illustrations, was available. Doubts remain, however, not least because of a factor that has so often bedevilled psychical research: gradually Ted's ability to produce 'thoughtographs' waned, until there was little for psychical researchers to investigate. Eisenbud had hoped that other 'thoughtographers' might come forward and thus demonstrate that Ted's abilities were merely the tip of a psychic iceberg, but so far this has not happened, and Eisenbud's experiments remain interesting but inconclusive.

Back in Mendon, Illinois, Ted Serios will still try, on request, to produce a 'thoughtograph', although none has appeared for some 15 years. The last successful print, with entirely appropriate finality, showed some drawn curtains. Today, all that appears on the Polaroids is the contorted face of the erstwhile 'psychic superstar' as he tries, in vain, to recapture his former, mysterious glory.

The interest shown in Ted Serios highlights how few people have the confidence to demonstrate their PK powers in public. So when a craggy New Zealander called Dr Rolf Alexander offered to show his skill at 'cloud-busting' to the British press in 1956, journalist Fyfe Robertson responded to the invitation by devoting several pages of the influential *Picture Post* magazine to the doctor's remarkable ability. He claimed he could dispel clouds in the sky simply by directing upon them 'a new kind of energy by which the human mind can act at a distance'.

This was, as Robertson laconically noted, 'a breath-taking claim', but with a few limitations: 'He cannot affect *all* clouds. He can do nothing with cirrus clouds, and almost nothing with stratus clouds. The reason, he believes, is that these are not charged with polarised electricity. His ideal clouds are well-formed, not overlarge cumulus clouds. These have a positive electric charge above, a negative charge below.

'Between forming and disintegrating, such cumulus clouds maintain a precarious state of equilibrium, and Dr Alexander believes that the energy he directs on them can cause disintegration precisely because equilibrium is delicate – a small amount of energy is enough to precipitate change. He suggests that the mind energy he uses disintegrates clouds by neutralising their electrical charges.'

This was not the kind of energy even an experienced practitioner could use every day, for 'It would be dangerous to try, he says, when he is off-colour or over-fatigued ... The effects on himself, he says, are un-mistakable; he feels a tightening about the diaphragm and behind the eyes.'

Fyfe Robertson, as millions of British television viewers know, is the proverbial canny Scotsman and therefore not easily fooled. He was impressed by the way clouds dispersed over Holne Tor in Devon when Dr Alexander demonstrated his powers: 'I really find it very difficult not to believe, startling and improbable though it may seem, and almost in spite of myself, that Dr Alexander can disintegrate clouds.' But he acknowledged that 'Nothing I have seen adds up to the kind of proof which scientists can legitimately demand.'

Several months before Fyfe Robertson's encounter with Dr Alexander on the Devon tor, tests of the New Zealander's claims had been started by Denys Parsons of the Society for Psychical Research. The vagaries of the English weather made it difficult for him to gather the data he needed, but Parsons used the waiting-time to assemble an impressive list of testimonials to the doctor's powers. 'It may not come during the life of Rolf Alexander,' wrote an American businessman who had witnessed a cloudbust in Mexico, 'but sometime he will be referred to in the mental and physical sciences as are Einstein and Pasteur in their respective fields.' When conditions for the test were at last propitious, the results were disappointing. Dr Richard Scorer of the Department of Meteorology at London's Imperial College of Science and Technology expressed his doubts in a letter to Parsons: 'He claimed that he could cause any chosen cloud to disappear before any two other "control" clouds which were of comparable size. His method was to stare at the chosen cloud. In the first test the cloud at which he was staring was the last of the three to disappear: in the second test it was the second of the three. I saw nothing unusual about the behaviour of any of the clouds.

'Apparently he only "works" with fair weather cumulus, and clouds of this type usually disappear in 15–20 minutes anyway. The point of interest is that when such clouds disappear their place is usually taken by new ones of very similar appearance, and unless this fact is known it is quite easy for an untrained observer to believe that what is seen is still the same cloud. If one cloud is watched with careful concentration it can be seen that it does disappear and that the new growth is to one side.

'If we assume that Dr Alexander was sincere and honest but misguided, then the simplest explanation of his behaviour is that when alone he has discovered that clouds of this type at which he looks intently disappear. When examining the rest of the sky, when he has finished, he finds that it

Dr Rolf Alexander 'cloudbusting' by mind-power from Holne Tor, Devon. *Left to right, top to bottom:* **The 'target' cloud is the one on the right of the group of three; the other two are 'controls'. The photographs, taken at 30-second intervals, show the 'target' cloud fading away, leaving the 'controls'.**

**Contorted cutlery:
The aftermath of a
metal-bending party.**

looks very much the same as before and concludes that he has been responsible for the dissolution of the cloud. The experiment can be repeated over and over again on a suitable day.'

As far as Denys Parsons was concerned, that wrapped the whole thing up: an explanation for the claimed phenomenon was far more likely to be found in the complex but understood processes of meteorology than in the shadowy realm of the mind.

Seventeen years later, however, in November 1973, when the Great Spoonbending Controversy broke in Britain, no such neatly argued dismissal of psychic claims was possible. From the moment Uri Geller made his British debut, on a BBC television talk show, there were scientists who took his work seriously. Moreover, an excited public lost no time in adding the weight of its testimony to the Israeli's claims that he could bend metal not only in the studio but also at long-distance. From homes throughout the country came reports of how watches which had stopped years before had suddenly started again, how cutlery had been found in strange contortions and how keys had bent in locks; even the family silver was not immune to Uri's paranormal powers.

Geller's extraordinary demonstrations inspired a field of study which still flourishes; in the jargon of parapsychology it is known as PKMB – Psychokinetic Metal Bending. In Geller's wake followed a Pied Piper's army of 'mini-Gellers' – children who claimed to be able to bend spoons, to create metal sculptures and to scrunch up paperclips inside glass globes by mind-power. Geller himself had a problem: wherever he went to show off his remarkable powers, the Amazing Randi was seldom far behind.

James Randi, a bearded, gnome-like figure of immense strength, is one of America's best-known magicians. For 30 years he has escaped from manacles, straitjackets and underwater barrels, caught bullets in his teeth, dazzled even Chan Canasta with his card tricks. Today, almost to the

**Uri Geller and** (*right*)
**James 'The Amazing'**
**Randi – sceptic**
**supreme.**

exclusion of his professional magic, he has become the most vociferous campaigner in the United States against what he sees as 'the profit and publicity-seeking ESP psychic crowd'. Since 1965 he has carried around with him a signed cheque for 10,000 dollars payable to 'anyone who can perform a single demonstration of a paranormal, supernatural or occult nature, under properly observed conditions'. Randi conducts his campaign from a bizarre wizard's den plonked insanely amid the suburban villas of Lennox Avenue out along the New Jersey Transit Authority's Bayshore line at Rumson. The door at the front opens the wrong way to the accompaniment of a witch's warning. The door at the back has a flap through which the raccoons come in to rob the fridge and once, unsociably, to slaughter Randi's parrot. Inside, an Egyptian Mummy, three cats and a skull and crossbones oversee Randi's relentless campaign against the 'flim-flam' of seers and psychics.

For his first meeting with Geller, in the New York offices of *Time* magazine in February 1973, Randi posed as a journalist, one of the simpler illusions of his career, for the only equipment he needed was the standard kit of yellow pad and pencil. By the end of the meeting Randi had found a new mission, and summed up the thinking behind it in his investigative book *The Truth About Uri Geller*: 'This writer is convinced that Geller is a clever magician, nothing more – and certainly nothing less . . . In my view, Geller brings disgrace to the craft I practice. Worse than that, he warps the thinking of a young generation of forming minds. And that is unforgivable.'

Even amongst conjurors Randi was exceptionally well-placed to challenge the Israeli 'boy-wonder'. More than 20 years earlier, using his real name of Randall Zwinge, Randi had himself succumbed to the temptation to pose as a psychic, and had confidently and successfully 'predicted' the result of the baseball World Series and the exact number of visitors to the 1950 Canadian National Exhibition. These 'feats' – smallish beer to a practised conjuror – resulted in newspaper stories which raved about 'The man with the mind which functions like a carbon copy of your own and maybe a little ahead of it.' Randi gave up trying to pass himself off as a miracle-worker but, after two years of 'close observation and careful analysis', he concluded that Geller had not been so strong-willed: the Israeli was doing no more than standard conjuring tricks which depended upon sleight-of-hand, the distraction of the audience's attention at crucial moments, signals from accomplices, and the substitution of one object for another. In fact, he realized, Geller's act consisted of tricks that had he been performing as a conjuror might have been considered rather trivial. But, unlike ordinary stage magicians who merely rejoice in their ability to deceive the eyes and wits of members of their audience, Geller claimed to have genuine paranormal powers.

Early on, Randi decided that the most effective way to prove his point would be by example; within a short time he claimed that he could replicate any 'miracle' in Geller's repertoire. Assiduously, he sought out journalists who had written starry-eyed articles about the Israeli's abilities, and his admonitions were always accompanied by a dazzling 'psychic' display. On one famous occasion, at the height of the British public's craze for spoonbending, Randi posed as an unknown psychic and hoaxed Britain's leading spiritualist weekly, *Psychic News*, into printing an enthusiastic report of the miraculous mayhem he had wrought on a visit to their offices when spoons, forks and a paperknife were bent. Just because an event or action *seems* to defy normal explanation, there is no reason, Randi believes, to class it as a miracle or evidence of paranormal phenomena: if a conjuror can out-Geller Geller, or at least equal him, trickery must always be involved.

Sometimes, frustratingly, this argument does not convince PK-believers; Randi is weary of people who, after seeing him perform, insist that he must have psychic gifts, despite his protestations to the contrary. He is impatient, too, with scientists who believe that their training and experience qualify them to judge whether fraud is involved: 'Scientists are the people least qualified to detect chicanery,' he told one reporter. 'They're the easiest to fool of all. If you want to catch a burglar, you go to a burglar, not to a scientist. If you want to catch a magician, go to a magician.'

Many of Randi's exposés of the 'Geller Effect' have been both damning and hilarious. For example, he once got his assistant to masquerade as a psychic on a radio show and asked listeners to ring in with reports of any strange manifestations that occurred during the broadcast. The calls that began to flood the switchboard showed that the assistant's non-existent 'powers' were every bit as dramatic as Geller's: mirrors cracked, cats ran amok, a light bulb exploded, cracks appeared in a window, an air-conditioner and a refrigerator stopped working, toilet paper fell off the roll, and somewhere in the catchment area of radio station WMCA, New York City, a spaniel began to sneeze, and a piggy bank broke open, disgorging its hoard of pennies into the night.

Randi is happy to confront scientists and parapsychologists. He even offers annual awards called 'Uris'. Categories include 'the scientist who says or does the silliest thing relating to parapsychology in the preceding twelve months' and 'the "psychic" performer who fools the greatest number of people with the least effort'. The trophy is a bent spoon, tastefully mounted in perspex, and 'Winners are notified telepathically and are allowed to predict their victory in advance.' However, he is careful not to offend his fellow magicians and is reluctant to explain how PK tricks can be done. Fortunately, two sociologists from New Zealand, David Marks and Richard Kammann, operate under no such restraints.

After observing Uri Geller both at close quarters and on stage, the New Zealanders listed the methods used by the man they call 'as slippery as an eel and as cunning as a fox, but, oh, so phony!' Here is how, they say, Geller contrives to alter the time shown on a watch belonging to a dupe in his audience: 'While handling a watch borrowed from the audience member, Geller moves the hands around, using the winder in the normal manner. He then places it face down in the hand of a small child, too nervous to turn over the watch and check that the time is still true. Distractions galore, and a good delay between the physical wind-on and the final time check, make this an easy but effective feat of mind power.'

They also marvelled at the number of people who offered their watches for paranormal repair, 'like a group of crippled pilgrims on their way to Lourdes'. Jewellers pointed out that about half the watches they are asked to mend are merely clogged up with dust and old oil, and showed that more than half would start if warmed in the hand. Marks and Kammann add: 'Probably they do not tick for very long as, in most cases, they need cleaning and lubricating. But that doesn't matter, as most people accept the sound of the ticking as a miracle of psychic power.'

Finally, they analyzed Geller's most famous *tour de force*, metal-bending. Their conclusion: 'There are many ways of making small objects bend:

'(1) Distract everybody, bend the object manually, conceal the bend, then reveal it to the now attentive onlookers. This is his usual method. The bend is made either by a two-handed tweak, or by levering it in something tough like a belt buckle or the head of another key with a hole in the top.

'(2) Geller (or an accomplice) pre-stresses the object by bending it many times until it's nearly at breaking point. Later it can be used to dazzle unsuspecting audiences as it bends, appears to melt, or even snaps in two pieces following the slightest pressure from Uri's wiry fingers.

'(3) Quite often collections of metal objects (e.g. a bunch of keys or a drawer of cutlery) contain one or more items that are already bent. Geller tells you he'll bend something and, when you examine the whole set of objects carefully, the bent item is found and Uri takes credit.

'(4) When an object is already bent, Geller will often say that it will continue to bend. He may move the object slowly to enhance the effect, or place it on a flat surface and push down on one end. But many people will believe they can see an object slowly bending purely as a result of Geller's suggestion that it is doing so.

'(5) Substitute objects already bent for the ones provided.'

Although by the mid-1970s there were already doubts about Uri Geller's powers, nevertheless he had really started something in the groves of academe. In universities throughout the world – in physics laboratories as well as in parapsychology institutes – research into PK and its manifestations became urgent and fashionable and, for the first time since J. B. Rhine's dice-throwing days at Duke, experimental results were eagerly anticipated and widely discussed.

Among the British scientists galvanized into starting investigations into PKMB after meeting Geller were two London University professors, John Taylor of King's College and John Hasted of Birkbeck College. Taylor, a leading theorist in applied mathematics, was so enthusiastic about metal-bending and the feats of the 'mini-Gellers' who emerged after the Israeli's first television appearances, that he wrote a fulsome book about them called *Superminds*. Later, however, he seems to have changed his mind, and is now convinced that their powers are not paranormal.

Not so Professor John Hasted, the kindly and respected chairman of Birkbeck's physics department. He is well aware that his pursuit of the true nature of PK has caused the raising of many an academic eyebrow, but persists in his work, noting wistfully that 'adverse circumstantial evidence' about Uri Geller's public performances has made life uncomfortable for him and his co-workers:

'This exercise,' he says, 'has created an atmosphere in which not only Geller but also the researchers into metal-bending have come to be regarded as suspect by the scientific community. Colleagues have been polite, but blasts of icy wind have often reached me.' Nevertheless, undaunted, Hasted has taken refuge from those icy blasts in his specially equipped laboratory deep inside the physics department, cramming his experiments into a busy round of teaching and administration, bolstered by his own conviction that paranormal metal-bending is a proper field of study for a physicist: 'Once I became committed by my own observations to recognizing that these peculiar physical phenomena really took place, I started to spend time on observations, in the belief that the phenomena demanded a new approach in physics in order to explain them.'

Aware that it is 'easier to make mistakes in psychic research than it is in physics', Hasted has taken great pains to ensure that experimental conditions are as watertight as possible. At an early stage, he decided to concentrate on 'no-touch' experiments, which, as the term suggests, means that the PK subjects attempt to bend the metal without having any physical contact with it. Using the practical laboratory expertise of the trained physicist, Professor Hasted has devised all kinds of experimental apparatus, including latchkeys with built-in strain gauges sensitive enough to register the smallest of changes in the shape of the metal. Progress has been slow but, over the years, Hasted has claimed a string of successes – one of them, a series of experiments with a teenage boy, Nicholas Williams, who was able to cause bends in keys hung up in a room while he sat well away from them in a chair making model aeroplanes.

Sometimes, the chart recorders attached to the keys displayed signals which showed that several keys were being bent at once. Other tests also gave dramatic results: Hasted left some thin strips of aluminium in a room, and when he and Nicholas returned to it after waiting outside for a few minutes, tight concertina folds had appeared in the metal.

Another of the children investigated by the professor produced weird 'scrunches' from paperclips which were encased, apparently out of reach, inside a glass globe. It was what Hasted calls an 'impossible task' – an experiment in which the precautions against fraud are so stringent that any successful bending of the metal must be due to paranormal agency.

However, Hasted does acknowledge that not all the problems were eliminated: no scientist actually witnessed the production of the 'scrunches', which took place away from the laboratory. More crucially, a tiny hole was left in the globe, since experiments in which it was completely sealed yielded nothing (perhaps because the glass acted as a barrier to psychokinetic powers). This meant that an 'impossible' task became just possible after all: one of Hasted's colleagues was able to produce a comparable though less tight-knit 'scrunch' by poking tools through the hole, and so was the ever-vigilant Denys Parsons.

Today, the globes are kept in a cupboard of Hasted's Birkbeck Laboratory, testimony to his ingenious attempts to discover the truth about PKMB, and symbols, too, of the countless questions that still have to be answered before this distinguished physicist can convince the scientific community that he has found any clear-cut answers.

Meanwhile, attempts to replicate and confirm earlier experimental results continue. In 1977, John L. Randall, the British author of a history of PK, and a colleague, C. P. Davis, did a clever experiment with a schoolboy named Mark Briscoe. The original experiment, which they were now trying to repeat, was conducted by Dr Eldon Byrd of the US Naval Surface Weapons Center, Maryland, with Uri Geller in 1973. Byrd had used a kind of metal called 'nitinol' with one peculiar quality: if twisted into a shape then heated to a high temperature, it will 'remember' that shape no matter how it is later deformed, and will always revert to it if placed in hot water. Before being given to Geller, a length of nitinol wire was straightened and heated, but after he had stroked the wire and produced a kink in it, the nitinol seemed to have lost its 'memory' and would not straighten out in hot water. Byrd could only conclude that Geller had somehow altered its 'memory' – a feat which physicists stipulated could be done only by heating to 500°C.

In their experiment with Mark Briscoe, Randall and Davis taped a short strip of nitinol wire on to a sheet of stiff white paper laid out on a laboratory bench. The wire ran over the edge of the paper and was sellotaped to the bench-top. Things began to happen almost at once: after Mark had been stroking the wire for only about ten minutes, Randall, who was sitting opposite him, noticed that the wire was gradually rising from the table. It twisted away from Mark's fingers and, the experimenters noted, 'The unstroked portion reared up like a snake, curling over at the tip. This was quite an impressive effect, since bending was obviously occurring in parts of the wire which had not been in contact with the subject's fingers.'

Intriguing though Randall and Davis's findings are, however, they have not been deemed conclusive by other parapsychologists. The questions they have raised, which include the possibility that nitinol can be shaped without using heat – with pliers, coins or even teeth – mean there is more work to be done before the issue can be resolved.

There had been a surprising, if less encouraging, outcome to a series of experiments reported to the prestigious science journal *Nature* by two researchers from the University of Bath. Dr Brian Pamplin and Dr Harry Collins tested six young 'mini-Gellers' between May and September 1975. The children, referred to only by letters of the alphabet, for reasons which will become apparent, were contacted through the local press and tele-

Concealed behind this one-way mirror, Bath University researchers caught 'mini-Gellers' cheating. One child bent a rod underfoot, others used two hands to twist spoons.

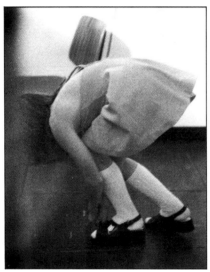

vision. A, B and F were all 11-year-old girls, C was a girl of 13, while D, aged ten, and E, 11, were boys. All of them had successfully bent cutlery and other metal objects at home. Because the scientists wanted to see paranormal metal-bending, they decided to try to create the most relaxing environment possible, while still maintaining the necessary rigorous experimental conditions. Bath University's psychology department had the ideal laboratory, containing three one-way mirrors. The scientists could watch from behind them and observe the metal-benders, whose concentration would be undisturbed by cameras and experimenters. In each test except one an observer also sat discreetly in the room itself.

In their letter to *Nature*, Pamplin and Collins reported the near-farcical events that followed: 'The subject was handed the spoon or rod after its outline had been drawn on a sheet of paper and was allowed to stroke it in the approved manner between forefinger and thumb of one hand and to report what they felt was happening. B reported that the spoon 'felt soft' before bending. C stated that it 'felt like plaster, then running water'. The running water feeling occurred, it was said, just before bending occurred.

However, at no time did C bend anything for us while experimenters were watching. The others all succeeded in bending spoons and B bent a rod of mild steel as well.'

Every so often, after the first 20 minutes, the observer in the room with each child was instructed deliberately to relax vigilance. Behind the mirrors, the scientists watched with growing amazement: 'The experimenters were specially alert during these periods and in all cases except C they observed and photographed cheating by the subjects. A put the rod under her foot to bend it; B, E and F used two hands to bend the spoon using considerable muscular power, while D tried to hide his hands under a table to bend a spoon in both hands out of sight of the observer.'

Neither of the Bath scientists had embarked upon the experiments in the hope or expectation of catching the children out, but as they said in their paper: 'We can assert that in no case did we observe a rod or spoon bent other than by palpably normal means.' And, although they added, 'We cannot, of course, conclude that all instances of the so-called Geller Effect are due to cheating', their photographs and videotapes held damning proof that, in PK experiments, not even the innocence of children can be taken for granted.

Because paranormal metal-bending challenges the accepted principles of their branch of science, much of the research into the phenomenon has been conducted by physicists. Mainstream parapsychologists, meanwhile, have also been trying to establish the truth about PK and, in recent years, have reported many, often bizarre, attempts to do so. One Italian professor, for example, has suggested that some people could use PK to make sense of jumbled fragments of sound. Another researcher, from the University of Amsterdam, has devised a PK test for babies, using his own children as subjects.

In a second series of these experiments, a British scientist, Dr Susan Blackmore, has been sitting her baby daughter, Emily, in front of an Apple computer for PK sessions. The computer plays a tune and shows a smiling face at intervals determined by a random number generator. The idea is that Emily will enjoy the 'programme' so much that she will induce the computer by mindpower to show it more often. Using a baby like Emily is in

Dr Susan Blackmore and her daughter Emily experiment with a PK test for babies.

line with some modern theories of PK which say that a child does not have to be able to try to invoke PK powers deliberately: they may be there from birth, and fade or are educated out of people as they grow older.

Growing awareness of PK has prompted other researchers to re-examine the origin of some séance-room phenomena – the raps, creaks, table-turnings and levitations – claimed to be caused by the spirits of the dead.

In the late 1960s, a Mrs Fewell wrote to the Society for Psychical Research to explain the odd behaviour of her dining-room table. Some guests (including a company chairman and other business people) had decided it would be fun to try to make the oak table rise from the floor; to everyone's amazement, it did so. Mrs Fewell wrote: 'At the end of our first sitting the table rose completely off the floor and was suspended there for some seconds, creaking and tossing to such an extent that I thought the table would fall to pieces, and requiring it for our lunch the next day I got down underneath the table and pulled it back to the floor. By this time everyone was standing up in order to keep their hands on top of the table.'

Mrs Fewell and her husband were keen to investigate further, but the weird manifestations included rappings in response to questions, and when these began to distress one member of the group, the sitters gave up. The story might have gone unrecorded had not psychologist Kenneth Batcheldor published the results of some experiments which suggested a table

**Table levitation: The moment of lift-off captured on video during one of a series of experiments conducted by Dr Kenneth Batcheldor** (*inset*).

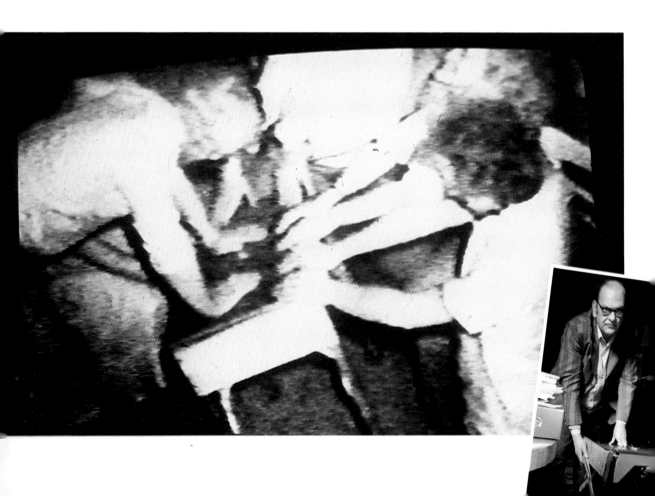

could, indeed, be made to levitate, not only without trickery or unconscious muscular action on the sitters' part, but also without a medium.

Batcheldor had held 200 sittings, usually with two close friends present. All of them felt considerable scepticism: 'the sittings commenced, therefore, almost in a spirit of amusement, but this attitude changed sharply in the eleventh meeting when the table, instead of merely tilting or rocking on two legs as it had done so far, rose clear from the floor. The explanation of unconscious muscular action was suddenly no longer applicable, since one cannot push a table into the air, either consciously or unconsciously, when the hands are on the top of it.' Predictably, 'it came as quite a shock. It seemed that we had stumbled upon a genuine paranormal force, and we determined to continue the meetings and find out all we could.'

All kinds of astonishing things happened at the sittings that followed: the table's antics included gliding along silently, beating 'an enormous tattoo', or tilting up on two legs. At times, it rotated slowly, at others it went so fast 'as to take the breath away'. It would rush from one end of the room to the other with the sitters in hot pursuit; at other times, it seemed glued to the floor and nothing would shift it. Further investigations revealed more oddities; for example, the table would tilt and lift someone sitting on top of it; strange breezes blew around the sitters' hands and sometimes the chairs on which they were sitting were suddenly pulled back.

Kenneth Batcheldor is the first to acknowledge that sceptics can easily find fault: for one thing, the table would only perform in darkness or near-darkness, presenting countless possibilities for fraud if one member of the group were determined to hoax the others. He also found that the more relaxed the atmosphere, the more likely the manifestations they wished to study were to appear: again, something that the hard-line sceptics would question. But against this Batcheldor staunchly maintains that neither he nor his friends were cheating; he also has photographs of many of the reported phenomena, and a videotape of the table-tipping recorded in infra-red light. The most telling confirmation of all, however, came when other researchers published similar results, notably the late Colin Brookes-Smith, who designed a table complete with instruments which could provide detailed measurements to supplement mere observation.

George and Iris Owen, investigators of the paranormal. They invented a 'ghost', Philip, but at their séances 'Philip' made his presence felt.

Such extraordinary events demand a theory to explain them and although Batcheldor is still developing one, he has concluded that to lift tables or produce raps the sitters are probably having to pool their individual powers of PK and that the right psychological atmosphere is essential if this is to happen. These ideas appealed to a group of enthusiasts in Toronto, Canada, and inspired one of the most colourful experiments in the history of PK research: the evocation of Philip the Imaginary Ghost.

In the autumn of 1972, some members of the Toronto Society for Psychical Research, led by George Owen and his wife, Iris, a couple with an established reputation as investigators of the paranormal, began to hold weekly meetings in the hope of producing a collective hallucination. So that their thoughts should all be directed towards the same goal, they decided to invent a 'ghost' whom they called Philip. According to his fictitious biography, Philip had lived in England in the mid-17th century. He had married a local beauty, Dorothea, but, since she still resisted his advances, he took a mistress, a raven-haired gypsy called Margo whom he installed in a gatehouse in the grounds of his Warwickshire home, Diddington Manor. When Dorothea discovered what was going on, she accused Margo of witchcraft and robbery. The accusation stuck and Margo was burned at the stake. Later, the distraught Philip committed suicide.

Although the sitters enjoyed discussing and embellishing this swash-buckling yarn, the tragic Philip never materialized, despite concentrated meditation. The experiment seemed doomed to failure but then Batch-eldor's theories, which Iris Owen came across, gave it a new lease of life. The eight members of the group were particularly impressed by the suggestion that: 'The ability to produce phenomena is not a mysterious capacity conferred on a few rare individuals called "mediums" but a *psychological skill* which can be acquired through aptitude and experience by virtually all human beings,' and at once changed their methods.

Instead of meditating, they concentrated upon creating the kind of relaxed and carefree atmosphere in which the British researchers had produced their results. They sang songs, told jokes, recited poetry – and waited for something to happen. Soon they were rewarded. 'One evening, during the third or fourth new session, the group felt a vibration within the table top, somewhat like a knock or rap . . . As the sitting proceeded other raps came, as if someone had struck the table a light blow. These knocks or raps became louder and louder until there was no doubt but that they were *heard* by everyone in the group. Each one of the group assured himself or herself that nobody was in any way, either deliberately or inadvertently, producing the raps which were proceeding from the top of the table.'

That was just the beginning. As the weeks went by, the table around which they sat would levitate and move about the room, and Philip (for the sitters had decided that it was he) would respond to questions about himself with loud raps. Sadly, an actual apparition of Philip, the tragic cavalier, never materialized, but they did seem to get repeatable phenomena, in full light and often in the presence of eye-witnesses and film cameras. Their results give psychical researchers hope that the cause of such PK effects, whether normal or paranormal, may one day be established.

There is less enthusiasm in the parapsychological community for reports of the strange goings-on in the town of Rolla, a small and unprepossessing township in the American state of Missouri. Rolla is the home of W. E. Cox, a former associate of J. B. Rhine and a pioneer of PK research. Nearby lives Cox's associate, Dr J. T. Richards. Both are members of SORRAT, the Society for Research into Rapport and Telekinesis, which has been conducting research into PK and other psychic phenomena for more than 20 years.

The focus of SORRAT's research programme, and of all the controversy, sits in Cox's cluttered garage on top of an old washing machine: it is an inverted glass fish-tank. Inside is a random selection of objects, including coins, lengths of wool and envelopes. Although the tank may look like something waiting for the refuse collector it is, in fact, one of the latest devices for detecting PK ability: a tiny laboratory known as the 'mini-lab'.

Each mini-lab constructed by SORRAT is scrupulously sealed before the experiments and the master lock plugged with superglue – Cox has legal

Still-frames from one of SORRAT's films of their sealed 'mini-lab' experiments to test the powers of PK. *Below:* Watched by W. E. Cox and J. T. Richards, locksmith Ron Henson seals a 'mini-lab' containing a letter addressed to Arthur C. Clarke, which was mysteriously delivered in Sri Lanka 3 weeks later.

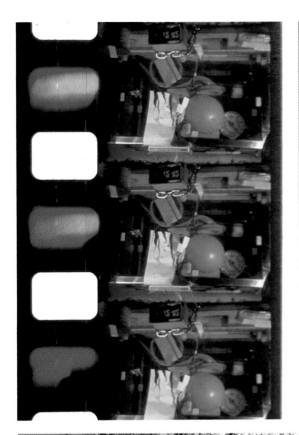

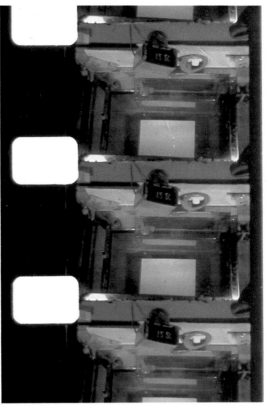

depositions to that effect – but many of the objects inside have been said to move about. He claims that a balloon, for example, inflated itself when no one was near, that pens have risen up and written messages, that leather rings have linked together, that metal has apparently travelled into the mini-lab right through the glass, without breaking it, and that letters from inside have turned up on the doormats of researchers in other countries. Indeed, one such letter, addressed to Arthur C. Clarke and placed in a locked and sealed mini-lab in September 1983 under the watchful eye of the television series film crew, reached his home in Colombo, Sri Lanka, a few weeks later.

Cox's trump card is that he has captured many of these astonishing events on cine film: he knew that verbal or written reports alone of such wonders would be hard to credit and would have little validity in the eyes of scientists. These films have excited intense (and not always polite) argument whenever they have been shown, and many leading researchers have travelled to Rolla to inspect for themselves the mini-labs and the experimental conditions. This can be a disconcerting business for, in Tom Richards's house, conversations tend to be accompanied by strange rappings.

Certainly, the SORRAT work raises many questions among sceptics: what, for example, is the agency that causes the objects to move – PK powers exercised by Dr Richards, discarnate spirits or something quite different? How greatly is the validity of the experiments undermined by the fact that outside researchers like Tony Cornell of the Society for Psychical Research have managed to produce films of similar 'manifestations' by normal means? Not surprisingly, at the Society's Centenary Conference in Cambridge, such arguments raged late and acrimoniously into the night, while the calm, pipe-smoking W. E. Cox stuck firmly to his belief that strange powers are indeed at work in Rolla, Missouri.

In the years since J. B. Rhine encountered the young gambler and formulated his first dice-rolling experiments, such controversy has relentlessly dogged PK research. Indeed, allegations of fraud, the protests of conjurors and the weird and wonderful stunts pulled by 'psychic superstars' have overshadowed many fundamental problems. There is, for example, no clear agreement about how PK experiments should be conducted and what safeguards should be used.

When George P. Hansen of the Institute for Parapsychology tackled the problem, he uncovered a litany of second thoughts about well-intentioned experiments and their results. It goes, in part, like this: 'Franklin used an electron miscroscope to examine several metal fractures produced by Uri Geller. He concluded that the fractures were highly unusual and that they would have been extremely difficult to produce by normal means. Later Franklin retracted his statement after additional consultation and admitted that for the most part the fractures were of a well-known type. Mattuck and Hill reported that Jean-Pierre Girard seemed to be able to slightly stretch an aluminium bar by PK. However, after further study they decided that strain-gauge slippage was the most likely explanation. Taylor claimed several children were able to bend objects within carefully sealed tubes. Randi seemed to have demonstrated the inadequacy of the seals, but Taylor disputed this; however, Taylor now seems to disavow his earlier work.'

There were plenty of rueful second-thoughts early in 1983 when that scourge of the spoonbenders, James Randi, announced that two of America's 'psychic superstars' were, in fact, conjurors. It was all part of a plan codenamed 'Project Alpha', which Randi had put into action in 1979. That year, James S. McDonnell of the McDonnell-Douglas aircraft company had donated $500,000 to establish a parapsychology laboratory at Washington University in St Louis, Missouri.

Randi enlisted the help of Steve Shaw and Michael Edwards, two young fans who had written to him for conjuring tips. At Randi's suggestion, they offered themselves to the new lab as 'guinea-pigs', claiming remarkable psychic powers. At the same time, Randi wrote to Peter Phillips, the director of the McDonnell Laboratory, with some advice on how to conduct tests on metal-benders and how to avoid being duped. Phillips accepted Shaw and Edwards's offer, but not Randi's advice.

Randi had warned Dr Phillips not to allow the 'psychics' to control how the tests were run or to change experimental procedures in any way. In fact, Shaw and Edwards were able to do as they wished from the start. When the experimenters brought in television cameras to monitor the tests, the two young 'psychics' complained that the equipment gave them headaches and sapped their powers. A favourite ploy to distract the observers' attention was to ask for a glass of warm water. The trick worked time and again. In these favourable conditions, Shaw and Edwards were able to pull off some apparently amazing feats. They bent objects in sealed containers (by opening them when no one was looking and expertly replacing the seals), they twisted keys after momentarily distracting the attention of onlookers, and even produced 'thoughtographs' by spitting discreetly on the camera lens. Although Phillips was always cautious in his claims, research papers about the two prodigies issued from the lab, while the popular press hailed their 'dazzling mental abilities'.

When Randi finally revealed the existence of Project Alpha, Phillips and his colleagues took the news philosophically, but there was no avoiding the fact that the testers had been tested and found wanting: the claims of psychical researchers for PK, and metal-bending, had taken a serious knock.

PK holds a curious place in the realm of the paranormal. There are no 'spontaneous cases', there is no history or legend. The idea of PK as a field of study was first put forward by J. B. Rhine in 1934, yet in the 1980s PK has become fashionable – spoonbending parties are all the rage in the state of Virginia. Moreover, some researchers believe that most paranormal phenomena can be explained in terms of PK: someone who 'foresees' a winner in a horserace might really be using PK to make the horse win; firewalkers might be able to cool the brands beneath their feet; and poltergeists, of course, might just be PK in action. Yet there is no hard proof that PK exists at all. In fact, parapsychology has little to show for five decades of research into psychokinesis, apart from canteens of twisted cutlery in five continents, a few tables tipped, some vanished clouds, a baby bemused by a computer, columns of statistics, batteries of random number generators, and reams of argument and counter-argument.

No doubt the young gambler who swaggered into J. B. Rhine's office half a century ago knew a good bet when he saw one; there is little evidence that the same is true of Rhine and those of his successors who chose to study PK.

# 5

# Life After Life

WHEN NEWS CAME that the Lady of the Woods had appeared once more in Porter County, Indiana, no one under 20 paused to let the grass – or even the soya bean crop – grow under their feet. They were off on one of the strangest and possibly most dangerous ghost hunts of modern times.

It was a few days after Halloween in 1965 and rumours of the apparition of a faceless woman on a lonely gravel track running between the towns of Chesterton and Liberty in this usually sleepy rural community in northern Indiana set in train a series of events both bizarre and near-farcical. A local student, Deborah Koss, followed the story. Her first conclusion was that the ghost could hardly have chosen a creepier spot for her distraught pacing and wailing: 'A dense, ominous wood is sliced in half by this country road where the trees appear to drape a black canopy over the dusty lane. Isolated within the wooded area is a murky pond encased by a dreary swamp.'

The Lady of the Woods had long been a well-known 'inhabitant' of the area, even though few people could agree upon the details of her tragic story. 'Several years ago, a Porter County woman and her baby allegedly died in the swamp. Some people say by fire, others say they drowned in a nearby lake, and still others say they were both murdered. As the legend goes, the deceased woman's ghost appears faceless and in white carrying her child and moves about in the woods where their unfortunate deaths occurred. This ghost is said to scream hauntingly, "Save my baby!" at unwary passers-by and to scratch on car windows.'

Night after night, gangs of teenagers drove off into the darkness, many of them without headlights so as not to disturb the ghost. Out into the gloomy countryside the convoys roared, packed with people who hoped to catch a glimpse of the fearful apparition. Occasionally, they were rewarded, as one eyewitness from Chesterton, who had joined the hunt with some relatives, told Deborah Koss: 'We were all in the car together. And pretty soon this boy who lives out there said, "Ah, what are you looking over that way for?

*Opposite:* **The rakish Lord Lyttelton learns of his impending death from an apparition, see p. 105.**

The gloomy swamp in Porter County, Indiana, in which the Lady of the Woods and her baby are said to have perished.

Look over there." And just as we looked up about, oh, I'd say about 15 foot off the ground – here comes a white thing between the trees. And it took the form of a woman. And it was as white as snow. And it has no facial features, but it had a woman's form and it swung back and forth between the trees comin' right at us saying, "Save me!" It was just like moanin' – "Save my baby!" And it was the awfullest sound. Oh, it scared me to death!'

But, arguably, the most horrified reaction of all came from the local farmers (with the exception of the one who cannily levied a parking charge of $1 on the intrepid car-bound investigators). These people had been brought up on stories of the Lady of the Woods and had trodden the eerie forest paths of Porter County for years, unmolested and untroubled by any wailing apparition; no, it was the gun-toting ghost-hunters who got them rattled. The owner of one piece of land where the crowds gathered later recalled the events in painful detail: 'Well, there was so many people in that woods down there. A fellow had five acres of soy beans. They were just flattened down. Then there was one guy, he got a little bit too much to drink. He got in his car and he drove around all the cars, he goes a zigzaggin' around there, and he goes back to town. He comes back with a dog, and chains, and one of these here huntin' knives and he was goin' get it. He was gonna kill the ghost, you know . . . So of course it went so far that we had to get the sheriff out here and took everything from everybody. They had guns. It's a wonder somebody didn't get shot or get killed. They were carrying guns. They had revolvers. They had shotguns. They even had air rifles. The kids had air rifles. They were gonna shoot the ghost.'

Through the columns of one of the local newspapers, the Indiana State police appealed for an end to the madness. ' "Keep your kids at home," is the warning of Sergeant Al Hartman, who said this morning that the ghost hunt along Meridian Rd was "stupidity by a bunch of nuts", and must be stopped before someone is hurt. He said area schools had been contacted and asked to discourage the ghost hunt, which was working up a dangerous mob hysteria. Shot guns have been fired "to kill the ghost", the sergeant said, and someone might get killed if this doesn't stop.' And stop it did, but only after several frenzied days and 'a flock of arrests' by the police.

Ghost stories rarely provoke such civic unrest or violent passions as they did in Porter County, but popular curiosity about them, keen in all eras of history, is well-nigh insatiable today. Few people know this better than Richard T. Crowe, the ebullient operator of the Chicago Supernatural Tour. The success of his five-hour, 110-mile guided coach-trip round the city's haunted sites has allowed him to give up his job compiling a profile of Chicago's ethnic groups and concentrate on its less tangible inhabitants.

Every Saturday and Sunday afternoon, armchair ghost-hunters are happily lured to 'Chicago's most unique personal involvement tour' by a list of ghoulish attractions detailed in a yellow handbill:

Visit the haunted Robinson Indian Burial Ground.
See Jewish Waldheim Cemetery and the Melody Mill Ballroom, haunts of a flapper hitchhiking ghost.
Learn the real secret of Peabody's Tomb.
Did the Grimes Girls' murder leave psychic impressions upon German Church Road?
Ponder the miraculous preservation of the body of Julia Buccola at Mount Carmel Cemetery.
Can a ghost bend metal bars? See the handprints of a ghost!
See these and other psychic hotspots in the Western Suburbs.

The tour itself features a visit to the grave of Chicago's most notorious resident, gangster Al Capone, and explanations of spooky phenomena in Richard Crowe's lively patter: 'And why is there a light at the other side of the lake? Traditionally, in folklore, a ghostlight is caused by a headless ghost coming back with a lantern looking for his head.' There are vivid tales of confrontations with phantom monks: 'One of the best reports I have is from a Cook County police officer who, in late 1977, encountered eight or nine figures, as he described them, "milling about in the cemetery in

**The Chicago Supernatural Tour features Resurrection Cemetery among its attractions.** *Below:* **The cemetery gates were found damaged in 1976. Were its thick bronze bars bent by a ghost?**

monk-like garb". He called out to them to come on out and surrender. When they paid no attention he ran into the cemetery in hot pursuit with the shotgun he had grabbed from the squad car. He ran to the top of the hill where the church is located, got there just a few steps behind the monks. When he got to the top of the hill, the monks were suddenly gone . . .'

The climax of the trip comes with a visit to one of the largest burial-grounds in the entire United States, Resurrection Cemetery. Crowe wastes no time in telling his audience the reason for their visit to this vast parade-ground of the dear departed: 'It contains thousands of graves, and one most impressive ghost at least: that of Resurrection Mary, a beautiful young blonde Polish American girl, about five foot seven, shoulder-length blonde hair, blue eyes, seen in her white ballroom-type dancing dress; seen since the mid-1930s, encountered under all different kinds of conditions along Archer [Road], around the cemetery, at ballrooms in the area – just about anywhere a young lady would like to frequent a party; that's fair game for the ghost of Resurrection Mary.'

All kinds of people, it seems, have unwittingly taken a fancy to the alluring apparition: 'For instance, there was Jerry Palus, who in 1939 as a young man attended a dance at Liberty Grove and Hall at 47 and Mozart. Jerry met a very attractive young blonde who he danced with dance after dance. He offered to give the girl a lift home. She accepted. He drove her down Archer in the direction of which she told him to drive, and as they got in the area of Justice, Illinois, she had Jerry pull the car to the side of the road. He did, and as they sat at the kerb, she said, "I must cross the street at this point. You cannot follow." Jerry didn't understand what she was talking about: the only thing across the road was a cemetery – Resurrection Cemetery. The girl jumped from the car, ran towards the gates of the cemetery and disappeared before she reached them. It was only then, Jerry said, that he understood why the girl he was dancing with that night had been ice-cold to the touch. The only other time he'd ever felt anything like that was when he worked part-time at a funeral hall. The touch was the touch of death – the touch of a corpse.'

Most extraordinary of all is a story told to Crowe by a former policeman, Sergeant Pat Homer, who was sent to the cemetery during a patrol in August 1976. 'He had heard that a girl with blonde hair, white dress, was locked inside. He got there about 10.30 in the evening. There was nobody in the cemetery that he could see. He then spots that two of the bars on the left-hand side of the gate were curiously bent apart. When he went over to examine those bars closely he found that not only were the bars bent but there were strange marks on them – hand-prints. Hand-prints squeezed into the metal itself, and these are bronze bars, one-sixteenth of an inch thick. Well, Homer couldn't understand what could have happened. Couldn't understand how they could be bent, twisted in that fashion, how those marks could have been left in the metal. After a few weeks of search and research he came to the conclusion that no hoax was possible. And Homer came to the conclusion that the only hands that could have done that would have been the hands of a ghost; those bars bore incredible testimony to the possibility of Resurrection Mary's existence, physical evidence of the existence of a ghost.'

Richard Crowe has many predecessors as a collector and communicator of ghost stories. Accounts of strange spectres crop up in the earliest written texts and no doubt inspired in readers of those far-off times that delicious mixture of fascination and fear that the Chicago Supernatural Tour's customers happily pay to experience. Thus, apparitions are important dramatis personae in many a classical Greek or Roman epic. The great orator, Cicero, handed down a tale known as 'The Travellers of Megara', certainly one of the world's oldest ghost stories, incorporating many elements which recur over the centuries.

Two travellers decided to spend a night at a place called Megara. One was put up by friends, but the other had to stay in a nearby inn. As he slept, the traveller who was staying with friends had a dream in which his companion appeared to him and implored him to save him from being murdered by the landlord of the inn. Later, in a second dream, the man appeared again, but this time the situation was different. The inn-keeper had committed the foul deed and the murdered man now begged his friend to avenge his death. He told him that his body had been hidden in a wagon. When the surviving traveller went to the inn, he discovered his friend's mutilated body concealed beneath a layer of straw in a cart, just as the dream had foretold. The local forces of law and order were duly summoned, and the innkeeper was brought to book.

While revenge seems to have inspired the appearance of many classical ghosts, others merely wished for a decent burial. In one case, reported by Pliny the Younger, a hideous spectre, festooned with chains, beckoned an inquisitive philosopher into the garden of a haunted house in Athens and showed him the spot where he had been unceremoniously buried. After the proper rites and formalities due to the dead had been performed at the graveside, the ghost disappeared for ever.

Even the Venerable Bede, some 700 years later, related several ghost stories in his *History of the English Church and People*, although their inclusion undoubtedly owes more to Bede's desire to provide proof of the miraculous powers of God than to any wish to send a shiver down holy or heathen spines. Thus, after a pair of missionaries had been murdered by barbarians who dumped their bodies in the Rhine, the corpses floated 40 miles upstream to where their companions were. A great ray of light shone to mark their arrival: 'Moreover one of the two appeared by night in a vision to one of their companions, a distinguished man of noble family named Tilmon, a soldier turned monk, and told him that their bodies would be found at the spot where he saw the light shining from heaven to earth. This happened as he said: their bodies were found and buried with the honour due to martyrs, and the day of their death, or of the finding of their bodies, is observed in those parts with fitting respect.'

In the 17th century the mere reporting of ghost stories, often at second or third hand, began to give way to more organized collection, personal investigation and analysis. For example, Robert Plot, the first Keeper of Oxford's Ashmolean Museum, sent out a questionnaire to assist him in compiling his *Natural History of Oxfordshire* of 1677: 'Are there any ancient *Sepulchers* hereabout of Men of Gigantick stature, *Roman Generals* or *others* of ancient times? Has there ever been any apparitions hereabouts?'

Pre-eminent amongst these early collectors – pioneers of many of the techniques of psychical research – was Joseph Glanvill, chaplain to King

Charles II and author of a widely-respected book called *Sadducismus Triumphatus: or, a full and plain evidence concerning Witches and Apparitions*, which was published after his death in 1681. A distinguished philosopher and divine as well as a prolific writer, Glanvill seized the opportunity to investigate psychic phenomena at first hand when he heard of the case of the Phantom Drummer which plagued the Mompesson family of Tedworth, Wiltshire in 1662–3.

'The Drummer of Tedworth' from *Sadducismus Triumphatus*.

The trouble began after a drum, which John Mompesson had confiscated from a vagrant, was delivered to his home. From that time on, drumbeats echoed through the house, and the ghostly 'concert' was repeated day after day to the acute distress of the family. Although on one occasion Squire Mompesson encountered 'a great Body with two red and glaring Eyes, which for some time were fixed steadily upon him, and at length disappeared', the Phantom Drummer had all the trappings of a thorough-going poltergeist, with thumpings, rappings and scratchings which Glanvill himself heard during his visit to the house: 'I searcht under and behind the Bed, turning up the cloaths to the Bed-cords, graspt the Bolster, sounded the Wall behind, and made all search that possible I could to find if there were any trick, contrivance, or common cause of it; the like did my friend, but we could discover nothing. So that I was then verily perswaded, and am so still, that the noise was made by some Daemon or Spirit.'

On the whole, however, 17th- and 18th-century phantoms were useful fellows, keen to tie up loose ends and complete business unfinished during their earthly life: the collectors of ghost stories came across many tales of murderers receiving their come-uppance, of the bereaved gaining their rightful inheritance, or of the dead delivering dire warnings to the living. John Aubrey, more a lover of a good anecdote than a serious collector of ghost stories, included many weird and wonderful examples in his *Brief Lives*. In one he tells of the time when the ghost of Sir George Villiers, father of the first Duke of Buckingham, appeared to his old school-fellow Nicholas Towes. He made his purpose clear: 'Said Mr Towes to him, Why, you are Dead, what make you here? Said the Knight, I am Dead, but cannot rest in peace for the Wickedness and Abomination of my Son George at Court. I do appear to you, to tell him of it, and to advice and dehort him from his Evil ways. Said Mr Towes, the Duke will not believe me, but will say, that I am Mad, or Doat. Said Sir George, Go to him from me, and tell him by such a Token (some Mole) that he had in some secret place, which none but himself knew of. Accordingly Mr Towes went to the Duke, who Laugh'd at his Message. At his return home, the Phantome appeared again; and told him, that the Duke would be Stab'd (he drew out a Dagger) a quarter of a Year after: And you shall outlive him half a Year; and the Warning that you shall have of your death will be, that your Nose will fall a-bleeding: All of which accordingly fell out so.'

In the 18th century, warning apparitions were still at work. In 1779 one unfortunate recipient of a ghostly visit was Thomas, the Second Baron Lyttelton, known throughout the land as 'the wicked Lord Lyttelton'. The authoritative *Dictionary of National Biography* compiled the following chilling summary from contemporary accounts:

'. . . at his house in Hill Street, Berkeley Square, Lyttleton dreamed that a bird flew into the room and changed into a woman, who warned him that he had not three days to live. He told the dream, and the story at once became the talk of the town. Though he affected to make light of it, the occurrence weighed on his mind, but on the morning of the third day he said that he felt very well and believed he should 'bilk the ghost'. Passing a graveyard with his cousin, Hugh Fortescue, he remarked on the numbers of 'vulgar fellows' who died at five and thirty [his own age] adding 'But you and I, who are gentlemen, shall live to a good old age.' The same day, accompanied by Fortescue, Captain [afterwards Admiral] Wolseley, and some ladies, he drove down to Pitt Place, Epsom, where he dined, and passed a cheerful evening in apparently good health. He died the same night [Saturday 27 Nov.], shortly after getting into bed at a quarter past eleven.'

Naturally, the incident inspired much wonder, gossip and speculation, despite the mutterings of the sceptics that Lyttelton's demise was due to a heart-condition and to his habitual drug-taking, rather than to some pre-ordained plan known only to those who had gone before him into the realm of death. The great Dr Samuel Johnson announced however 'I am willing to believe it,' pronouncing the occurrence 'the most extraordinary thing that has happened in my day'.

The foundation in London of the Society for Psychical Research in 1882 brought a new attitude: curiosity and amazement were not enough; accounts of phantoms and apparitions were thenceforth to be subjected to painstaking scrutiny in the search for the truth about paranormal phenomena. Investigative committees were set up to review evidence. They included the Committee on Haunted Houses, and the Literary Committee, which collected and analysed accounts of all other types of apparitions. The members of the committees believed that their main task was to establish the facts about apparitions, as far as this was possible. Once they had done this, they could begin to theorize. 'What is really needed,' declared the Literary Committee in its first report, 'is a far larger supply of first-hand and well-attested facts . . . Knowledge can never grow until it is realized that the question "Do you believe in these things?" is puerile unless it has been preceded by the inquiry "What do you know about them?"'

In the first ten years of its existence the Society for Psychical Research collected an extraordinary number of cases of apparitions, some from friends, others from newspaper readers; and books, especially biographies, provided still more. Most useful of all were the first-hand accounts from an international survey known as the Census of Hallucinations.

Between April 1889 and May 1892, 410 collectors took part in the project, which drew 17,000 answers. The interviewees had, initially, been asked to reply 'yes' or 'no' to a single question: 'Have you ever, when believing yourself to be completely awake, had a vivid impression of seeing, or being touched by a living being or inanimate object, or of hearing a voice; which impression, so far as you could discover, was not due to any external physical cause?' If the answer was 'yes', the collectors had instructions to ask further questions about the percipient's state of health when the apparition was seen, whether he or she had ever had a similar experience and, most important of all: 'Please state what you saw or heard or felt, and give the place, date and hour of the experience as nearly as you can.'

Of the 17,000 people questioned, 1,684 or 9.9% answered that they had

had an experience of the kind specified. Although the administrators of the Census discounted hallucinations that had occurred during feverish illness, seen out of the corner of the eye or during the uncertain and illusion-prone borderland between waking and sleeping, and all those suspect for various other reasons, there still remained a substantial number of cases which could not be explained away.

One particularly striking feature of the material collected by the founding fathers of the Society of Psychical Research is that many apparitions were seen at the precise time at which the real flesh-and-blood person was dying. For example, Mrs May Clarke of Upper Norwood reported: 'In the month of August 1864, about 3 or 4 o'clock in the afternoon I was sitting reading in the verandah of our house in Barbados. My black nurse was driving my little girl, about 18 months or so old, in her perambulator in the garden. I got up after some time to go into the house, not having noticed anything at all – when this black woman said to me, "Missis, who was that gentleman that was talking to you just now?" "There was no one talking to me," I said. "Oh, yes, dere was, Missis – a very pale gentleman, very tall, and he talked to you, and you was very rude, for you never answered him." I repeated there was no one, and got rather cross with the woman, and she begged me to write down the day, for she knew she had seen someone. I did, and in a few days I heard of the death of my brother in Tobago. Now, the curious part is this, that *I* did not see him, but she – a stranger to him – did; and she said that he seemed very anxious for me to notice him.'

Mrs Eleanor Sidgwick, wife of the Society's first President, recorded a baffling account of an apparition which coincided with the death of a young English aviator. On 7 December 1918 Lieutenant David E. M'Connel left Scampton Aerodrome in Lincolnshire to fly a 'Camel' aircraft to the Yorkshire brewing town of Tadcaster some 60 miles away. Another plane went with him to bring him back to Scampton after the delivery had been made. Soon, both pilots found themselves enveloped in a thick blanket of fog, and M'Connel's companion had to make a forced landing. M'Connel himself carried on, wrestling with his bucking aircraft, peering into the fog and trying to maintain a safe height. About a quarter of a mile from Tadcaster the plane nosedived and crashed. M'Connel was killed when his head hit the gun mounted in front of the cockpit: his doubled-up cigarette case which was recovered from the wreckage, testified to the force of the crash. His watch stopped at 3.25 p.m.

Back at Scampton, M'Connel's friend and mess-mate Lieutenant James J. Larkin sat writing letters in his room, unaware of his fellow-officer's struggle on the journey to Tadcaster. He later described what happened in a written statement, made at the request of M'Connel's father:

> I heard someone walking up the passage; the door opened with the usual noise and clatter which David always made; I heard his 'Hello, boy!' and I turned half round in my chair and saw him standing in the doorway, half in and half out of the room, holding the door knob in his hand. He was dressed in his full flying clothes but wearing his naval cap, there being nothing unusual in his appearance. His cap was pushed back on his head and he was smiling, as he always was when he came into the room and greeted us. In reply to his 'Hello boy!' I re-

**Ted Simon, who experienced an apparition of a living person in Essex.**

marked, 'Hello! Back already?' He replied, 'Yes. Got there all right, had a good trip.' . . . I was looking at him the whole time he was speaking. He said, 'Well, cheero!' closed the door noisily and went out.

Larkin did not have a watch, but estimated that the visit had happened between a quarter and half-past three: just when the earthly David M'Connel was meeting his death 60 miles away in Yorkshire. That evening, in the Albion Hotel, Lincoln, Larkin learned of his fellow-officer's fate, to his acute distress and amazement: 'As you can understand . . . I was at a loss to solve the problem. There was no disputing the fact that he *had* been killed whilst flying to Tadcaster, presumably at 3.25, as we ascertained afterwards that his watch had stopped at that time. I tried to persuade myself that I had not seen him or spoken to him in this room, but I could not make myself believe otherwise, as I was undeniably awake and his appearance, voice, manner had all been so natural. I am of such a sceptical nature regarding things of this kind that even now I wish to think otherwise, that I did not see him, but I am unable to do so.'

Perhaps the oddest discovery made by the SPR pioneers when they classified cases was that more apparitions of living people were reported than of dead. To give an example of one such today: writer Ted Simon reported in *The Times* in 1983 that he had gone with his wife and son to visit a friend of his mother's, 'a kindly middle-aged widow' who lives 'in one of the world's more boring places', near the Essex seaside town of Southend-on-Sea. 'Her house lights were on and we rang her bell several times. Through her window I saw her walk from her kitchen and across her living room towards the front door. "Here she comes," I said. She was back-lit by the kitchen light and I could not see her face clearly, but she was solid enough otherwise and I recognized her distinctive gait.'

But she did not answer the door. Ted Simon rang the bell again and again, but the door stayed shut. Eventually, he gave up. When he tried to telephone her from his mother's house, there was no reply. 'I went back, perplexed, and rang her door bell again. Through the window I then saw her once more, less clearly, going back through her kitchen door, the light making a halo of her fluffed out hair style. She resolutely refused to answer . . .' Mystified, Ted Simon telephoned her the next day and, to his amazement, learned 'that she had been away all day to visit her daughter, leaving the house empty and the lights on "for the burglars".'

The SPR committees found that the reported cases divided into various broad classes. Hallucinations of those long dead they called 'revenants'; David M'Connel's appearance at Scampton was a 'crisis apparition'. One theory that had many supporters on the committees was that telepathy – the exchange of thoughts between two people – was the root-cause of many such apparitions. Thus, David M'Connel's fear as his plane crashed could have impinged upon the mind of his friend Lieutenant Larkin with such intensity that it was projected on to the surroundings at Scampton although – oddly, in the circumstances – the M'Connel of the apparition seemed calm and much as usual.

Certainly, many of the reported cases provided beguiling support for the idea that apparitions resulted from the transmission and reception of strong emotion. Mr John Hopkins of Carmarthen wrote: 'One evening, in the early spring of last year [1883], as I was retiring to bed, and whilst I was in the full enjoyment of good health and active senses – I distinctly saw my mother and my younger sister crying. I was in Carmarthen, and they were away in Monmouthshire, 80 miles distant. They distinctly appeared to me to be giving way to grief, and I was at once positive that some domestic bereavement had taken place. I said to myself, "I shall hear something of this in the morning." When the morning came, the first thing which was handed to me was a letter from my father in Monmouthshire, stating that they had, on the day of writing, had intelligence that my nephew had just died.'

Telepathy on a more elaborate scale might also help explain apparitions seen by several people at the same time. Another Victorian witness, Mr C. Colchester of Bushey Heath, reported a ghost which appeared to three people in two separate rooms. 'Forty-two or three years ago my father was with a detachment of his regiment, the Royal Artillery, stationed at Montreal, Canada. He had left his mother some months before in England in an indifferent state of health. One evening he was sitting at his desk, writing to her, when my mother, looking up from her work, was startled to see *his* mother looking over his shoulder, seemingly intent on the letter. My mother gave a cry of alarm, and on my father turning round the apparition vanished. On the same evening I and my brother (aged about six and five years) were in bed watching the bright moonlight, when suddenly we saw a figure, a lady with her hands folded on her breast, walking slowly, between the bed and the window, backwards and forwards. She wore a cap with a frill tied under her chin, and a dressing-gown of the appearance of white flannel, her white hair being neatly arranged. She continued to walk, it seemed to me, fully five minutes and then was gone. We did not cry out, and were not even alarmed, but after her disappearance we said to each other, "What a nice, kind lady!" and then went to sleep. The children mentioned what they had seen to their mother next morning, but were told not to talk about it. The news of their grandmother's death on that same evening arrived a few weeks afterwards. "I may add," Mr Colchester concluded, "that neither I nor my brother had ever seen our grandmother till that evening, nor knew of what my mother had seen till years after." ' Conceivably, if telepathy exists, Mr Colchester's mother could have 'tuned in' to the grandmother's death agonies and then telepathically conveyed the image to her children as they lay in bed upstairs.

Early psychical researchers reported several experiments which apparently demonstrated that it is possible to project an apparition using ESP. In more modern times, one such test was carried out by Lucian Landau and his wife Eileen, who now live on the Isle of Man. One night before they were married Landau arranged that Eileen, who was sleeping in the same house but in a different bedroom, should attempt to visit him as an apparition. He awoke suddenly at dawn, and there in the room was the figure of Eileen, clad in a nightdress, her face drained of all colour. 'The figure was moving slowly backwards towards the door, but it was otherwise quite motionless; it was not walking.' Landau followed. 'I could then clearly see the moving figure, which was quite opaque and looking like a living person, but for the extreme pallor of the face, and at the same time the head of Eileen, asleep in her bed, the bedclothes rising and falling as she breathed.' She was still

Georgina Feakes and her cousin Owen Howison, whom she saw in a vision, after his death, carrying a blue orchid. Later it was discovered that Owen had secretly picked the rare flower on Table Mountain.

asleep when the figure finally vanished. The ESP theory is far less convincing, however, when it is applied to apparitions of people who are newly dead. Francis J. Pain told the London *Daily Express* of one strange encounter. 'The year is 1942. I was then flight lieutenant in a fighter squadron in the Western Desert. On the morning of July 3 my squadron took off to intercept a wave of Stuka dive-bombers with a top cover of ME109 fighters high above them. After the combat the squadron was separated over a large area of sky, and we made our own way back to base in ones and twos.

'I started strolling over to the mess tent about 100 yards away. Flight Lieutenant Ginger (——) came towards me from my right – "Hell of a party, Derna," he said, "I never saw them until they hit us." I had my cigarettes out and offered him one and for the first time since I had known him he refused saying, "No thanks, old boy, I don't need one now." He branched off to his tent, which was 10 or 12 yards away to our right. I continued to the mess. Squadron Leader J —— came into the bar and said to us, "Bad show about Ginger, they cut him to pieces as he pulled out from under those tail-end Stukas." "Derna" was a nickname that Ginger attached to me and at that time was used only by him.'

By the time the two airmen 'met', Ginger was already dead. The theory is that, just possibly, Ginger might have transmitted a powerful thought which, for some reason, was not received by his friend until later, but this seems to be stretching a point in favour of the telepathic theory of apparitions too far.

Explanations are even more difficult to find for the countless cases involving an apparition of someone who has been dead for some time. One of the most colourful and convincing accounts of recent years comes from Mrs Georgina Feakes of Kent.

In 1944 a cousin of Mrs Feakes named Owen Howison was killed in action in Italy. He had been guarding engineers repairing a blown-up bridge. Mrs Feakes heard of his death from Owen's mother, who lived in South Africa. One day, sitting in her house in Tilekiln Lane, Old Bexley, Mrs Feakes' cousin appeared to her in a cloud of golden mist. She says: 'His lips were moving but I could hear no words except the last two which were "Tell mum."' A few days later, he appeared again. 'This time his voice was clear and distinct. He said his tank had been blown up, but he still felt very much alive. Would I tell his mother, and would I please send his love to poor Helen?' When Mrs Feakes asked Owen for proof that it really was him, he said 'Watch,' and at once produced from inside his shirt an exotic blue orchid. Its sweet, heavy scent filled the room. Quickly, he put the flower back inside his shirt, but then repeated the action, showing the unfamiliar bloom once more to the spellbound Mrs Feakes. Then, with a last, urgent, 'Tell Mum, please. Goodbye dear cousin,' he was gone.

Although Mrs Feakes knew of Owen's death at the time of her vision, several significant details of his life were revealed in the uncanny encounter which, in the view of Owen's surviving family, Mrs Feakes could not conceivably have known about. The most remarkable revelation of all came when Mrs Feakes asked her aunt about the blue flower and the odd way in which Owen had handled it. Back from South Africa came the explanation:

'On Owen's last leave he climbed Table Mountain and stole the blue flower which is protected by law and may not be plucked. He tucked it inside the chest of his shirt to bring home and had just taken it out to show (as I can't climb and had never seen one) when there came a knock. He was nervous of discovery (a heavy fine for picking it) and put it back inside his shirt, but it was only sister Cynthia. He showed me again, when the front door banged and he popped it for a second time into his shirt. This time it was brother Peter coming from work, so now I could really have a good look at this marvellous flower.' Wartime censorship meant that letters were read by the authorities, so they had not written about the blue orchid for fear of prosecution. Owen's mother told Mrs Feakes she was absolutely certain 'He never mentioned this to anyone outside the family, and for Owen to re-enact this scene for you, proved to us he still lives.'

Owen's plea to be remembered to Helen puts paid to the possibility that the apparition was created through a telepathic link-up between Mrs Feakes and her aunt. Owen had, indeed, had a friend called Helen. He wrote her romantic letters and poems, but no one in the family knew of her existence when Georgina Feakes saw him. Helen introduced herself to them later, when the story of Owen's weird reappearance with the blue orchid was circulating in Cape Town. One theory is that Mrs Feakes had unconsciously acted as a medium and had enabled Owen's surviving spirit to make contact. All that can be said is that the tale of the Blue Orchid of Table Mountain provides interesting evidence for advocates of survival after death, but not the proof that psychical researchers have sought so eagerly in the analysis of apparitions and in the shadows of the séance room.

The rare and protected Blue Orchid.

Apparitions are easier to explain away than to explain, as sceptics discovered long before the telepathic theories were advanced. In 1841, Charles Mackay published a book called *Extraordinary Popular Delusions and the Madness of Crowds*, which included many stories of 'ghost' trickery. One tale concerned six monks who had generously been put up in a large house at Chantilly by the King of France. They decided between themselves, however, that they would prefer to live in an abandoned royal palace. Soon, there were reports of strange events at the palace: shrieks, coloured lights, the sound of clanking chains, a horrible spectre with a long white beard and the tail of a serpent appearing at a window and frightening passers-by. The monks, naturally, announced that they would try to rid the castle of the diabolical intruders, and the grateful king agreed to their suggestion that they should be allowed to live in the palace. To nobody's surprise – least of all the wily monks' – the hauntings ceased at the moment when the deed making over the palace to them was signed and sealed.

In modern times, examples of people mistakenly believing they have seen or heard a ghost are plentiful. Richard Crowe includes a timely warning during his Chicago Supernatural Tour. In the city's Woodlawn Cemetery there's a section known as Showman's Rest: this was inaugurated to take the bodies of more than 60 circus people who were killed in a train crash in 1918. It is a picturesque spot, dominated by some unusual carved stone elephants. Over the years visitors have reported hearing strange animal sounds: 'You can hear elephants and other circus-type animals on the night-time breeze.' Although they are, indeed, very spooky, the sounds are entirely explicable in normal terms. The case was solved by an enterprising policeman, Sergeant John O'Rourke. Crowe explains:

'He was out here a few years ago and, as he walked round the area, he suddenly began to hear strange animal sounds. It was midnight, and he couldn't understand what was going on. Just before his knees gave out from under him, the solution dawned on him. What he was hearing – what so many other people had been hearing over the years – were the sounds of elephants and other circus animals all right, but not the animals killed in that tragic train wreck of 1918, but the very-much-alive animals from Brookfield Zoo a mile-and-a-half away to the south and west. You see, at night, when the factories close down and the hustle-and-bustle of daytime activity ceases, those sounds could carry a great distance. We're just the proper distance from Brookfield Zoo to hear those animal sounds at night.'

Milbourne Christopher, the American magician, has a similar tale to tell about a house in Union, New York State. Several families were driven out of the place by a fearful wailing sound before a man who wished to study a haunted house was allowed to stay there for several days. He later returned to the estate agency with the answer to the mystery in his pocket. The wailing sounds had been caused by draughts blowing through a small metal whistle which had been stuck into a hole in the attic by a tenant's child. Another 'ghost' had been well and truly laid.

Sometimes a 'ghost' may turn out to be no more than an optical illusion. In 1964, after Anglia Television screened a programme about the paranormal, several viewers got in touch with the company to point out that they had actually seen a ghost on the film. A hooded monk, they said, was standing to the right of a man who was being interviewed on location about the alleged haunting of derelict Morley Hall. Everyone concerned with the making of the programme was baffled, for they could see nothing. Eventually they enlarged some single frames from the film, and found that marks on the stonework of the window looked rather like the outline of a figure.

The uncertain state between waking and sleeping has often given rise to convincing but explicable illusions, so common they have names: a hypnagogic illusion is one that precedes proper sleep, in which a thought or image which has been in the percipient's mind during waking hours may assume an apparently solid form. A hypnopompic illusion is one that follows sleep and may be the continuance of a dream. The Rev. E. H. Sugden of Bradford in Yorkshire told of this disconcerting experience: 'Once I had a most vivid dream about a man whom I knew well. On suddenly waking I saw him, in the light of early morning, standing at my bedside in the very attitude of the dream. I looked at him for a second or two, and then putting my foot out, I kicked at him; as my foot reached him, he vanished.'

There have been cases, too, when a 'ghost' turned out to be a living person all the time. In her centenary history of the SPR, Renée Haynes gives a good example. During the Second World War, when petrol was short, she used to hitch-hike ten miles to work and back. 'I used to stand in a country main road, shining a torch onto my left hand (which wore a red ski-glove) and making the hitch-hiker's sign. But cars and lorries, most helpful by daylight, refused to stop after dark, and indeed even seemed to accelerate. In the end I returned to wait an hour for the regular bus to go slowly lurching homeward through mud, rain or snow. It was two months before the explanation came to me. Someone said at a local party, "You're interested in ghost stories. Did you know there's a very well authenticated one of a luminous red hand being seen in mid-air, evening after evening, on a particular stretch of the Witney road?" I authenticated it still further!'

Even the secret infiltration of a living person into a sedate household has been advanced as an explanation of ghost sightings. In a house in Cheltenham, Gloucestershire in 1882 a girl named Rosina Despard, later to become a distinguished doctor, spotted a tall woman, dressed in black, her face concealed by the handkerchief which she held in her right hand. There were further encounters, and the strange figure was also seen by other inhabitants of the house. At the time, the apparition was thought to be the ghost of a 'Mrs S.' who had lived in the house before her death a few years before. Miss Despard submitted various 'proofs of immateriality', such as the woman's apparent ability to walk through fine strings stretched across the stairs, but Peter Underwood, a leading authority, has described the Cheltenham ghost as 'one of the less convincing cases of haunting in the records of psychical research'. He believes the woman may have been a real person, an illicit lodger living there with the permission of Captain Despard.

Among the arguments Underwood cites in support of his theory are the fact that Mrs Despard was known to be 'a great invalid', so that the Captain might reasonably have wished to seek 'consolation, companionship and an intimate relationship with another woman'. Certainly, the figure always appeared extremely lifelike, and the handkerchief over her face may have been to prevent recognition or being seen plainly. In this light, the reluctance of Captain Despard to allow investigation adds fuel to the suggestion that another woman was leading a secret life in the house, her presence betrayed only by an occasional mistimed walk or by footfalls in the night.

The possibility of fraud, sadly so prevalent in the psychic world, must always be considered. In 1956 the Society for Psychical Research published a devastating report on the phenomena recounted of 'the most haunted house in England', Borley Rectory in Suffolk. The report called into question the reputation not only of the rectory's ghosts but also that of their tireless publicist and investigator, Harry Price. The authors, Eric J. Dingwall, Kathleen M. Goldney and Trevor Hall, contend that Price got hold of a potentially good story and exploited it for all it was worth (which was quite a lot, since he derived a couple of best-selling books from it). They suggest that he deliberately obscured facts that would have enabled outside observers to judge whether the apparently strange events that made the rectory famous were of normal or paranormal origin; that he suppressed evidence failing to support his thesis that the house was haunted; and that he may have stooped to fraud on several occasions to provide 'good copy'.

Borley Rectory's reputation, according to the report, became established locally during the incumbencies of the Rev. Henry Bull and his son Harry. The Rev. Harry, may have held spiritualistic beliefs and was certainly eccentric. He appears to have spent an abnormal amount of time sleeping, and he may have had hallucinations which inspired stories of sightings of a nun, a spectral coach, an old family retainer and, perhaps, a headless man.

Borley achieved national fame when another rector, the Rev. Guy Eric Smith, asked the London *Daily Mirror* to investigate the rectory's haunted reputation. The editor called in Harry Price. Price noted after his first visit to Borley: 'The Smiths took the rectory living in September 1928, finding the place in terribly bad repair. There are rats in the house, and toads, frogs, newts etc in the cellars. They themselves refuse to believe in ghosts and know nothing about them.' But no sooner had Price appeared on the scene than strange things began to happen: bells rang, apparently without human agency, some medallions materialized, keys jumped clean out of locks, a vase suddenly smashed, footsteps echoed in empty corridors, the house was filled with whisperings.

The arrival in the autumn of 1930 of a new rector, the Rev. Lionel Algernon Foyster and his much younger wife, Marianne, brought new and still more sinister phenomena. Messages appealing for help from Marianne were found on walls, fires appeared to break out spontaneously, furniture was thrown about, small objects were propelled through the air, and Mrs Foyster's bedclothes were often disturbed by apparently unseen forces. Given Price's interest, and the tendency for things to happen in his presence, the rectory's continued fame was inevitable.

The authors of the SPR report present the other side of the coin. Unwilling to accept the 'facts' as described by Price without challenge, they subjected the evidence for the haunting of Borley Rectory to a rigorous re-examination. Their main finding was that the case failed to stand up to careful scrutiny in almost all respects. For example, they established many perfectly normal explanations for so-called paranormal occurrences: the footsteps and whisperings were due to a strange acoustical effect which relayed sounds from an adjacent cottage into the house; air pressure may have made keys jump from locks; and the bells could just as well have been rung by rats and mice, which infested the place, or by hoaxers, as by invisible agents. The house could be entered by two doors or a trap door in the courtyard which led to the cellar, and there were three staircases, allowing anyone who wished to play tricks in the rambling building to do so. Dingwall, Goldney and Hall also point out that Marianne Foyster may well have been depressed by living in the run-down country rectory, and coping with an ailing husband twice her age (he had officiated at her baptism). She could well have been producing the 'phenomena' herself, drawing on her knowledge of a famous poltergeist case, known as the Great Amherst Mystery, for some of the weirder effects. The Foysters' previous incumbency had been in Canada, a few miles away from the scene of the mystery, which was an often-told local story.

The 'villain' of the whole piece, however, in the eyes of the report, was Harry Price, who eventually took on the tenancy of the rectory himself to further his investigations. The report's authors maintain that he prejudiced the objectivity of the research by appealing for help from people with no previous experience of psychical research, and that his 'Blue Book' of instructions for them contained too many suggestions of what they might see: 'The design of the experiments was faulty, the overall conduct of the enquiry deplorably lax, and the absence of any central control fore-doomed the investigation to failure from the scientific point of view. These things did not matter to Price. He got what he hoped and expected to get from his body of untrained observers who constituted the bulk of the witnesses during the period under review. All he had to do was to write up and carefully edit their stories for publication.'

## SUFFOLK & ESSEX FREE PRESS

THURSDAY, JUNE 13, 1929

Circulated extensively in South Suffolk and North Essex.　PRICE TWOPENCE

Offices : Station Road, Sudbury, Suffolk.

# BORLEY GHOST FACTS

I CANNOT UNDERSTAND
TELL ME MORE

*Marianne*,

I STILL CANNOT UNDERSTAND
TELL ME MORE,

**Vicki Branden with Hound, her dog. She met a phantom motorcyclist on the lonely road.**

More damagingly, perhaps, eyewitnesses came forward to testify that Price had done more than bias the results: a newspaperman told of the time he had seized Price after mysteriously being hit by a stone and found that the great ghost hunter's pockets were crammed full of pebbles. And, when *Life* magazine published a picture of a brick apparently teleported into the air at Borley, why did Price 'forget' that demolition work was in progress and that the brick had actually been thrown by a labourer who was hidden from the camera lens?

Publication of 'The Borley Report' (as it became known) aroused a storm of controversy, and by no means all members of the parapsychological community were disposed to accept its findings. But in the late 1970s Iris M. Owen and Paulene Mitchell of Toronto's New Horizons Foundation, added further controversy when they interviewed Marianne Foyster, by then almost 80 years old. Marianne put much of the blame on her husband. The Rev. Foyster, it seemed, had been writing a largely fictitious account of goings-on at the rectory in the hope of earning enough money through its publication to ensure that she would be adequately provided for after his death. Marianne described several 'incidents' that the Rev. Foyster manufactured to test the reactions of his visitors. Price, however, by no means escaped criticism, for Marianne Foyster believed that he was not fooled by the fiction. Whether Price played a principal or a secondary role in the events that made Borley Rectory notorious, the claim that it was 'the most haunted house in England' has, like the building itself, been demolished.

There are, of course, many apparitions which do not result from trickery or distortion of the evidence. State of mind may often be a factor predisposing people to hallucinate. In a paper in *The British Medical Journal* in 1971, Dr W. Dewi Rees, then a general practitioner in mid-Wales, reported that almost half the widowed people within the catchment area of his medical practice at Llanidloes had experienced hallucinations of their dead spouses, especially during the first ten years of their widowhood. They were not generally frightened by the apparitions; on the contrary, they found them friendly and comforting.

Not so Vicki Branden, a writer from Toronto, Canada. While driving home from a long trip in December 1974, she parked at the side of the road to let her dog out. Suddenly she was confronted by a terrifying vision. 'It was very dark and lonely and fairly late, and there, in the headlights, I could see this man, and I had no idea that he wasn't real.' He was standing menacingly astride a motorcycle. 'He was extremely solid and vivid, and so dangerous-looking: a stereotypical biker figure. He had no shirt on, but one of those little waistcoat things. I thought "I'm gonna be murdered," and I'd hardly had time to think and he was gone.'

Afterwards, both Vicki Branden and her dog were violently sick – but not, as it turned out, from fear: 'Finally, we staggered back to the car and, as soon as I opened the door, having been out in the fresh air, I realized that the car was full of fumes. I had bought this tin of starter spray, and the top was defective, and it had been leaking ether, or something like that, in the car. So we were both half-gassed when it happened.'

Although the fumes from the starter spray had brought on the hallucination, why had Vicki Branden seen a phantom motor-cyclist and not something more familiar to her? She cannot, of course, be certain about the answer, but she does remember a similar image coming into her consciousness one night sometime earlier when she was drifting off to sleep. She was also worrying about her 15-year-old son's growing interest in motorcycles for, as he put it when she returned home, ' "You don't like motorcycles," he reminded me, "and you're scared of the motorbike-gang type of guy. Lately you've been afraid that I'll want a bike as soon as I'm sixteen. So all this stuff has been going on in your head." ' Fear and fumes had almost certainly stimulated her imagination so violently that she had projected her thoughts on to that lonely roadside at the dead of night.

Many medical conditions induce hallucinations. One of the most graphic reports of such phenomena was written in the 18th century by a Berlin bookseller called Nicolai: 'I saw, in a state of mind completely sound – and, after the first terror was over, with perfect calmness – for near two months, almost constantly and involuntarily, a vast number of human and other forms, and even heard their voices; though this was merely the consequence of a diseased state of nerves, and an irregular circulation of blood.'

The 'phantasms', mainly of people Nicolai merely knew slightly or only by sight, began appearing in February 1791, and 'appeared to me contrary to my inclination; as if they were presented to me *from without*, like the phenomena of nature, though they existed nowhere but *within my mind*. I could, at the same time, plainly distinguish between phantasms and real objects; and the calmness with which I examined them enabled me to avoid the commission of the smallest mistake. I knew, exactly, when it only *appeared* to me that the door was opening, and a phantasm entering the room; and, when it *actually* opened, and a real person entered.'

Some apparitions seem to be attached to particular places. Ghost hunters have compiled gazetteers of them, but the search for acceptable theories to explain them has been less successful.

For more than 30 years, Harry Martindale has been trying to figure out a spectacular apparition he experienced in the cellar of the Treasurer's House in York in 1953. He was installing central heating in the building and was knocking a hole in the cellar ceiling. Suddenly, he heard a trumpet call and, a few moments later, a Roman soldier marched straight through the wall, followed by another on a horse, and then an entire column of soldiers. The astonished Martindale watched as they went past. 'They were all dressed exactly the same,' he says. 'The first thing I looked at was the helmet. It came straight underneath the chin. From the bottom of the helmet I could see there was a growth of hair; most of them had beards. On the top half, they wore broad bands of leather joined together to form a jerkin. On the bottom half they wore a skirt.' They all carried a short sword and one soldier a large round shield with a raised boss in the middle.

Later, when he recounted his story, Harry Martindale discovered a curious thing. A Roman road runs under the Treasurer's House, and the ladder on which he had been working had been positioned in a hole excavated to the level of the original Roman paving. This explains a strange aspect of the soldiers' appearance: 'I couldn't see any of them from the knees down until they came to where the hole had been excavated in the centre of the cellar floor. Then, for about

**The Treasurer's House, York, built on the site of a Roman road. Harry Martindale says he saw Roman soldiers marching through its cellars.**

two paces, I actually saw them walking on the surface of the Roman road.'

Explanations for hauntings of this kind usually lean heavily upon the so-called 'stone tape' theory. The idea is that scenes or events from a place's history have become trapped in that very spot. Later, over the years, the moments from the past are rerun, like a sound or video tape, and appear fleetingly to witnesses from our own times. York was a major city of Roman Britain and legions of soldiers must have trodden the road that now lies beneath the Treasurer's house. The 'stone tape' is a convenient idea, but many questions remain unanswered: for example, what causes the tape to be made in the first place and what decides when it should play?

Could this theory conceivably apply to a No. 19 bus? Conductor Trevor Pease saw a ghost on his double-decker in Plymouth. The bus was empty, Pease recalls, when it drew up at a stop on a main road into the town. 'Two ladies – in their thirties, I should imagine – got on the bus followed by two gentlemen. Up the stairs the four of them went. And there was another lady, rather older than the other ones, but as far as I was concerned she was the mother of the two ladies because the three of them looked so much alike. I assumed the men were the husbands. As the lady got on the bus-platform, for some reason or other she stopped. She looked at me, and her face broke into a nice big grin. She looked up, gave her shoulders a shrug and she walked upstairs. I rang the bell – you know, "Ping, ping. Hold tight, please!" – and looked up to see and noticed they were going right up to the front seats. There was nothing at that moment to suggest anything was wrong, because they were five human beings getting on a bus. The only thing that struck me as odd was the fact that they were not very sociable in letting the poor old lady get on last, while they hopped on first.'

Pease rang the bus straight through the next stop, and it was when he went up to collect the fares that he realized: 'There's one missing. Where's the old lady gone?' She was nowhere to be found, so Pease asked one of the four remaining passengers about the old lady and described her: 'She was medium build, slightly smaller than medium height – I would have put her at about five feet four. She was wearing – believe it or not – a leopard-skin two-piece suit, with matching hat and handbag. And she had a diamond – or diamond-like – butterfly brooch in her lapel. Her hair was greyish, and very well groomed. I said, "There's no question about it, she looks too much like these two ladies not to be their mother." '

Sure enough, one of the women told him: 'The woman you've described to us was our mother. The outfit she was wearing was mother's. In fact, we bought it for her. Last time she wore it was when she went out with us. But she died 14 months ago . . .'

Trevor Pease on a Plymouth bus. Did a ghost travel on the upper deck of the No 19, the ghost of a woman who had died 14 months earlier?

Why should a monk-like figure have haunted Sharon Grenny's council house on the Nunthorpe Estate in the fishing port of Grimsby? One night, as she was tucking up her two-year-old son Jamie in bed, she heard a shuffling sound and, when she turned to see what had caused it, there stood a man, dressed in a brown robe. Most terrifying of all was the fact that his face was completely featureless. She at once fled from the room, leaving the child. Her elder child, Stacey, had also seen the terrifying figure. Eventually, unable to face spending any more time in the house, Sharon Grenny was allowed by an understanding town council to change houses.

Stephen Dimbleby encountered his apparition in the eerie tunnels of a Yorkshire coalmine, Silverwood Colliery, near Rotherham. It was a Sunday, around midnight, and Stephen was working at the coalface with two other miners. Suddenly, as he went up a tunnel to collect some equipment, 'It just appeared from nowhere – the figure of a body, and I couldn't see through him. He was just like an ordinary bloke, and my first instincts were that it was just somebody mucking about. And then it hit me: he's come from nowhere, just appeared.'

The horrified young miner grabbed his helmet-lamp in the hope of identifying the figure: 'And when I shone my light in his face, there were no features on his face. And then I just dropped everything, and set off running out . . .' Stephen has never gone back down the pit. His terror at the very thought led to sleepless nights and a plea, which was accepted, for a much less well-paid job on the surface, far away from the faceless horror underground.

Just as puzzling is the story of the phantom hitch-hiker Roy Fulton encountered on a deserted road near Dunstable in Bedfordshire. At about nine o'clock one night in October 1979, Roy was heading home after a darts match in Leighton Buzzard. He took his usual route down the quiet backroads, it was a journey he had made countless times before in the little minivan he used for his job as a carpet-fitter. This journey, however, was to prove totally, frighteningly different:

'As I was passing through the village of Stanbridge, going out of the street lights, there was a young lad thumbing a lift. I should think he was about 19 – maybe 20 – years old: dark trousers, dark jumper, with a white shirt, with a rounded-off collar. So I thought to myself, I'll stop and give him a lift. So I stopped in front of him, so he had to walk back towards the car – and I picked him up in my headlights. That's why I could distinguish all the markings on him. He opened the door. I never touched the door. He

Roy Fulton sought sanctuary in his local pub, The Glider, in Dunstable, Bedfordshire, after giving a lift to a 'phantom hitch-hiker'.

got in, sat down, and I asked him where he wanted to go. He never said a word – just pointed up the road, so I assumed that he wanted to go to Dunstable or Totternhoe.'

The hitch-hiker's silence didn't worry Roy. 'I thought to myself, well, he might be deaf or dumb or something like that. So I never thought a lot more of it. I just started driving off, doing about 45 miles an hour. About four or five hundred yards before we reached the street lights at Totternhoe, I picked up my packet of cigarettes that I had on the dashboard and offered him one. And that young lad wasn't sitting there. And, believe me, I froze. Then I really braked sharp: I thought he might have fallen out. And then I thought to myself, Well, he couldn't have fallen out 'cos the interior light would have come on in the cab. He couldn't have got in the back, because I'd have seen all the movements. I never even got out of the car. I just put it in first gear, and I went like a bat out of hell, to be honest with you. It frightened the life out of me.'

A few minutes later, the shaken Roy Fulton reached the sanctuary of The Glider, his local pub. Never before had he quite so badly needed a double Scotch or the comfortable conviviality of his favourite bar. His friends crowded round. One of them said, 'What's the matter, Roy? You look like you've seen a ghost!'

Many stories of phantom hitch-hikers seem to be apocryphal and belong more to modern folklore than to real life. In 1982, for example, no less a luminary than the Archangel Gabriel was reported to be regularly flagging down motorists in southern Germany, telling them that the world would end in 1984, and disappearing from their moving cars. The local police could do no more than refer the troubled drivers to the Munich episcopate, where a spokesman announced, reassuringly, that 'It is inconceivable that an angel would ever appear in the form of a hitch-hiker. And it is not in the interest of God to issue such a message of doom.' Yet Roy Fulton is certain that he gave a lift to a ghost. Indeed, he will not drive down that road in the dark today, preferring a longer trip via the busy main highways.

In the face of stories like these even the most articulate of theorists fall silent. It is impossible to dismiss them out of hand, when they are reported by sincere and often terrified people.

Actor Telly Savalas, known to television viewers world-wide as 'Kojak', has one such baffling tale to tell. One night he was driving through a remote area when he ran out of petrol. It seemed unlikely that anyone would pass by, but a man in a black Cadillac turned up and offered him a lift. In the course of conversation, the driver mentioned that he knew a certain athlete. Telly was somewhat surprised to discover from the newspaper the next day that this athlete had died in strange circumstances in the exact spot where he had been given the lift. And when Telly called a telephone number his rescuer had given him, to repeat his thanks, a distressed woman on the other end of the line told the embarrassed Savalas that, although the driver of the Cadillac seemed to bear him a striking resemblance, her husband had been dead for the past three years.

Volumes and shelves of volumes have been filled with stories of ghosts and apparitions seen by people with little reason to attract attention to themselves, patently sincere, and willing to answer the most searching questions posed by investigators of the paranormal. As the writer and researcher Andrew Lang acknowledged: 'Only one thing is certain about apparitions, namely this, that they do appear. They really are perceived.'

But are any apparitions real? If anyone had seen a ghost and taken a good clear photograph, then we should be a long way towards establishing their objective reality. So far, however, nothing like proof has emerged from the darkroom. Indeed, the activities of the charlatan photographers who produced portraits allegedly of the spirits of dead people between the 1860s and the 1930s have inspired a wary approach from researchers ever since. The spirit photographers may have brought some consolation to the bereaved, who were provided with 'evidence' of the survival of their loved-ones after death: they certainly provided investigative journalists with some entertainment and some frank and fearless exposés. Mrs Ada Emma Deane, a former charlady, became famous for her photographs of the Armistice Day Ceremony at London's Cenotaph war memorial in the 1920s. Amazingly, the pictures contained faces, presumably of the dead, looking down on the proceedings. Unfortunately for Mrs Deane, however, she was caught out by a press agency which told the world that the faces actually belonged to living sportsmen, and that identical portraits, minus the Cenotaph, were in its files.

Some thirty years before this fiasco, however, on 5 December 1891, a photograph was taken which appeared to provide proof that the dead did return to haunt their former earthly abodes. The photographer, a Miss Sybell Corbet, set up her camera in the library of Lord Combermere's mansion, Combermere Abbey near Nantwich, Cheshire, at two o'clock in the afternoon. She intended to take a picture of the room and, because the exposure of the plate was a long one – an hour – Miss Corbet did not stay by the camera throughout. The photograph turned out well, for it showed a comfortable, book-lined Victorian library in sharp focus. It also turned out very curiously, for there, on the left of the frame, was a mysterious person sitting in a high-backed armchair. To the best of Miss Corbet's knowledge, no other living person had been in the library that afternoon, and certainly not the distinguished gentleman whom the figure in the photograph most closely resembled. For Lord Combermere, the owner of the library, had just died. He had been run over by a cab while crossing a London street and an injury to his leg had brought about his death. His funeral was taking place at the time the picture was being taken.

Miss Corbet was adamant that the plate had not been exposed before, and she was equally sure that the figure was that of a gentleman and not of a servant, for the footmen at the house always wore livery. The butler was consulted; he also was certain that no stranger had entered the library at the time in question. But Professor William Barrett who, with a Mr Gordon Salt, investigated the case, thought differently; indeed, he managed to produce an almost identical photograph. He wrote: 'I believe that one of the servants came into the room, sat down in the chair, crossed his legs and then uncrossed them, looked down for a moment and then at the camera, saw that he was being taken, so got up and went away, having been in the chair about 20 to 30 seconds. This will give the ghost of an apparently older

**Film star Telly 'Kojak' Savalas tells of an encounter with a 'dead' motorist who gave him a lift.**

Sybell Corbet's photograph of the library at Combermere Abbey. The mysterious figure – which some people believed was Lord Combermere's ghost – can be made out in his lordship's favourite chair in the left foreground.

man from a young man, *with no legs*, and a semi-transparent face, &c.' When an expert on spirit photography took a close look at the picture and pointed out that the outlines of many of the parts of the figure's body were blurred, everyone agreed that the man in the picture, despite his resemblance to the dead Lord Combermere, was not a ghost but an interloper or a hoaxer caught in the act.

There are a few photographs, apparently of ghosts, taken by reputable people, which have not been explained away. One was snapped by the Rev. Kenneth Lord in Newby Church in North Yorkshire in the summer of 1954. The church is in an exceptionally picturesque setting in the leafy grounds of one of England's stately homes, Newby Hall, near Ripon.

Mr Lord had been appointed vicar of the parish and wanted some photographs of his church to send to some friends. Of the 12 photographs Kenneth Lord took with his Rolleicord 4 that day, the most striking was frame 5, which showed the inside of the church and, by the altar, something else: a tall cloaked and hooded figure with a skull-like face. The Rev. Lord is certain that there was no one else in the church during the photo session and that the place appeared quite normal through the viewfinder. When he found the weird apparition on the printed film, he sought the opinions of experts. 'The film went to Kodak,' said his wife, 'because it was a Kodak film. It went to an independent photographer – and various other bodies – and they could find no possible way in which it could have been faked.'

Ghostly figures have also appeared in photographs taken in many other churches. A holiday portrait of Lady Palmer taken by her friend Miss Townsend in the Basilica at Domrémy, France in June 1925, reveals a pair of spectral priests standing near her ladyship. Just as invisible to the naked eye but captured on film by a local solicitor was the 'person' kneeling at the altar of St Nicholas's Church, Arundel. Gordon Carroll found a similar interloper in his picture of St Mary's, Woodford, Northamptonshire in 1966; the head and shoulders of an immaculately-dressed gentleman can be discerned in a picture taken of the choir stalls in Gloucester Cathedral early in this century. Mrs Hilda L. Wickstead was amazed to discover a pair of embracing lovers in the middle of her souvenir shot of Holly Bush Church, near Malvern, Worcestershire, taken during a spur-of-the-moment visit to the deserted graveyard. Yet, despite the credentials of the photographers, and the precautions taken by them against any technical faults, the camera can lie, and this kind of evidence for the existence of ghosts has, up to now, proved frustratingly inconclusive.

The problem posed by apparitions was concisely expressed by H. H. Price, Wykeham Professor of Logic at Oxford University and a leading authority on psychical research. 'Whatever explanation we offer,' he wrote, 'we soon find ourselves in very deep waters indeed.' The subject remains as fascinating and as enigmatic as another ghost John Aubrey described in the seventeenth century:

'Anno 1670, not far from Cyrencester, was an Apparition: Being demanded, whether a good Spirit, or a bad? returned no answer, but disappeared with a curious Perfume and most melodious Twang.'

**The Rev. Kenneth Lord's photograph of Newby Church. He cannot explain the presence of the skull-faced hooded figure on the right.**

# 6

## Sympathy of Souls

IT WAS A CLASSIC LAST MESSAGE, crackling desperately and indistinctly through the polar skies:

'Motor on right side giving trouble . . . We are flying against a 100-kilo-metre-an-hour wind velocity . . . and have lost altitude from 6,000 metres to 4,300 metres . . . We are going to land in . . .'

Then the pilot's words were no more than a meaningless jumble in the ether, and contact with his aeroplane was lost.

The pilot was Sigismund Levanevsky, a pioneer Russian aviator who, with five companions, had set out from Moscow on 12 August 1937 on a flight over the North Pole to Fairbanks in Alaska. Two other flights – one to Washington State and the other to California – had shown that air travel between Moscow and the United States was possible, despite the treacherous weather-conditions of the Arctic. Levanevsky's was to have been the last test run before the introduction of a regular service.

In the days that followed Levanevsky's SOS, the drama of the lost aircrew grew with every edition of the newspapers, every wireless news bulletin. Radio stations in Siberia reported transmissions, frustratingly faint, that could have come from a ditched aeroplane; a Consolidated flying boat, chartered from the Americans by the Russian Government, zigzagged over the frozen ocean on runs that often lasted for more than 1000 miles. Speculation about Levanevsky's fate, the position from which he had broadcast his last message, and his chances of survival in the Arctic wastes, was intense, but, after 30 days, the flying boat returned, having found no trace of the missing men.

Such disasters were an all-too-familiar feature of pre-war aviation and the struggle to open up new long-distance routes. There is perhaps only one man alive today who has good reason to remember, in detail, the story of Levanevsky's disappearance and the curious events that followed. By the late 1930s Harold Sherman was one of New York's most prominent sports

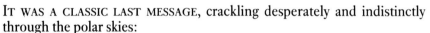

124

The Russian aviators who disappeared in the Arctic in 1937; Sigismund Levanevsky is third from left. No trace of their plane, pictured below at Scholkovo Aerodrome, Moscow, was ever found. In a remarkable ESP experiment, Harold Sherman (*inset left*) monitored the progress of the search party led by Sir Hubert Wilkins (*inset right*).

journalists, and a writer with sixty novels and two Broadway plays to his credit. A member of the City Club of New York and a devotee of the lively conversation at its round table, Sherman was on nodding acquaintance with the Australian explorer Sir Hubert Wilkins, a fellow-member and the man the Russians had commissioned to search for Levanevsky.

Wilkins had been the obvious choice, with almost a quarter of a century of Arctic and Antarctic aviation behind him. He had led the first fruitless search in the flying boat and, when the Russian Government decided there was still a chance some survivors might be found, he agreed to try again. The problems were formidable. The original expedition had been conducted in daylight but now the long Arctic winter night had set in; the moon, stars and the Northern Lights would be the only navigational aids. The sole factor compensating for the rigours of long stretches in a freezing cockpit and the poor visibility that winter flying brings, was the knowledge that tiny human figures would be easier to spot silhouetted against the snow in moonlight than in the uniform whiteness of the daytime landscape.

A Lockheed 10E aeroplane, with extra fuel tanks and navigational aids for night-flying, was being made ready for the resumed search when, in the late autumn of 1937, Wilkins was button-holed by Sherman in the City Club of New York. Sherman, now in his eighties and living contentedly with his wife Martha on a 200-acre estate in the beautiful Ozark Mountains in Arkansas, remembers every word of their conversation:

'I said to him, kind of half seriously and half humorously: "Sir Hubert, what would happen to you if, on your flight to search for those Russian fliers, your plane were forced down and your radio went out of commission, as the Russians' radio apparently did?" Sir Hubert said: "If that happened to me, it'd be a long walk home."

'Then I said: "Wouldn't it be great, Sir Hubert, if the mind of some humans could be developed to such a point that all you'd have to do, if you were forced down and your radio went out of commission, would be to sit and think of your latitude and longitude, transmit that information to a human receiver, and he would send a rescue plane to pick you up at that point.'

'Sir Hubert smiled and said: "You're jesting, of course, Sherman, but I wouldn't say that, in perhaps fifty to a hundred years, the minds of some humans will not be developed to the point where that could be done."'

Both men, it emerged, believed in the possibility of telepathy – the direct and unspoken communication of thoughts between individuals miles apart. At home in Australia, Wilkins had been astonished by the Aborigines' apparent ability to describe events which occurred beyond the range of their sight or hearing; while Sherman had been conducting his own private investigation into the phenomenon since his schooldays. During the conversation in the City Club of New York, the two men realized that Wilkins's expedition to the far north would provide the opportunity for a unique experiment. Sherman recalls:

'He suggested that three nights a week – Mondays, Tuesdays, and Thursday nights – between 11.30 and 12 midnight Eastern Standard Time – he'd get off by himself if he could and relive and review in mental imagery form the outstanding things that had happened to his expedition that day. I would, in my study in my New York apartment, record my impressions of what I felt had been happening to him.'

Theirs was an unlikely partnership – the dashing Arctic aviator and the contemplative writer – but the tests offered a chance to prove that thoughts could be transferred from one mind to another at will and over vast distances.

The Wilkins–Sherman tests were, in fact, to be a careful and systematic study of a phenomenon which has been remarked upon with wonder by people of all cultures from the earliest times. The mechanics of the operation – the way in which the thoughts have been transmitted and received – may have varied, but the essential element has always been the same: precise thoughts or impressions are claimed to have been communicated by mental energy alone.

Twins often claim a telepathic link. For example, in January 1984 Christine Young of Mexborough in South Yorkshire described how she felt her sister's labour pains when her twin, Carol, was producing a baby son. Many other people believe that they can receive the thoughts of members of their family – often over considerable distances. Mrs Joicey Acker Hurth, who lives in the picturesque town of Cedarburg, Wisconsin, tells a particularly remarkable story.

One day in 1955, her five-year-old daughter, 'little' Joicey, came home from a birthday party to find that her father and brother had gone to see the latest Walt Disney movie at the Rivoli Cinema a block and a half down the road. 'She flew out of the door and up the street to join them,' recalls Mrs Hurth. 'I went on back to the kitchen and I was standing in front of my sink washing a dish or two. All of a sudden I froze and dropped the plate I was holding. I just raised my eyes to heaven and said, "Oh God, don't let her get killed." I just knew something was wrong. I immediately went to the phone to telephone the theatre and a young girl answered. I said, "My daughter has had an accident, is she badly hurt?" and the girl stammered and almost dropped the phone and said, "J-j-just a minute, it just happened, how did you know?" Then the manager came to the phone and he said, "Mrs Hurth, your daughter was hit by a car. She got up and ran to the side of the road and your husband is with her now. He's going to take her immediately to the doctor. She doesn't seem to be seriously hurt."' Later, after being

'Little' Joicey Hurth in 1955. When her mother (*inset*) sensed she had had an accident on the way to the cinema, she telephoned manager Ray Nichols, who verified that 'little' Joicey had been hit by a car.

pronounced fit by the doctor, and returning to the Rivoli to see the Disney film, 'little' Joicey told her mother that after the accident she had run to the side of the road and had sat down on the kerb, 'crying and saying "Mama, Mama, Mama"' to herself, for so great was the shock that she was, as she later put it, 'screaming inaudibly'.

To get to the Rivoli Cinema, 'little' Joicey had had to run a long way – up Portland Avenue from her house, left along Columbia for about 50 yards and then on to Washington Avenue. Her mother could not possibly have seen the accident or heard it.

Both 'little' Joicey and the cinema manager, Ray Nichols, still remember the incident well after almost 30 years and still wonder how it was that Mrs Hurth knew about the accident and was on the telephone only moments after it had happened.

Sometimes, a wife has 'called' to her husband at a time of crisis. In about 1610, the metaphysical poet John Donne travelled to France on a diplomatic mission, leaving his pregnant wife at home in England. According to Donne's biographer, Izaak Walton, Donne was found by the Ambassador Sir Robert Drury two days after his arrival in Paris 'in such an ecstasy and so altered as to his looks, as amazed Sir Robert to behold him'.

When Donne could bring himself to speak, he said: 'I have seen a dreadful vision since I saw you: I have seen my dear wife pass twice by me through this room, with her hair hanging about her shoulders, and a dead child in her arms . . .' When Donne insisted he had seen the vision, despite Sir Robert's suggestion that it was 'the result of some melancholy dream', a messenger was sent to England to establish 'whether Mrs Donne were alive; and if alive, in what condition she was as to her health'. Twelve agonizing days passed before the messenger returned to report 'that he found and left Mrs Donne very sad, and sick in her bed; and that after a long and dangerous labour, she had been delivered of a dead child. And, upon examination, the abortion proved to be the same day, and about the very hour, that Mr Donne affirmed he saw her pass by him in his chamber.'

Biographer Walton's reaction, incidentally, has been echoed many times since by other commentators on telepathy, if not quite so quaintly: 'And, though it is most certain, that two lutes being both strung and tuned to an equal pitch, and then one played upon, the other, that is not touched, being laid upon a table at a fit distance, will – like an echo to a trumpet – warble a faint audible harmony in answer to the same tune; yet many will not believe there is any such thing as sympathy of souls; and I am well pleased, that every Reader do enjoy his own opinion.'

During the Second World War, there were many well-attested cases of mothers receiving telepathic news about their sons at the front long before conventional channels of communication had reported events. In 1940, when British forces were being evacuated from Dunkirk, Mrs Carrie Thomas of Coalville, Leicestershire, woke up one night and saw a vision of her son, Jack:

'And when I opened my eyes,' she later told a researcher, 'he was at the side of the bed. He was in the Royal Engineers, but the clothes he had on, I had never seen the like.' The next morning Mrs Thomas told Jack's wife about the vision and the very odd clothes he was wearing: '. . . He wasn't in khaki nor hospital blue, [I] had to say he had on a teddy bear suit.'

When Jack Thomas finally reached home, he told his family the dramatic story of his escape from Dunkirk. Like thousands of other beleagured British servicemen he had had to swim through the water, beneath the enemy bombardment, in the hope of scrambling aboard one of the armada of 'little ships' which had sailed from the south coast of England in the most extraordinary rescue operation of the war. To make swimming easier he had stripped off most of his uniform, with the result that clothes had to be found for him when he reached the safety of the rescue ship. He was given an officer's night suit. It was exactly what his mother had seen him wearing in her vision: a yellow outfit which made him look just like a teddy bear.

After the war in 1947, Leslie Boughey received a remarkable telepathic message from his wife. He was on a tour of duty with the Royal Air Force, stationed at RAF El-Firdan in Egypt. His wife was in England, working in a factory near Stoke-on-Trent. Leslie Boughey remembers that despite the separation he was enjoying the posting, and was in excellent health.

'Then, for no reason at all, I woke up one night with the most excruciating pain in one of my hands, centring mainly on one finger. My tent mate got some water and I sat with my hand in it as the sweat poured off me. There was no mark on my finger, no swelling, inflammation, or anything, yet I just wanted to hold it and scream. After a few hours, towards dawn, the pain eased and eventually disappeared, with no after-effects except the memory of the worst pain I had ever experienced.'

The Bougheys were in the habit of writing to each other every day. They numbered each letter in sequence so that they would know if one had gone astray. Leslie's letter telling of his painful finger crossed in the post with one from his wife. 'My wife explained that she had had a fragment of brass swarf in her finger, which had turned septic. Eventually she had to be taken to the doctor's surgery to try to relieve the pain. The infection had to be lanced which, the letter said, brought almost instant relief. The extraordinary thing was, the time of her operation coincided exactly with my painful experience: the same hand, even the same finger.'

From time to time, from baffled but unimpeachable sources, come reports that whole groups of people have learned to use telepathy. Conveniently they usually live in places where there are few, if any, telephones.

The Director of Kenya's National Parks, Colonel Mervin Cowie, told a remarkable tale to a *Times* reporter in April 1962: 'A family of Africans in Tanganyika [Tanzania] was widely thought to be using telepathy to control lions and terrorize villages. There was "a certain measure of proof" that a number of Africans and lions were living together in the remote Singida Province. The men almost "hunted" with the lions and shared their prey.

'Recently one of the "lion-controllers" was gaoled by a chief after villagers protested about killings by lions. The man told the chief that unless he was freed by nightfall he would get his lions to kill the chief's cattle. The chief refused. Next morning fourteen of his cattle lay dead.' Colonel Cowie added: 'I have reason to believe this story. There seems to be something, maybe mental telepathy, between the natives and the lions.'

Reg Iverson, radio operator for the New York Times, who tried to keep contact with Wilkins's search party in the Arctic.

Although Sir Hubert Wilkins and Harold Sherman had heard many such stories of spontaneous telepathy, and knew that it was an elusive phenomenon, they were convinced that a properly set-up experiment might produce convincing evidence. Dr Gardner Murphy, Head of Columbia University's Psychology Department, agreed to monitor their tests. The arrangement was that each night Sherman would record his impressions of what Wilkins had been doing and then post a copy of his notes to Murphy who would annotate and file them until Sir Hubert's own log could arrive for comparison.

For Wilkins, the events that followed his departure for the far north in search of the Russian fliers were to provide the most rigorous but exciting adventures of a lifetime of exploration: there were chancy landings on the pitted surfaces of frozen Arctic rivers; 'blind' sorties in which the Electra, the Lockheed plane, was enveloped in seemingly endless and near-impenetrable cloud; often mountain peaks would suddenly loom up out of the unfriendly night.

For Sherman, keeping his thrice-weekly vigils in the silence of his New York study, the search for Levanevsky turned out to be equally exciting, if far less dangerous: 'The very first night I was electrified at getting the sensation that a circuit had been closed between Sir Hubert Wilkins's mind and my own! . . . I had never felt this way before and, with the sensation, came a rush of impressions which I commenced to record in a notepad on my desk. It did all seem incredible, as I wrote, since one impression followed another, almost without a break . . . as though I were a Western Union operator, taking down a series of messages being telegraphed to me by some distant sender.'

While *The New York Times*'s radio operator, Reg Iverson, was able to contact Wilkins only thirteen times in five months, Sherman received so many telepathic communications that he hardly had time to record them: his notebooks, which he has carefully preserved, are filled with staccato phrases, scrawled in thick pencil for page after page.

When Wilkins's log arrived, spasmodically, from 3000 miles to the north, Sherman realized that he had made an extraordinary number of 'hits', although many of the things he 'saw' Wilkins doing had seemed most unlikely at the time. He remembers writing one night: 'I had a feeling you were taking off on a flight this morning for some place that seemed like Saskatchewan. I had the feeling you've been caught in a blinding snow-storm and can probably make a forced landing at some place that sounds like Regina. I see you, Wilkins, roped in on an officer's ball that appears to have been held there this evening. I see many men and women in military attire and evening dress. You, Wilkins, are in evening dress yourself . . .'

It sounded hopelessly unlikely, because, as he told his wife, 'I know he didn't fly north to attend any social event. He was going for a serious rescue mission . . . I am sure that Wilkins didn't fly north equipped with an evening dress suit; and yet I saw him in my mind's eye in an evening dress suit . . .'

But Sherman had disciplined himself to record even the most apparently bizarre impression and, when, some weeks later, Wilkins' account of that day came through, he read: 'This morning took off on flight. Hoping to reach Saskatchewan. Was caught in heavy blizzard. Propose to turn back and make a landing in Regina. Was met at the airport by the Governor of the province who invited me to attend an officers' ball being held there this evening. My attendance at this ball was made possible by the loan to me of an evening dress suit.'

Some sessions yielded an astonishing run of 'hits'. One of the most striking was on 7 December 1937.

*Sherman*: 'Don't know why, but I seem to see crackling fire shining out in darkness of Aklavik – get a definite fire impression as though house burning – you can see it from your location on ice – I first thought fire on ice near your tent, but impression persists it is white house burning, and quite a crowd gathered around it – people running or hurrying toward flames – bitter cold – stiff breeze blowing . . .'

Later Wilkins added his comments:

*Wilkins*: 'While I was in Radio office at Point Barrow, the fire alarm rang. A long ring on the telephone. [There are only four telephones at Barrow.] It was an Eskimo's shack on fire. The chimney blazed up, and the roof took fire, but it was soon put out. Some damage resulted, mostly from the efforts of the zealous firemen. Was pretty cold that night with a light wind.'

*Sherman*: 'Your plane looks like a silvery ghost in moonlight – I seem to be almost under nose of it – standing in snow, looking up – it towers over me – I've never seen plane, of course, but it seems to have high bow, with two huge propellers either side of cabin or cockpits – motor concealed in great silver metal tube-like cylinders or encasements – don't know technical names for purposes of description – a rounded metal door seems to lift up to admit entrance to cockpits from top of plane – big instrument board front cockpit – seats for two – pilot and co-pilot or navigator – rear cockpit and space beyond for another passenger and storage – separate rounded metal door with glassed-window covering each cockpit – plane rests on giant skis – dark in colour . . .'

*Wilkins*: 'Description of plane *practically exact*.'

*Sherman*: 'Windows in plane seem of slit nature – wide panels that go around front and sides – as well as observation opportunity through top of plane – even though doors clamped shut – Everything fastened down – compactly packed, plane not yet equipped or stored with things as it will be on actual search hops . . .'

*Wilkins*: 'Okay, as previously stated.'

*Sherman*: '17th comes to mind as real take-off for search flight – day later than you had originally contemplated – this different sort impression involving time dimension – seem foresee unfavorable weather conditions arising to prevent action on 16th . . .'

*Wilkins*: 'Weather was and remained unfavorable over whole moonlight period, 15th to 17th inclusive.'

*Sherman*: 'Lights in town on high, thin poles – cast weird reflection over none-too-attractive landscape – with frozen spots of what seems to be lake or water areas back beyond town . . .'

*Wilkins*: 'Several electric lights at Barrow on high thin poles. One on high mast is kept burning constantly as guide to trappers and travellers Barrow-bound. It is claimed that this light may be seen from a distance of thirty miles, if the air is clear.'

*Sherman*: 'There is a road that seems to run a little distance back from river bank – making a turn around curvature of land as river seems to widen out beyond Aklavik into quite a bay – which stretches on and on as far as eye can see – this is main road in Aklavik – most of houses and stores of any consequence along it . . .'

*Wilkins*: 'This is more or less a description of the lagoon, with the river-like entrance at Barrow.'

*Sherman*: 'A prominent citizen in Aklavik has died – and I seem to catch glimpse of funeral service – strange sensation – this connection that an Aklavik doctor is also an undertaker – or somehow associated . . .'

*Wilkins*: 'There was a funeral service. A baby died. [Eskimo.] The natives act as their own undertakers.'

*Sherman*: 'Is there some man you deal with in Aklavik by name of Webb or Weber? Name came to me and man seems medium height, heavy set, heavily clad – hooded garb.'

*Wilkins*: 'An owner of a store at Aklavik is PEFFER – about as described.'

As the transcript shows, Sherman was by no means always right in his impressions – here, as on other occasions, for example, he correctly described some of the events of the day, notably the house fire and the baby's funeral, but got the wrong location: Wilkins was not at his expedition base at Aklavik but at Point Barrow, some 500 miles away. Similarly, Sherman failed to discern the day on which Wilkins made his final but fruitless sweep for the Russian fliers: an epic flight which took the search party more than 3000 miles in 20 hours and to within 150 miles of the North Pole. But Sherman found that on most occasions he was able to pick up moments of emotion, whether engendered by the dangers of Arctic flying, tensions between members of the expedition, or routine accidents, such as the time Wilkins and his crew members bumped painfully into the overhanging stovepipes in their quarters. 'Feelings generate the power behind thought,' concludes Sherman.

The results of their long-distance telepathy experiment, which was carefully monitored and witnessed in sworn affidavits by some of New York's most prominent citizens, astonished both Sherman and Wilkins, although they had embarked upon it in the belief that communication between minds was possible. It is no exaggeration to say that it radically changed Harold Sherman's life and today, from Mountain View, Arkansas, he continues to propagate his views on the paranormal in a stream of books, instruction manuals and cassettes.

Dramatic as the Sherman–Wilkins results were, they were not totally without precedent; in 1930 the American writer and would-be social reformer, Upton Sinclair, published a book which differed strikingly from the campaigning works that had brought him fame. Entitled *Mental Radio*, and distinguished by a kindly though non-committal preface by Albert Einstein, the book recounts a series of experiments in which the author's wife, Mary Craig Sinclair, had tried to reproduce drawings prepared by her husband, his secretary and her brother-in-law.

Sometimes Mrs Sinclair held the drawings, which were in sealed envelopes, over her abdomen; on other occasions the drawing she had to

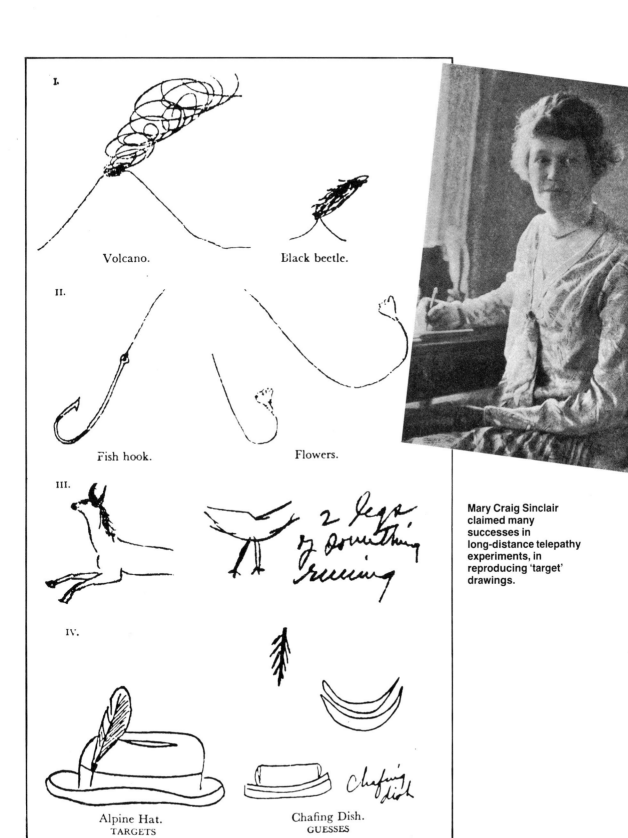

I.

Volcano.

Black beetle.

II.

Fish hook.

Flowers.

III.

2 legs
of something
running

IV.

Alpine Hat.
TARGETS

Chafing Dish.
GUESSES

Chafing dish

Mary Craig Sinclair claimed many successes in long-distance telepathy experiments, in reproducing 'target' drawings.

copy was executed many miles away. The results achieved by his 'witch-wife' astonished Sinclair into writing the book, even though he liked to think of himself as a hard-nosed reporter of the world's realities. Out of 290 drawings used in the experiments, only 70 completely eluded her, and Sinclair judged 155 to be partial successes and 65 as direct hits.

It is not the kind of experiment that modern psychical researchers deem acceptable, for Sinclair did not bother to ensure that the 'target' drawings were chosen at random. He just drew 'anything that came into my head'. Since he obviously knew his wife very well, the likelihood that they would both think of the same thing without any question of telepathy being involved was great indeed. Sinclair, however, was totally convinced.

To the inevitable suggestions that the distinguished writer had been hoaxed, Sinclair reacted with indignation: 'I assure you I am as cold-blooded about the thing as a man can be. In fact I don't like to believe in telepathy, because I don't know what to make of it, and I don't know to what view of the universe it will lead me, and I would a whole lot rather give all my time to my muck-raking job which I know by heart.'

The evidence Sinclair and his wife had collected was all the justification needed: 'We present here a mass of real evidence, and we shall not be troubled by any amount of ridicule from the ignorant. I tell you – and because it is so important, I put it in capital letters: TELEPATHY HAPPENS!'

On the other side of the Atlantic, however, few researchers felt able to make such cocksure assertions. One of the earliest decisions made by the fledgling Society for Psychical Research had been to establish a committee to investigate telepathy. They called it 'Thought-Reading' or 'Thought-Transference' and the committee's deliberations occupy many pages of the Society's earliest *Proceedings*. Their diligence was exemplary, but the findings were by no means conclusive, and the experiences often unhappy.

In 1881 the scientific investigation of the phenomenon appeared to have got off to a near-perfect start: the first subjects were the Creery sisters, the five daughters of a clergyman from the Derbyshire spa of Buxton and, according to the committee's report: 'All thoroughly healthy, as free as

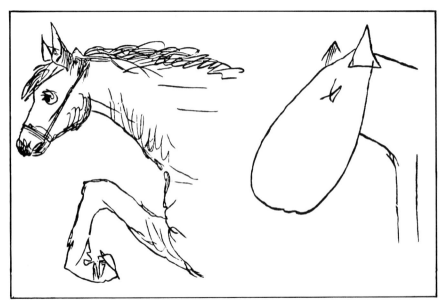

Fraudulent 'telepathists' often fooled the investigating committees set up by the Society for Psychical Research. George Smith of Brighton scored this apparent 'hit' in trials in 1883. Later, his accomplice Douglas Blackburn confessed he had used a code and sleight of hand to tell Smith what was in the 'target' drawings.

possible from morbid or hysterical symptoms.' Their ability to describe exactly which playing card someone had in mind, for example, appeared astonishing. The initial tests, which were conducted in various places in Buxton, greatly impressed the investigators, who included some of the Society for Psychical Research's most eminent founding-fathers: Frederick Myers, Edmund Gurney and Sir William Barrett, Professor of Physics in the Royal College of Science for Ireland.

The girls were aged between ten and 17 and, although their background was of the utmost probity, the experiments were conducted in accordance with a strict scientific protocol which Barrett described:

'Having selected at random one child, whom we desired to leave the room and wait at some distance, we would choose a card from a pack, or write on paper a number or a name which occurred to us at the moment. Generally, but not always, this was shewn to the members of the family present in the room; but no one member was always present, and we were sometimes entirely alone. We then recalled the child, one of us always assuring himself that, when the door was suddenly opened, she was at a considerable distance [in their own house, at the further end of a passage], though this was usually a superfluity of caution, as our habit was to avoid all utterance of what was chosen. Before leaving the room the child had been informed of the general nature of the test we intended to select, as "This will be a card," or "This will be a name." On re-entering she stood – sometimes turned by us with her face to the wall, oftener with her eyes directed towards the ground, and usually close to us and remote from her family – for a period of silence varying from a few seconds to a minute, till she called out to us some number, card or whatever it might be.'

Undeterred by the committee's eager scrutiny, Mary, Alice, Maud, Kathleen and Emily Creery and their maid-servant demonstrated their powers with charm, confidence and success. In Buxton, in Cambridge, and in Dublin they identified, with precocious aplomb, playing cards, names written on concealed pieces of paper, and objects like penknives and a box of almonds. Sometimes, it is true, their talent seemed to fail them completely, and at others they merely came up with impressive near-misses, such as 'Amy Freemore' for 'Amy Frogmore' or 'Albert Grover' for 'Albert Snelgrove'. But all in all, it was hardly surprising that the committee should have been impressed – 'Absolutely unexceptionable and conclusive' was how Barrett described a couple of the early experiments.

So when, in 1888, two of the sisters admitted they had been using a simple code – coughs, movements of the head and other secret signals – it was a bitter blow, and the astonishing results from the early tests by which the committee had set such store were discredited for ever. That was the first, but sadly by no means the last, instance in psychical research of the wiles of apparently innocent children making a mockery of the best-prepared protocols of learned and honourable men of science.

Intrigued by the writings of distinguished British students of the paranormal like Sir Oliver Lodge, the physicist, and Sir Arthur Conan Doyle, creator of Sherlock Holmes, and encouraged by the doyen of American psychologists William McDougall, Joseph Rhine espoused parapsychology with a passion that sustained him through half a century of controversy. In the early days, particularly, he was eager to examine any extraordinary claim, however outrageous. Thus, he sat in on one of the séances held by the medium Margery Crandon in Boston and was scandalized by the crude trickery to which he saw her resort. He travelled to Richmond, Virginia, to visit a Mrs Fonda and her remarkable horse, Lady Wonder, which was supposed to be able to read minds. When asked a question, Lady Wonder obligingly tapped out answers on a 'typewriter' equipped with horse-sized keys. Other allegedly psychic pets which came under Rhine's scrutiny included a dog called Chris from Rhode Island, who had a talent for predicting the next day's winners at Narragansett; and Sugar, a cat which had allegedly followed its owners for 2000 miles when they moved house from California to Oklahoma.

To finance his studies before going to Duke University, he had stoked boilers and sold aluminium pots and pans from door to door, and to further his knowledge of psychical research he did not shrink from buttonholing the most distinguished experts of his era.

With the great Swiss psychiatrist C. G. Jung he discussed the strange episode of a knife which had suddenly broken into pieces while inside a locked sideboard at Jung's home. Later, in compliance with some of the weirdest military contracts ever awarded, Rhine advised the US Army on whether hypnosis could be a war weapon, and whether dogs could detect mines without being given any sensory clues.

But these mostly inconclusive episodes lay outside the mainstream of Rhine's work, which was to test the existence of telepathy – or Extra-sensory Perception (ESP) as he came to call it – and to establish its characteristics, in the strict conditions of the laboratory. To test for ESP Rhine used a set of cards, like playing cards but with special symbols. There were five symbols – star, cross, square, circle and wavy lines – and five cards with each symbol, making 25 cards in the pack or 'run'. In a typical run the experimenter would look at the 25 cards one by one and the guesser would, without looking, say what he thought each card was. Any guesser could expect to score five 'hits' in a run: he could, for example, say 'square' for every card and be sure of being right five times. But whatever he called, he should score an average of five by chance alone. Anything better might indicate that there was a hidden power involved: the faculty of ESP.

Early in his trials, and before the Duke laboratory had been formally set up, Rhine struck lucky. In 1931 he tested a volunteer economics student, Adam Linzmayer. The results were astonishing. In the first experiment Rhine placed nine cards face down and out of Linzmayer's field of vision. Patiently, Linzmayer described the symbol on each card and each time he was right. This extraordinary start – the odds against Linzmayer naming each card correctly were roughly two million to one – was followed the next day by another spectacular success: in 12 'runs' of cards – 300 in all – Linzmayer called 119 cards correctly. Since the theory of chance allowed a subject to make five correct guesses in 25, Linzmayer could have been expected to score 60. Instead he had achieved almost twice as many 'hits'. In further tests, including one conducted, bizarrely, in Rhine's car, Linzmayer produced the occasional outstanding result, but his powers seemed rapidly to wane (although he is said to have won several thousand dollars at the gaming tables of Las Vegas).

Rhine's next success, after many fruitless trials with other people, came with Hubert Pearce, a divinity student. Most of these tests were conducted by J. Gaither Pratt, Rhine's trusted associate. After a poor start, Pearce emerged as a true psychic 'star'. Pratt ran hundreds of separate trials, and Pearce's performance improved to a point at which his average number of 'hits' in a 'run' was nine out of 25. Once, in an experiment with Rhine, Pearce scored a straight 25. But when Pearce left Duke to take up his ministerial duties in a run-down parish in Arkansas, his powers, like Linzmayer's, seemed mysteriously to desert him.

For Rhine and Pratt, though they worked long hours for little pay, those were heady days. Proof of the existence of ESP seemed to be within reach: 'Our plan,' said Rhine, 'has been to try to catch what looks like ESP and, gradually improving the safeguards as we go, bring the phenomenon, if possible, up to the point where there can be no question about the interpretation of the results.'

What Rhine got for his pains was criticism: it came from his colleagues, from visitors to the laboratory and from the scientific community at large. Psychologists throughout America had been sceptical since the start about the establishment of the laboratory and Rhine's attempts to further the acceptance of ESP research as a branch of science. A few had openly challenged and denounced him. On the very campus where his department stood, there was lingering hostility. The celebrated European writer and philosopher Arthur Koestler noted much later in a sympathetic article in the London *Observer*, after a visit to Rhine and his wife Louisa at Duke:

'In McDougall's day the heads at the university acquired lasting merit by enabling Rhine to establish his laboratory: but this does not alter the fact that the members of the various faculties still consider the parapsycholo-

Lady Wonder, the 'mind-reading' horse, tapped out her answers to visitor's questions on a giant 'typewriter'.

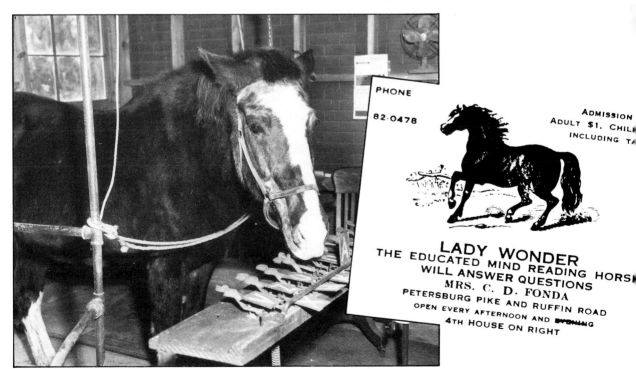

PHONE

82·0478

ADMISSION
ADULT $1. CHILD
INCLUDING TA

**LADY WONDER**
THE EDUCATED MIND READING HORSE
WILL ANSWER QUESTIONS
MRS. C. D. FONDA
PETERSBURG PIKE AND RUFFIN ROAD
OPEN EVERY AFTERNOON AND EVENING
4TH HOUSE ON RIGHT

**J. B. Rhine** (*right*)
**testing Hubert Pearce**
**in 1933. Pearce is trying**
**to guess the symbols**
**on each card; he was**
**not allowed to touch**
**the pack, which is**
**face-down on the table**
**in front of him.**

J. B. Rhine (*right*) testing Hubert Pearce in 1933. Pearce is trying to guess the symbols on each card; he was not allowed to touch the pack, which is face-down on the table in front of him.

gists as outsiders, beyond the academic pale, and I had ample opportunity to notice this. To say that the Rhines are ostracized would be to put it too dramatically; but they are lone figures in the landscape, and they are resigned to it.'

Even more worrying were the attacks on Rhine's methods and findings which persisted throughout his career, almost from the moment when he first described them in print. The main problem was that Rhine and his team had still been working out their procedures while their best ESP subjects were notching up their most convincing results. Had the safeguards during the early experiments been good enough to exclude cheating or mistakes? Could the above-average scores have been achieved through an agency other than ESP? At least one British researcher thought so.

Mark Hansel, formerly Professor of Psychology at the University of Wales, is a formidable analyst of claims for ESP. Unlike many of his peers, he thought it important not to shun the work of the parapsychologists but to examine it carefully, because, he wrote, 'if their claims are justified, a complete revision in contemporary scientific thought is required at least comparable to that made necessary in biology by Darwin and in physics by Einstein. On the other hand, if ESP is merely an artifact, it is then important to understand how conventional experimental methods can yield results leading to erroneous conclusions.'

Hansel took direct action and, at Rhine's invitation, he travelled to Duke in 1960 to examine the laboratory's most remarkable findings. The effect of the visit was devastating: 'Judging by the flak it produced,' Rhine's biographer Denis Brian wrote many years later, 'Hansel's raid was parapsychology's Pearl Harbor.'

One of the experiments that had come under Hansel's scrutiny was the series that Gaither Pratt had conducted with the divinity student Hubert Pearce. At Duke, Hansel set about reconstructing the conditions under

**Rhine's assistants,
J. Gaither Pratt and
Charles E. Stuart** (*right*)
**check the results of an
ESP test.**

which the tests had been held and, in doing so, made a remarkable discovery. Everything had been designed so that Pratt and Pearce should work well away from each other – this was to avoid any suggestion that factors like involuntary whispering or identifying the cards from their backs had been involved. Pearce, therefore, sat in a small room in the university library, while Pratt operated from a building about 100 yards away.

The tests went like this: Pratt would shuffle and cut a pack of ESP cards, and put it face-down on the table. At the appointed moment, he would start to work through the pack, picking up each card in turn, concentrating on it, and then placing it face-down on top of a book. Simultaneously Pearce was supposed to pick up the telepathic signal and identify the card. When he had got through each pack, Pratt would wait for five minutes and then begin another 'run' with different cards. At the end of the tests, he would turn each card face-up, record the order in which they had been dealt and send a copy of his list to Rhine. Meanwhile Pearce, 100 yards away in his library cubicle, finalized his score-sheet. Later, the results would be compared.

It had all seemed perfectly foolproof to Pratt, and to Rhine; but not to Hansel who, in his reconstruction of the tests on the Duke campus, found a fatal flaw and demonstrated it in true British fashion – with a practical joke. Hansel persuaded a member of the laboratory's staff, Wadhi Saleh, to sit in a locked office and go through a pack of ESP cards just as Pratt had done. Hansel told him that he would go and sit in another office down the corridor. When the experiment was over Saleh found, to his amazement, that Hansel had correctly identified 22 out of 25 cards. He was even more astonished to discover that Hansel's success was in no way due to ESP. Once Saleh started work, Hansel said, 'I slipped back to Saleh's room and saw the cards by standing on a chair and looking through a crack at the top of the door. I had a clear view of them . . . Saleh's desk was about sixteen feet from the door, and he had no suspicion of what I had done until I told him.'

The implication was obvious: Pearce could have left the library while Pratt was doing the experiment, peered through a crack in the top of the door and either copied out or memorized the order of cards before rushing back to the library and filling in his scoresheet. Each experiment was carefully timed; Pearce would have known exactly how long he had, and that the opportunity to see the cards would occur when, after going through the pack, Pratt turned each card up to record the symbol printed on it.

Hansel cast further doubt on the safeguards against fraud; for example, he queried the decision to allow Pearce to suggest changes in the way they were conducted. All in all, Hansel's stern attack on Pratt's experimental methods must have made uncomfortable reading back at Duke: 'These experiments were not a first-year exercise. They were intended to provide conclusive proof of ESP and to shake the very foundations of science. If Pratt had some misgivings, there is no evidence that he ever pressed them. He took no precautions to ensure that Pearce stayed in the library or to prevent the cards being visible to anyone looking into the room.'

By the time Hansel had voiced his criticisms Hubert Pearce was dead and could not throw light on any of the issues raised, although he had always denied cheating. But since controversy had become as constant a presence in Rhine's working life as the ESP cards he carried round with him for spontaneous tests, the work of the Duke laboratory was defended with a pugnacity which may have been quite alien to the cool objectivity cultivated by scientists in other fields but was, nonetheless, effective in maintaining public interest in work on ESP.

The problem was that the voices of the critics were not easily stilled: long before Hansel's revelations about the Pearce–Pratt series and his sceptical evaluation of many of Rhine's other keynote experiments, other researchers had published their doubts. One, for example, demonstrated that it was possible to see through the cards used for the tests. (Indeed, the packs still obtainable from the Society for Psychical Research and patented by Rhine carry a sticker which says: 'Care should be taken using ESP cards, as if held at a certain angle and in certain light the symbols can be perceived through the back of the card.') When Rhine riposted that he had used home-made cards for the early tests, his critics showed that these often made things easier, since the symbol on each one could often be detected by carefully studying its edge. Another problem was that the Duke findings were difficult to repeat elsewhere. Furthermore, as experimental conditions became tighter, there were far fewer spectacular scores.

Even so, beleaguered but undaunted, J. B. Rhine continued his research right up to his death in 1980. In the eyes of many he may not have achieved his dearest wish and proved the existence of ESP beyond reasonable doubt, but he did at least provide a framework for experiment and discussion that may one day answer many of the questions he was the first to try to tackle in a systematic fashion.

Such credit, however, cannot be given to Rhine's equivalent in Britain, the London University mathematician, Dr Samuel George Soal. Soal was noted for his careful and critical approach to ESP research, and had conducted a meticulous experiment on a stage mind-reader called Frederick Marion. Marion's act was sensational. He could discover an object hidden in a cluttered room in seconds and unhesitatingly identify which of six tin boxes concealed a gold ring. Soal concluded that Marion had learned to read unconscious muscular signals from the people testing him. It was a rare and amusing talent but by no means paranormal.

Soal tried many Duke-style card-guessing experiments, but when these yielded nothing convincing, Soal was brutal in his criticism of Rhine and his methods. His attitude changed, however, when a new theory advanced by a psychical researcher inspired him to re-examine the voluminous but apparently fruitless results of his card tests. The theory argued that there was sometimes a 'displacement effect', which meant that although the subject failed to identify the 'target' card, he was, instead, calling either the previous one or the one that came directly after. When Soal went through the old score-sheets in 1939, he found to his gratified surprise that two sets of results showed striking 'displacement effects'.

The subjects had been Basil Shackleton, a fashionable professional photographer, who had claimed his psychic powers were at their best in the evening, especially after a drink or two, but who had failed to show any signs of telepathic ability; and Mrs Gloria Stewart, the wife of a consulting engineer from Richmond, Surrey. Soal's curiosity was aroused, and he decided to embark upon a new series of tests with Shackleton and Stewart. With his criticism of the Duke University methods in mind, he devised a

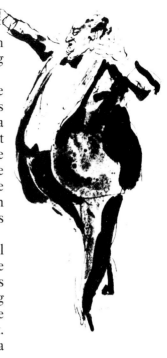

*Above:* **Dr S. G. Soal portrayed by Feliks Topolski.** *Opposite:* **Soal designed cards with animal symbols for his ESP tests, and for his investigation of 'mind-reader' Frederick Marion he constructed this extraordinary 'sentry-box' to conceal questioners, in order to determine whether Marion was helped by unconscious muscular signals from the people testing him.**

**Glyn and Ieuan Jones with Glyn's father, Dick. The two boys scored remarkable results in Soal's ESP tests.**

new and apparently stringent set of conditions under which the investigations were to be conducted. They were elaborate in the extreme: but then he was not going to lay himself open to criticism like the Americans.

Instead of cards printed with the symbols devised by Rhine, Soal introduced new ones which, he thought, might prove easier to visualize. They bore pictures of animals: an elephant, a giraffe, a lion, a pelican and a zebra. The experiments were usually held at Shackleton's studio and at Mrs Stewart's home in Richmond. The procedure varied in minor details, but the sessions followed roughly the same pattern.

The person who was going to try to receive the symbols by ESP was called the Percipient and the person attempting to transmit them was called the Agent. They sat in different rooms and were each watched by another person who was known as the Experimenter. The one with the Percipient was called EP for short, and the one with the Agent, EA.

In one room, then, the Agent sat at a table facing a screen which had a small hole in the middle. His Experimenter, EA, sat on the other side, almost completely hidden from the Agent's view, except for the tiny window in the screen. The Agent sat with the animal cards he was to try to send to the Percipient face-downwards in front of him. Soal had prepared a list of numbers from one to five, taken at random. The choice of card to be sent – they were numbered from one to five – was signalled to the Agent by EA opposite, who showed the number to him through the hole in the screen.

In the other room, the Percipient would then guess which card the Agent was concentrating upon and record his answer. As a further measure, copies of the Percipient's scoresheet, EA's analysis after the cards had been examined at the end of 50 runs, and Soal's random number tables, were sent to a distinguished and unbiased professor at Cambridge.

The results were highly impressive. Mrs Stewart scored many more hits than predicted with the target cards. This suggested that ESP did exist. Shackleton, on the other hand, was most successful in guessing the card which followed the target the Agent was actually trying to send him. Out of 3,789 cards, he scored 1,101 hits, when only 776 had been expected. Theory had become fact: the existence of the 'displacement effect' had been triumphantly established.

Soal was jubilant and his fellow-researchers showered plaudits upon him. In 1955, he discovered another pair of successful telepaths, 13-year-old cousins named Glyn and Ieuan Jones. Soal had come across them during his holidays at Capel Curig in Wales where he regularly went on flower-hunting expeditions.

The first experiment took place one afternoon after tea. Ieuan and Glyn sat at a table by the window in the front room of Ieuan's mother's house. Soal put a suitcase between them as a makeshift screen and produced a pack of the animal cards he had used with Stewart and Shackleton. Though the results of this first informal test were disappointing, Soal persisted and the schoolboys later began to produce high scores.

Between 1955 and 1957 Soal tested the telepathic abilities of the Jones boys in a variety of settings: in rural Snowdonia near the boys' homes; on the playing-fields of St Paul's School in London; and in the book-lined rooms of the Society for Psychical Research. The experiments attracted considerable attention; the boys appeared on television and in the newspapers, but sceptics were not impressed. Some queried whether the experimental conditions were tight enough; others pointed out that Soal had not eliminated all the possibilities for cheating. For example, in some tests the boys could see each other's feet, and if they had been so minded, they could have signalled to each other by changing the way they were positioned. Other sceptics wondered whether the boys, or accomplices, had learned to signal with a sheepdog whistle or a Galton whistle: both produce the kind of high-pitched squeak that dogs and children can hear with ease but which is undetectable to a middle-aged person.

On one occasion the boys admitted shamefacedly that they had, indeed, been using a code – sniffing, coughing or making their chairs creak, depending on what the cards showed. But Ieuan, now a hotel catering manager, and Glyn, an oil company engineer, maintain they cheated only once, to test the researchers' powers of observation and never did so again; to this day, they are mystified by the hostile criticism.

As far as the Shackleton–Stewart experiments were concerned, no one smelt a psychic rat until long after the results had been published. The indefatigable Hansel had suggested in 1960 that there might have been some trickery involved but the first inklings of general doubt were felt in 1971, when an episode which had taken place during the second series of sittings with Shackleton was revealed in full. Mrs Gretl Albert, who had acted as Agent in two of the experiments, said that she had looked through the hole in the screen that separated her from Soal who was acting as EA and had seen Soal changing figures on the sheet of random numbers. Whatever the reason for Soal's action, Mrs Albert reckoned it was, at the very least, not in the spirit of a well-regulated experiment. Fuelled by this and by other allegations, the case for and against the validity of the findings was hotly debated in the parapsychological journals during the last years of Soal's life; he died in 1975.

It is rare for such controversies to achieve any kind of final resolution, and for this one to have been resolved in the way it was must make it unique. For the answer – or at least the decisive clue to it – came in a dream.

Betty Markwick is a statistician. On the night of 31 March 1971 she dreamed she was visited by Dr George Medhurst, a mathematician and a prominent member of the SPR, who had recently died. 'Dr Medhurst,' she wrote later, 'appeared in the role of tutor explaining a mathematical-graphical problem which he wished me to work upon.' Five days later, Miss Markwick received a copy of an article by Medhurst, published after his death, about Soal and his ESP experiments. Since, she says, its subject matter 'seemed curiously linked with my dream', she began an intricate investigation of Soal's results, particularly those of the Shackleton tests.

Soal claimed to have used random numbers taken from books of logarithm tables to determine the choice of 'target' card. Dr Medhurst had realized that if the exact source of them could be found, allegations that Soal had changed the numbers would be unfounded. Miss Markwick followed this lead and began a complex analysis by computer. Her main findings astonished her. She found that some long sequences of numbers had been repeated in many experiments. This was not damning in itself but she went on to discover that these sequences of numbers were not absolutely identical: extra numbers had been interpolated. And time after time, it was these extra numbers which corresponded to the 'hits'. When these numbers were removed from the record, the results of the tests were not remarkable and not above chance.

Betty Markwick wrote, with obvious regret, that 'The sad and inescapable conclusion remains that all the experimental series in card-guessing carried out by Dr Soal must, as the evidence stands, be discredited.' Exactly how Soal managed to get away with changing the figures is not totally clear, but Miss Markwick's computer analysis has left no doubt that the erstwhile sceptic of ESP and Britain's foremost critic of the American card-guessing experiments had stooped shamefully to fraud.

In the last 25 years, high technology has taken over from simple cards in ESP tests, and the random number sheets so laboriously drawn up by the early experimenters have been replaced by generators designed to produce targets, for example, according to the decay of a radioactive isotope. Such use of machinery in tests, of course, ensures that the possibilities of human error or fraud are greatly reduced, if not eliminated.

One of the foremost exponents of such methods is Dr Helmut Schmidt of the Mind-Science Foundation in San Antonio, Texas. Using his machines, Schmidt has asked volunteers with apparent psychic abilities to fulfil various tasks, such as predicting which one of four lights would be switched on by a Random Event Generator. Some of the volunteers have produced striking results, thousands of times better than chance.

Many researchers believe ESP has a fleeting, delicate nature. The practitioners of what is known as the 'Ganzfeld technique' cater for this by testing people in rather bizarre but pleasant conditions. The idea is that our ESP faculty may lie hidden at a low level of our consciousness, and may all too easily be swamped by the general hubbub of life. The ESP 'guinea-pig' is encouraged to enter a meditative state: he lies on a bed bathed in red light, his eyes are covered with halved table-tennis balls and 'white noise' or the sound of the sea is played to him through earphones.

Once the busy world has been hushed the experiment can begin, and attempts are made to send him a picture by ESP. As he lies in his luxurious, altered state, the subject describes the images that come to him. These are later matched by referees with the target picture. At least nine major parapsychological laboratories have undertaken 'Ganzfeld' studies in the last ten years and many have reported results which show that ESP may occur, if not flourish, in these tranquil conditions.

The range and ingenuity of the ESP experiments reported in the past few years are enormous: for example, children have been tested through puppet-shows, and one astronaut, Ed Mitchell, even tried to communicate telepathically with people on Earth from the surface of the moon. All that has been missing has been unequivocal proof that telepathy exists.

What makes it all the more frustrating is that there have been so many cases of ESP reported outside the laboratory. The Society for Psychical Research's original Committee on Thought-Reading recognized the importance of collecting these strange stories, and published them alongside reports of their scientific endeavours. This account, vouched for by a medical man, Mr Ede of Guildford, and published in 1882, is a classic example:

'Lady G. and her sister had been spending the evening with their mother, who was in her usual health and spirits when they left her. In the middle of the night the sister awoke in fright and said to her husband, "I must go to my mother at once; do order the carriage. I am sure she is taken ill." The husband, after trying in vain to convince his wife that it was only a fancy, ordered the carriage. As she was approaching her mother's house, where two roads meet, she saw Lady G's carriage. When they met, each asked the other why she was there. The same reply was made by both. "I could not sleep, feeling sure my mother was ill, and so I came to see." As they came in sight of the house, they saw their mother's confidential maid at the door, who told them that their mother had been taken suddenly ill, and was dying, and had expressed an earnest wish to see her daughters.'

Gladys Wright, a midwife who says she answered a telepathic midnight call to a premature delivery.

In mid-December 1952, Mrs Gladys Wright of Norfolk also felt impelled to leave her bed to help someone facing a crisis. She was a country midwife and always on call to deliver babies, but on one particular night gales were blowing and her telephone was out of order. She writes:

'I retired to bed about 10.30 p.m., and in no way could I find sleep, becoming more and more agitated and convinced in mind that a certain patient needed me. My husband appeared very annoyed re my proposed arrangements, and remarked, "How stupid can you get? Surely they will come for you if you are wanted." However, the forceful feeling that I was needed was an absolute certainty. I dressed myself to pay the patient a visit. She lived about four miles from me.

'When I reached the house at about 2 a.m. lights were shining all over it. I literally ran down the garden path, opened the door, to find this patient standing by her kitchen table looking very anxious and obviously in strong labour. I said, "Where is your husband?" and she said, "He has just gone to phone you." Actually, he was in the shed getting his cycle ready.' All went well, and the premature infant, a boy, was safely delivered. Mrs Wright concludes: 'I was not expecting the call, and had never been sent for.'

Mrs Shirley Gray of Boston in Lincolnshire reported a similar experience in 1977. She awoke one morning to hear her name being called by a friend, and saw before her the head and shoulders of her friend Mrs Pat Craven. Mrs Craven looked 'haggard and in pain', but the oddest thing of all was that she was wearing a strange sleeveless garment with a square neck. Unknown to Mrs Gray, Mrs Craven was in hospital in Mombasa, Kenya, where she had gone for a holiday. At about the time Mrs Gray had the vision of her friend, Mrs Craven was taken to hospital after a serious accident. For the subsequent operation on her Achilles tendon, Mrs Craven wore a square-necked gown uncannily similar to the one Mrs Gray had seen.

Stories like these, from the experience of ordinary people, keep faith in ESP alive. This is why, when laboratory tests fail, or present no unchallengeable results, the quest for proof continues. No doubt it will go on even though, for the moment, the truth about telepathy seems as hard to find as those lost Russian aviators for whom Sir Hubert Wilkins searched in the wild and hostile darkness of the Arctic night.

# 7

# Blessings In Disguise

IN THE SPRING OF 1974 it fell to a class of schoolchildren in Oakland, California, to witness a strange and disturbing manifestation. The bleeding wounds of Christ – the stigmata – appeared on one of their classmates.

For at least 700 years, since St Francis of Assisi first manifested these signs, there have been cases where devout Roman Catholics have apparently found their bodies beginning to shed blood, as depicted in the statues and ikons of crucifixion to be found in almost every Catholic church, however small or poor. Invariably these people have found themselves propelled into the tempestuous waters of religious enthusiasm, hailed as saints, denounced as charlatans, the centre of healing cults, objects of pilgrimage, catalysts for flagellation. Some have been canonized, others exposed as frauds, or anathematized as heretics.

But Emery High School, Oakland, is as remote as can be from the feverish obsessions of European religion. The children are mainly black, their parents Baptists, their fathers longshoremen in the Oakland docks, or bus drivers across the bay in San Francisco.

In Easter week 1974 the Rev. Anthony Burrus was teaching the fifth grade – bright children whose families he knew well and who were keen to grab at education. It was mid-morning, and during a maths lesson, when the stigmata came in most dramatic fashion to twelve-year-old Cloretta Robertson, a chubby girl, always neatly dressed, with a round face and twin bobs in her hair.

Mr Burrus said, 'It just happened like she was shot with a machine-gun right across her forehead. Blood was flowing all down her face, all over her eyes. It was as though there was a crown of thorns around her head and she was just smiling and talking.' Antony Burrus had no doubt that he was seeing the final stage in an extreme case of stigmata – even St Francis had not displayed the signs of bleeding from the head – and a case unique in that it was happening to a non-white, non-Catholic girl.

*Opposite:* **Cloretta Robertson, who every year as Easter approaches, suffers the stigmata, the wounds of Christ on the Cross.**

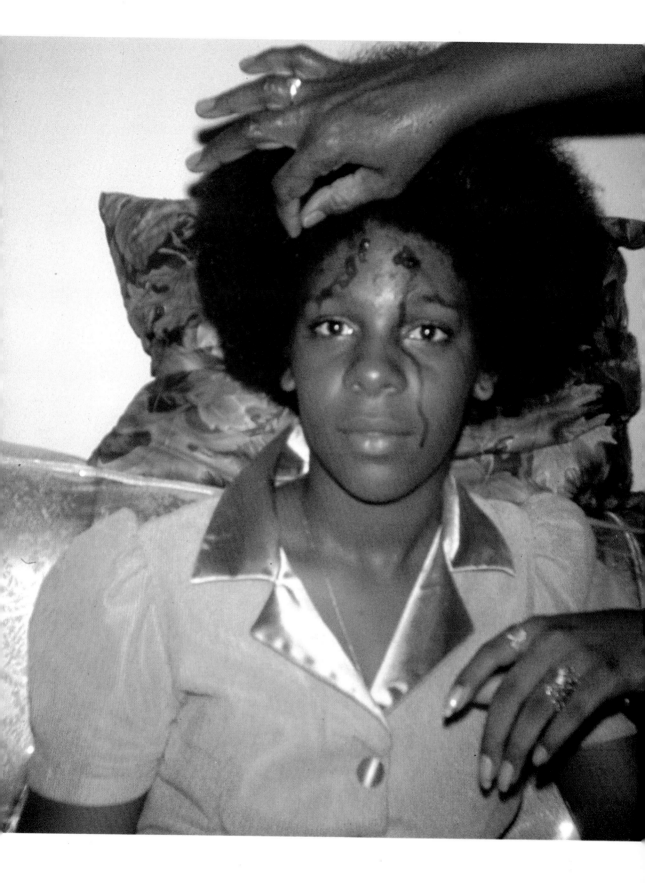

The first signs had in fact begun two weeks earlier. 'She started to bleed in her hands,' said Mr Burrus. 'She would open her hands and the blood was coming out like a natural oil well. We went into the Principal's office and it was shocking to him. He called Cloretta's mother and she took her away to the doctor.' Over the next few days, Mr Burrus was to become used to the appearance of the stigmata. 'Many times she would sit in class doing her work and, without warning, she would come to my desk and say, "Mr Burrus I'm bleeding and I have to go to the back room." We would just go into the back room and pray together. We would hold hands and when I opened mine they would be covered with her blood. Sometimes she would go round showing it to the children. It just paralysed them.'

The very first signs had begun two years before. And every year since, as Easter has approached, Cloretta Robertson has been struck by the stigmata, sometimes just in a hand, but sometimes in all the six places of the traditional wounds of Christ: the hands, the feet, the left side and on the forehead. She has been exposed to repeated medical examinations and tests. Cloretta's mother, on the very first occasion, took her to the local doctor who cleaned her up, could find no sign of a wound in her hand, and sent her home. When she bled again the same day, Mrs Robertson took her to the Kaiser Hospital in Oakland where she was seen by Dr Kaia. Again she was cleaned up, but her hand kept on producing blood. 'I think practically every doctor they could get to her came,' said Mrs Robertson, 'and all they could say was "This is strange, this is very strange."'

Cloretta was referred to Dr Loretta Early, paediatrician at the West Oakland Health Center. Cloretta was sitting in her office, drawing, when she felt her hand starting to bleed. She showed Dr Early two or three drops of blood in the palm of her left hand. The doctor then watched transfixed for three or four minutes as blood welled up from the centre of the palm and spread down the palm's creases. When she wiped the blood away there was no wound, only a pea-size bluish discolouration.

Dr Early conducted elaborate tests on Cloretta's blood and the blood from the stigmata, but could prove only that the two were identical. She summoned a psychiatrist from the University of California at Berkeley, Dr Joseph Lifschutz, but they could find no medical explanation for Cloretta's condition except psychogenic purpura, that is, psychologically induced bleeding. All they were certain of was the event itself, which by now had been witnessed by nurses, schoolteachers, hospital staff, numerous doctors and the children of Emery High School. It was two years before they published their theories, by which time Cloretta had become the centre of a wondering cult at the New Light Baptist Church on the corner of Grove and Parker Streets in Oakland, and had felt herself able to cure minor illnesses, to halt the asthma attacks of the pastor's son Mark, to touch her aunt Winifred's stiff neck and restore it, and to heal cut legs and hands. 'Our church,' Pastor Hester told his congregation, 'has been chosen for the most wonderful manifestation, which we must cherish and be worthy of. The wounds of Christ have shown themselves on our Cloretta.'

Today, and in film taken in 1974, it is very apparent that Cloretta has been a happy girl, plump, smiling, attractive, a little shy but enjoying the attention the stigmata have given her. The doctors confirm that the family is 'very close, warm, positive and apparently emotionally and physically healthy'. But Cloretta was deeply religious even at the age of ten – the Bible virtually her only reading, praying every night and sometimes feeling that she heard her prayers answered, spending all Sunday in church and singing with the choir. A week before the stigmata began, a television film about the crucifixion had left her with vivid dreams, and then she had read *Crossroads*, John Webster's highly-charged book about the crucifixion. It is not difficult to imagine its impact on an impressionable young girl. But, as Dr Lifschutz says: 'Millions of people have felt the traumatic shock of visualizing the nails being hammered into the body of Christ. Why should this thing happen to Cloretta? And more puzzling still – how?'

It was in September 1968 that the most venerated stigmatist of modern times, Padre Pio, was laid to rest at San Giovanni Rotondo in southern Italy. He had bled constantly from the hands and feet for more than 50 years and the process to have him declared 'Blessed' is already under way – the first stage towards what seems to be imminent sainthood.

The legends surrounding Padre Pio are legion. He is supposed to have had the gift of prophecy, even telling the present Pope John Paul II that he would one day be Pontiff. He is credited with innumerable miracles of healing, on a scale even larger than Lourdes: a girl born with no irises in the pupils of her eyes to whom he gave sight, paralyzed people walking, cancer victims cured. Even the accounts of his life, which carry the 'Nihil Obstat' of the official Roman Catholic censor, include tales of 'bilocation' when the Padre is believed to have been in two places at once – appearing to Italian soldiers in North Africa in the Second World War and standing beside the beds of sick women when he was known never to have left the cloister. But above all the wonder of the stigmata brought worshippers in their hundreds of thousands to San Giovanni Rotondo, waiting often days on end to have their confessions heard by the celebrated priest.

Padre Pio was born into a peasant family at Pietralcina near Benevento. He entered the Capuchin brotherhood, already in poor health when he was ordained, but still noted for the most rigorous fasting and prayer. The stigmata appeared on him at the chapel of San Giovanni Rotondo – then an isolated and primitive village – on 20 September 1918, three days after the Capuchins had celebrated the feast of the stigmata of St Francis.

Padre Pio was alone in the chapel, praying. Suddenly, outside, a piercing cry was heard. One of the monks, Father Leone, rushed in to find Padre Pio lying unconscious on the floor with blood pouring from five places – both hands, both feet and the left side. For the next 50 years, the wounds seemed never to close, never to become infected, never to stop bleeding.

The Capuchins and the Vatican acted swiftly. Photographs were taken. Dr Luigi Romanelli was despatched to examine Padre Pio; his report was, in essence, the same as the many that followed over the years, from Dr Festa, Dr Bignami and others. On the back and front of the hands, there were scabs, almost an inch across: the wound appeared to go right through them. The scabs always bled a little at the edges, and from time to time they came off, so that the wound bled more profusely. Both feet were in a similar state. Around the edges of the stigmata the flesh, even when examined under a magnifying glass, showed clear, almost translucent, with no sign of damage or inflammation. The chest stigma, like an inverted cross three inches long, gave the priest more pain than the other wounds, bleeding much more freely; Padre Pio reckoned he lost up to a cupful of blood on some days.

Almost immediately, as news of the stigmata spread, Padre Pio became the centre of an intense and enduring adulation. The Capuchins themselves carefully guarded their brother: none of the blood-stained garments was ever thrown away, but stored in a special room in the monastery. The Vatican was extremely circumspect, and in an ordinance which lasted to the end of his life, forbade him to publish any writings or to travel away from the

Padre Pio and (*below*) at the Church of San Giovanni Rotondo, the relics which fascinate the faithful: the chair in which he died; the cell in which he spent the last 30 years of his life; his shoes, made large to accommodate his bandages.

monastery. This last, however, merely ensured that an unending stream of pilgrims came to him, queueing at the confessional, covering the walls of the chapel with scribbled messages imploring help and intercession, arriving in their hundreds at 5 a.m. each day, wheeling the sick and the dying into the church in the hope of a blessing and to hear him say mass.

The daily offerings and contributions soon mounted so that a gigantic hospital could be built beside the monastery. A vast array of literature appeared. The official biographer, Father Charles Carty, reflected the atmosphere which surrounded the long, early morning Mass, often an hour and a half or more: 'During Mass many of those present are bathed in the wonderful scent that comes from the father. Why does Padre Pio's Mass last so long? We cannot tell what transpires in his soul, so burning with love for Christ that he wears imprinted on his body the sacred wounds. If he has been called to suffer for all, surely his sufferings must increase during the Holy Sacrifice of the Mass, especially in the moment when Our Lord mystically renews the bloody sacrifice of Calvary. Padre Pio seems to be transfigured with grief, and in certain moments of the Mass his face shows signs of suffering incredible pain, his eyes seem on the verge of tears, his lips move as though in colloquy with Our Lord, truly present on the altar from the Consecration to the Communion.'

In this atmosphere of intense piety and adulation it is not hard to imagine the extreme pressure on a man who even in his youth had been wont to punish his body with fasting and spiritual exercises, beyond the usual demands of his faith.

After the early years of the stigmata no medical examinations were published, but Padre Pio appeared daily with his hands bandaged and often covered with woollen mittens. Only in his final days, in the late summer of 1968, according to the Capuchins, did the stigmata diminish. Over the years they had changed from the quite small holes shown in the early photographs of his hands taken 'under obedience', to the extensive scabs and bloodstains shown in the later pictures.

Padre Pio was buried in the monastery where he had lived all the 50 years since his stigmata had arrived. In that time the primitive remote village had been transformed into one of the major centres of pilgrimage in Europe. More than 100,000 people attended his funeral; the procession took more than three hours to move the open casket a mile and a half from the church. 'I was reminded,' wrote one priest, 'of another procession I had often read about. In 1226 the body of St Francis was carried the mile and a half from Porziuncula to Assisi. He too was a stigmatist. Neither Assisi nor San Giovanni Rotondo was a town rich in material things, but both were honoured with a stigmatist, a holy man of God.' And, indeed, Padre Pio did follow a line of intriguing cases of stigmata.

More than 100 years ago, the Belgian Academy investigated the case of Louise Lateau who, in the course of ecstatic trances, was producing stigmata in her hands. The Academy arranged for the girl's hand to be encased in a glass globe, 'a tube from which was carefully attached round the arm and sealed so as to exclude the use of any sharp instrument'. The blood flow was, nevertheless, found to occur as before. By the time she died in 1883 she had revealed the stigmata 800 times.

Louise was a peasant girl prone to receiving visions of St Ursula and St Roch and other, obscurer, saints. During meditation and prayer she would suddenly be struck rigid or collapse into paroxysms; until, one Friday in April 1868, the stigmata appeared – on hands and feet and beneath her left breast. From then on the pattern was utterly regular. Each Tuesday burning sensations would appear at the stigmata points, culminating, on a Thursday evening, in shooting pains. Large blisters developed on Friday mornings, the blisters would burst and the blood flow. Louise would then be given the communion wafer. The routine after that was prayer, followed, as the clock chimed two, by a half-hour trance. Next, a session on her knees. Then, finally, she would lie face down on the floor, arms outstretched, for an hour and a half or more. Suddenly the ecstasy would seem to end and she would get to her feet. By Saturday the bloody areas would have disappeared, leaving patches of pinkness on the skin but the body otherwise unaffected, until Tuesday came round again.

For 15 years, until her death, Louise Lateau was studied by medical men and scientists. Dr Gerald Molloy, the rector of University College, Dublin in Ireland, described a visit to the Lateau house, which had already become half-shrine and half-circus: 'There is no wound properly so-called, but the blood seemed to force its way through the unbroken skin. In a very short time sufficient blood had flowed to gratify the devotion of pilgrims who applied their handkerchiefs until all the blood had been wiped away. This process was repeated several times during the course of our visit.'

'A true likeness of the wonderful servant of God, Gemma Galgani.'

The pattern of the Friday blood flow and the Saturday or Sunday restoration was repeated in two of the other cases which followed Louise Lateau. Gemma Galgani, who died at the age of 25 in 1903, acquired the stigmata after being, it was said, miraculously cured of tuberculosis. She was also endowed, her parish priest at Camigliani in Italy reported, with clairvoyant powers and with a talent for seeing ghosts. Her wounds appeared promptly at eight o'clock on a Thursday evening without any apparent preparation. 'The violence of the pain made her keep her hands convulsively closed, but the wounds seemed to go right through her hands and feet and were covered by a swelling that at first looked like clotted blood, whereas it was found to be fleshy, hard and like the head of a nail.' By Sunday, the marks were gone. Gemma in due course became St Gemma, without being too much molested by men of science, protected by 'reverential delicacy inspired by the ecstatic in her mysterious state'.

No such consideration was shown to Therese Neumann, the stigmatic from Konnersreuth in Bavaria. She died in 1962 after 37 years of attention from mystics, physicians and journalists. Therese was born in 1898 and by the time she was 20 had become bedridden, blind and paralyzed, apparently from hysteria after a fire at a neighbour's farm. When St Theresa of Lisieux was beatified in 1925, Therese Neumann was suddenly cured of her blindness and, after visions of the child-saint, seemed to lose all her old symptoms and got out of bed. By the end of 1926 bleeding had appeared.

The American dermatologist Joseph V. Klauder described the scene as he found it: 'The ecstasy began every Thursday between eleven and twelve o'clock and lasted until Friday afternoon. Therese would awaken suddenly from sleep, partly sit up and remain motionless for a short period. She

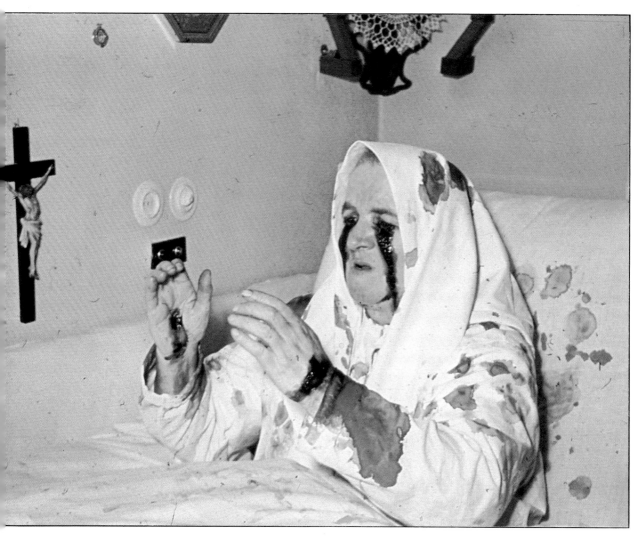

**Therese Neumann on Good Friday, 1953.**
*Below:* **As a young nun, and her chair, preserved as a holy relic.**

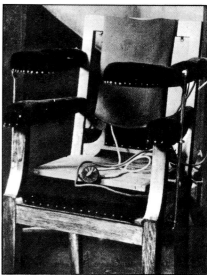

would become deadly pale, with eyelids half closed and hands stretched out; blood-tinged tears would run down her face and clot on her chin and neck. After five or ten minutes she would sink back into the pillows and appear exhausted. When asked questions she would describe in a low voice what she had seen. Apparently she would live the whole scene at Calvary, following Christ at each step. In the final hour when she would experience the Crucifixion, she would sit for the whole hour in a half-upright position with arms extended and eyes wide open and staring.' Therese had stigmata on hands, feet and brow but, as time went on, it was only the passion of Holy Week which could produce bleeding from all the places at once.

Fraud is always a possibility, and with stigmata, self-inflicted wounding cannot always be ruled out. Dr Martini, in 1938, saw Therese Neumann making 'strange and very intense movements with her arms and legs under cover of her bed clothes during the hours before bleeding appeared'. Even with Padre Pio sceptics thought the iodine he used to rub into his hands might have damaged them and prolonged the bleeding. Confronted with the stigmata, local clergymen are usually devoid of doubt. 'These are the wounds of Christ', says Cloretta Robertson's Pastor Hester in Oakland. The American Capuchin priest, John Schug, described Padre Pio's marks as 'The real and visible wounds of the Crucifixion'. He asserted that Padro Pio also had the mark of the scourges: 'Cleonice Morcaldi gave Padre Pio a white linen shirt. Three days later he gave it back to her for washing. She looked at it and gasped: "Madonna, it is one flagellation." It was splattered with blood from top to bottom, from front to back.'

However the blood appears, it seems clear that the marks do not accord with the actual wounds of the crucifixion. All the evidence today is that the Roman method of crucifixion was to tie the arms to the cross with ropes and to drive in the nails through the wrists. (If the body had been supported solely through nails in the hands, the weight would probably have torn right through the flesh.) The stigmata, therefore, accord rather with the wounds shown on church statuary and in Renaissance painting – Gemma Galgani's wounds seem to have appeared in exactly the same places as those shown on the crucifix in her parish church. The variety of parts of the chest in which wounds manifest themselves seems to reflect the indecision of artists on a matter on which the Gospels are silent – where exactly did the Roman soldier's spear thrust penetrate? St John merely said the spear 'pierced his side, and forthwith came there out blood and water'.

But it seems hard to doubt that stigmata do appear. An intense religious devotion allied to a traumatic childhood seems to be a common factor – though Cloretta Robertson appears to have come from a happy and normal home, and a Swedish girl, studied by Dr Magnus Huss, produced bleeding without any religious overtones. The girl, Maria K, was beaten up when she was 23 years old. Afterwards, every couple of weeks, she would produce bleeding from the head, the ear and eyelids. Supervised in the Seraphim Hospital in Stockholm, she continued to produce blood without any marking on the skin except for a pinkness and tenderness. Dr Huss eventually found that Maria could produce the bleeding at will, simply by picking á quarrel with some other patient in order to wind herself up to the necessary emotional pitch.

Oscar Ratnoff, Professor of Medicine in Cleveland, Ohio, reported in 1969 that he had seen blood oozing out of the hair follicles on a patient's thigh, over an area as big as a silver dollar, during a period of severe emotional distress. Careful examination afterwards showed no signs of any wound, self-induced or otherwise. As Professor Ratnoff says, 'To describe such things is not the same as to explain them,' but he and his team have documented more than 60 cases in which patients, almost invariably women with hysterical personalities and the most gruelling of private lives, have been able to produce bruises on their bodies without any external damage. The whole process often took only an hour or two, therefore the patient could be reliably observed. First, there would be a redness or puffiness, soon followed by a blue ring around the site or a bruise covering the spot. Some of the bruises were spectacularly large – up to six inches – and the process could go on for many years.

Tests by American researchers Frank Gardner and Louis Diamond suggested that these patients might be sensitive to some element in their own blood, what is known as autoerythrocyte sensitization. But Ratnoff was left with the strong conclusion that the bleeding and bruising under the skin in his patients was triggered by their emotions. 'Our patients had more than their share of the griefs of the living,' he said. Eight had alcoholic husbands, twelve were repeatedly beaten by their husbands and five had had similar treatment from their parents. Eight more related experiences 'in which they had been confronted with individuals with severe physical disabilities of the lower extremities'. They all showed 'a predilection for painful and humiliating experiences, and a proneness to accidents, injuries and surgery'. Hysterical and masochistic traits were dominant. The picture seems convincing: intense emotional drives can produce weals, bruises, even bleeding through the pores of the skin.

During the Second World War doctors and psychiatrists working with troops became acquainted with the extraordinarily severe effects of battle on the minds of even the toughest soldiers. Almost no one could last longer than 30 days in continuous combat without first becoming battle-happy – a stage in which they would become reckless and wildly expose themselves to danger – and then collapsing into the total lethargy of battle fatigue. Usually the result was nervous collapse, often requiring very long periods of recuperation, and psychiatric and drug treatment. But sometimes, the fear and panic of combat produced more dramatic physical effects.

One of the most desperate episodes of the war took place just before Christmas 1944 at Bastogne in Belgium. The Germans had broken through the Allied front in the Ardennes and were pushing with their panzers towards the Channel ports in what promised to be a dangerous thrust behind the invading forces. At Bastogne, units of the American Army found themselves the last barrier to the success of this German offensive; a bitter and relentless fight developed.

On the morning of 21 December one soldier, a circus artist in civilian life and a veteran of the North African campaign, was knocked over by a shell explosion. He had no external injury. But he was blind. Back at the base hospital neurological ward, it slowly became apparent that there was no physical cause for the blindness, so the surgeons decided instead to try psychiatric treatment under hypnosis. The technique was the fearsome process of abreaction, in which, sometimes helped by drugs, the patient is made to re-live his experiences with an intensity that drives him to the point of total collapse. One session sufficed to bring back the man's sight but in the course of conjuring up the vividness of the battle experience, the psychiatrist told the soldier that he had been struck on the hand by a shell fragment. After he was awakened from hypnosis the soldier complained of a burning sensation on his hand. About four hours later a substantial blister appeared which eventually sloughed off, leaving a raw wound that cleared up three days later. The doctors were fascinated and tried other tests on the unfortunate soldier: they found that they could raise cold sores around his mouth by suggestion under hypnosis; they made identical small cuts in the fingers on both his hands, telling him that the right hand would bleed but that the left hand would feel no pain and would not bleed. The left hand did not bleed.

Since those wartime days, it has become clear that the scars of the mind can be transmuted into lacerations on the body, often years after the events themselves took place.

Dr Albert Mason, a Harley Street doctor, told of a disturbing experience with a patient he called Mrs Stavely. She obviously had a considerable effect on him at first meeting: 'Large soft violet eyes, delicately chiselled features, perfectly shaped lips and rounded chin. A gay little hat suited her fair hair perfectly, her dark brown costume was expertly tailored, quiet and expensive, a large python had provided skin for her neat shoes and handbag. Her figure was trim, and I imagine that her vital statistics would have been applauded by the connoisseurs.' She also had a bad back.

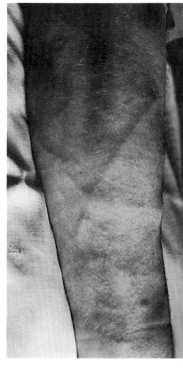

Can scars of the mind be transmuted into weals, even lacerations, by their sufferers?

Mason concentrated on treating the back trouble by hypnosis; it duly disappeared, only to be followed by a skin rash. Mason banished the rash, only to find the appearance of fibrositis. Clearly, there was some deep-seated problem and Mason set about discovering it. Mrs Stavely had by now developed an inability to hold anything hard or metallic, even a knife or fork. Once she was in deep hypnosis, Mason gave her a 'jerk' hammer to hold and told her to recall the experiences which had made hard objects repellent to her. 'Then occurred one of the most extraordinary things I have ever seen since I began to study as a medical student.

'Mrs Stavely began to move as though she were uncomfortable; she began to rub her shoulders on the couch and soon she started to scratch them. And as I watched with fascination, an urticarial weal began to form on her neck and on the part of her chest which I could see above her dress. It was a fantastic sight. There was this beautiful woman lying on the couch holding my hammer, and as the minutes went by a long raised weal, white in the centre and with inflamed red edges, tailing off into a flare of angry scarlet appeared on her neck and chest.'

The cause of the eruption soon emerged. As Mason puts it: 'Her husband was one of those unfortunate creatures who can get sexual feeling only through dressing up in women's clothes. He also found it necessary to suffer pain, and he kept asking his wife to hit him with a stick. She, highly sensitive, had shrunk from such brutish lovemaking, but had finally agreed and suffered for it by taking the pain to herself in her mind.'

*Opposite:* **The self-styled Pope Gregory the Eighteenth, and** (*below*) **his church at Palmar de Troya. Otherwise known as Clemente Dominguez Gomez, he too claims to suffer the stigmata.**

Cases of weals, even blisters, appearing without physical wounding or damage are at least comprehensible to conventional medical science, for there is a rare condition known as dermatographia which has some similarities: sufferers react to the slightest touch. Anyone can write their name on a victim's back using only a feather. Even in normal people there is a rapid reaction to quite light touch: run a pencil down the arm, and immediately a white line appears as the blood vessels contract to minimize any blood loss. Then the line turns bright red as the blood rushes back. Next a ridge shows up where histamine has leaked to start the healing process. The result is a striking weal, even from such a small 'injury'.

It is conceivable that a vividly imagined wound might initiate the same process and produce the still extraordinary sight of weals or blisters appearing without any physical cause. Dr Robert Moody reported in *The Lancet* a wartime case of an officer who in the past had been tied to his bed by the wrists to prevent him from sleepwalking. Years later, during his nightmares, he produced weals which bled.

Over the years the power of the human mind to produce physical changes in the body has produced some extraordinary, even comic, testimony. Thinking, it would seem, really can increase your sexual attributes.

Dr Richard D. Willard of the University of Chicago in 1977 set about trying to increase the breast size of a number of women – by mind power. The women were hypnotized then treated to luscious images of full and rounded breasts, visions of ripe and fruitful bosoms, suckling from erect and fulsome nipples, pictures of Hollywood perfection. After twelve weeks Dr Willard reported to the American *Journal of Clinical Hypnosis*, that 46% had found it necessary to increase brassière size, and all but 15% had noted a significant increase in their breast size. 'This report shows that through hypnosis and visual imagery the size of an organ can be affected and, specifically in this experiment, enlarged,' pronounced Dr Willard.

In 1960 another doctor had tried a similar treatment on a small-breasted girl. Two years later Dr Milton H. Erickson was able to report breast development of 'one inch thick on one side and one and a half inches on the other side'. The other results he claimed for these experiments may perhaps have been more useful: the girl broke off her engagement to a 47-year-old unemployed alcoholic and took up weekly reading of those encouraging passages in the Song of Solomon:

> O Prince's daughter, the joints of thy thighs are like jewels, the work of the hands of a cunning workman.
>
> Thy navel is like a round goblet which wanteth not liquor; thy belly is like an heap of wheat set about with lilies.
>
> Thy two breasts are like two young roes that are twins.
>
> Thy stature is like to a palm tree and thy breasts to clusters of grapes.

Engagement to a more suitable young man was soon reported.

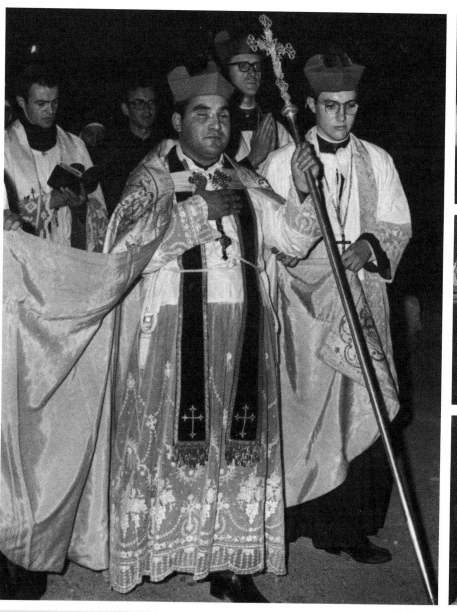

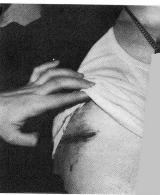

However they are produced, the stigmata at least can be very profitable. In southern Spain, at Palmar de Troya near Seville, there is currently a rival Pope, calling himself Gregory the Eighteenth, otherwise Clemente Dominguez Gomez, an ex-insurance clerk.

Gomez claims that at six o'clock in the morning on 2 April 1971 Christ came down and touched him on the forehead with a crucifix that was dripping blood. Since then, Clemente Gomez has from time to time exhibited the chest wound and the crown of thorns wounds on his forehead. He also persuaded a real archbishop to ordain him, first as a priest and then as a bishop – thus allowing him to ordain hundreds of others, mostly appealing youths – and then get himself elected Pope. He has a large green plastic cathedral in a field in which 12-hour Masses are conducted every night for the thousands of pilgrims who come to the site. He now owns an array of property in Seville and in Palmar de Troya. The Vatican has excommunicated Clemente Gomez, but the stigmata continue. So do the pilgrims. And so do the donations.

In the same year that Cloretta Robertson's wounds manifested themselves, another American girl, Lucy Rael from Questa, New Mexico, exhibited the signs of stigmata which launched her on a spectacular career of Pentecostal evangelism. Through Texas, California, and the states of the south and west Lucy packs in the crowds, with the special bonus that her daughter Angelica now shows signs of bleeding too.

A reporter from the *Atlanta Journal* wrote: 'When Sister Lucy lifted her blood-stained hands, the crowd went wild. Mrs Callie Taylor of Hartford Avenue said, "I touched her hands, there were holes there and blood was coming out. Her feet also had wounds."' There is an air of revivalist show biz surrounding Lucy Rael's stigmata, which seem to appear without warning at the emotional height of her crusade meetings. She has never been reported to have undergone detailed medical examinations in hospital, but a Texas doctor, Charles Melenyzer from the Lutheran Hospital in San Antonio, saw her during a service. 'I've never seen anything like it before and I'll remember it for a long time. The blood was more the texture of serum, but it congealed as normal blood does. There was no evidence of any puncture of the skin.' More than ten years on, Lucy Rael is still running a flourishing healing ministry, and still bleeding. As her posters say: 'See for yourself this miraculous sign of blood that was foretold by the prophet Joel and confirmed in the second chapter of Acts. Thousands have been amazed by this stigmata. The deaf hear, the blind see, the lame walk.'

There are other signs of holiness, as well as the bleeding wounds, claimed by stigmatics. Therese Neumann, Louise Lateau and others are also supposed to have gone for months or years without taking food or drink (one of Louise Lateau's investigators did find bread and fruit in a cupboard in her room) but such claims are notoriously easy to make and serious investigation is liable to end in tragedy, as happened in 1869 with the little Welsh girl, Sarah Jacob.

Sarah lived in a remote one-storeyed farmhouse at Lletherneuadd in south Wales, but she became a national celebrity when the local vicar wrote to the papers claiming that she had 'not partaken of a single grain of food for 16 months. She did, occasionally, swallow a few drops of water during the first few months of this period; but now she does not even do that.' Within weeks the local boys were greeting trains at the nearest station with placards proclaiming 'Fasting Girl' and offering to guide visitors to the bedside where they found 'a very pretty little girl of 12 reclining fancifully dressed, crowned with a wreath and decked in all sorts of gay ribbons, who smiled upon them and was very pleased to be admired'. Shillings and half-crowns were, it seems, not infrequently left behind in appreciation.

Sarah had already emerged from two weeks of day and night supervision by a local committee without them detecting any evidence of deceit or chicanery when she had the misfortune to be visited by Dr Robert Fowler, vice president of the distinguished English scientific body, the Hunterian Society. Dr Fowler wrote indignantly to *The Times* demanding an investigation. Sarah's parents raised no objection, and so a medical committee was set up with four nurses brought down from Guy's Hospital in London – one Welsh-speaking – to supervise the girl under strict instructions.

The result was sadly predictable. For four days Sarah was fine and cheerful. Then she went into a decline, with a racing pulse, sunken eyes and insomnia. The London *Daily News* did complain about the 'grotesque proceedings which are taking place at the bedside of a little girl in Wales' but the medical magazine *The Lancet* and most of the press seemed quite content. No one on the medical committee or among the nurses seems to have thought of trying to make Sarah eat, nor of abandoning the vigil, even when she was 'threatening to sink'. On the second Friday she seemed to lose the power of speech and at three in the afternoon she died.

There was a posthumous uproar. Five of the doctors on the committee were charged with killing the girl, but they were released by Carmarthen magistrates. The parents were not so lucky. Mr Justice Hannen sent them both down to hard labour. All the evidence suggests they had truly believed in Sarah's powers. A little girl's fantasies had exacted a terrible price.

Llethernoyadd-Ucha, Carmarthenshire, the home of Sara Jacob.

# 8

# Taking The Heat Off

THE POWER TO DEFY PAIN – even to embrace it – is a badge of faith for many creeds around the world. But if there is one place above all others on this Earth where the flesh is gladly mortified and the body macerated for the love of God, then it lies in the remote jungle of south-east Sri Lanka at Kataragama. There, the mutilation, the laceration, the suffering, go on all year at this temple sacred to Hindu, Muslim and Buddhist alike.

It is in the month of August that the year-round rituals attain an apogee of ecstasy. As dawn comes it is already stiflingly hot: the sun itself would be enough to endure through the day, but the faithful are already taking on the travails which they will carry through till evening. One man stands calmly as a huge steel skewer is thrust through his cheek. There seems to be no sign of blood. Slowly the skewer is driven onwards, continuing right through his tongue and out through the other cheek – two or three inches projecting on either side. Mouth open, with the sacred ash on his forehead, he begins the long slow dance which will go on till dusk.

The bell deep within the Kataragama temple tolls slowly. To its rhythm, a group of three men is being scourged, each lash opening up the flesh. Another man is slowly forcing knives through the skin of arms and legs. Yet another is surrounded by a dozen or more helpers carefully inserting metal hooks into his back. The sacred ash covers him like talcum powder. Eventually, there are 40 or 50 hooks embedded in the flesh of his back, each with a cord attached. Then, like a temple bullock, he is harnessed to a cart loaded with gifts and offerings, and he must pull: on the long slow journey to the temple, he is to be the draught beast for the gods. Amid the milling crowds, jostled by the bearers of less painful burdens – the great wooden structures decorated with peacock feathers and forest flowers also on their way to the temple – his journey seems an impossible undertaking.

In the August festival it is mainly Hindus who bear the flagellation, but

How is it possible for
people to walk across
firepits at temperatures
that would melt steel?

The August festival in Kataragama, Sri Lanka, where Hindus and Muslims perform extraordinary acts of self-mutilation without apparent suffering.

even then, at the mosque at Khizr Thakya, Muslims can be seen slashing themselves with knives and swords, driving steel spikes into their bodies. As darkness closes in, the focus of ecstasy moves, drawn towards the glow and the seared air of that most mysterious ritual of all, the walk across fire.

The pit, 20 or 30 feet long, has taken days to prepare. The smoke, the flames, finally, the white-hot radiation, confront the penitents with the promise of ultimate communion with the fierce gods of the Hindu pantheon. In years past, practical, perhaps sceptical, men have taken to Kataragama thermocouples, temperature gauges and the paraphernalia of the metallurgical laboratory. There is no doubt that the temperature of the stones in the pit reaches 800 or even 1000 degrees Centigrade.

The candidates for the ordeal, 50 or more, make their way in line first to the stream of Menik Ganga, to wash their whole bodies in the Hindu way. Then, slowly and deliberately, they turn to the fire pit. The incantation is a simple repetition of the prayer, '*Haro Hara, Haro Hara*'. The heat from the stones is intense enough to keep spectators several yards distant, but the Hindu priest who leads the penitents steps without hesitation into the fire. Neither dawdling nor hurrying, he makes the journey to the other end and then, untroubled, the return. The others follow. No sign of fear is discernible nor, at the end, any sign of burning or blisters or injury – only a drained expression, as through the exhaustion, or the exaltation, of emotion. Then, like a crowd leaving the cinema, they go quietly home.

Kataragama is as extreme a shrine of bodily suffering as any in the world,

but penance of the flesh is not the monopoly of any one faith, or of any country. The Catholic flagellants of Spain, the ecstatics of the American Appalachians, the fakirs of India, all find a way to holiness through apparently incredible tortures of the body which have always fascinated, and usually repelled outsiders. The British in India made constant and fruitless efforts to limit the displays of the fakirs. In the 1930s, according to *The Times*, the Italian Fascists found themselves upset by the practices of their new subjects, the Zanies, in Libya: 'The perforation and burning of the flesh, walking on fire, the swallowing of poisonous animals, broken glass, nails and prickly pear leaves, and the placing of rings through the noses of children, must be considered repugnant to the principles of morality and of modern civilization.'

Among these practices there are things which can be explained, as physics students attending the 1981 fall semester of the University of Montana were to discover. The class was settling down in the main lecture room on the college campus at Bozeman, when the two big doors swung open and the strains of Gregorian chant filled the air. Two men in black monkish robes appeared and processed slowly towards the lecture dais. Between them they carried a bed of nails and, prostrate upon it, a man dressed only in boxer shorts. Thus was Professor Larry D. Kirkpatrick of the Physics Department, Montana State University, introduced to his new students. The bed was laid on the dais and a block of concrete placed on the professor's body. A girl student was invited to break it with a sledge

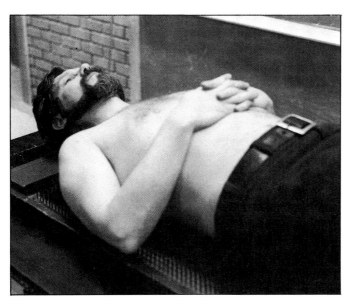 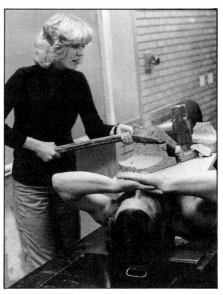

**Demonstrations in practical physics from Professor Larry D. Kirkpatrick, University of Montana.**

hammer. 'Sometimes they miss,' said Professor Kirkpatrick. 'Then it does hurt!' Then, the final scene. In through another door trots a football player in full uniform, clearly a blocker and of daunting proportions. He proceeds to sit on the professor's chest. 'Normally I hardly feel a thing,' says Professor Kirkpatrick, 'but last year I got one who must have weighed 260 pounds and I said to him ever so quietly "You can get off now."

'They may forget a lot of what I teach, but I guess they don't forget that. What I'm trying to show is the concept of weight distribution, of pressure, and of Newton's ideas on inertia. There's an ordinary carpentry nail every half inch, say 2700 in the whole bed. I guess there's about 800 supporting the upper part of my body. If you reckon that weighs 100 pounds, then you're talking about one-eighth of a pound per nail. I figure I'd have to have at least a pound per nail to puncture my back – that's why I think I could still do it with one-fourth as many nails. One thing I didn't realize in building these things is that you really should sort the nails, so that you get the same length nails in any one portion of the bed. The high ones do hurt, let me tell you. Actually, we've dulled a couple of them. So it's a little bit of dishonesty there – but I usually tell the students that. As for the girl and the concrete block, well, you know about inertia. The larger the mass of the object, the more the tendency to remain at rest. So if I get hit by something, my body just doesn't move very much. It doesn't really press down on the nails and it doesn't really hurt.' The academic exegesis is convincing. Indeed, in 1982, a Welshman, Ken Owen, lay for five days on a bed of nails two inches apart, without injury.

Few of the other feats of the fakirs or the Zanies conform so dramatically yet straightforwardly to the laws of physics or the precepts of human physiology, but some inkling is emerging.

In October 1981 Dr Wolfgang Larbig reported to the magazine *Electroencephalography and Clinical Neurophysiology* another of the strange scenes which, it appears, now add interest to academic life. Dr Larbig's object was 'to identify special psychophysiological strategies to cope with stress and pain that modern civilized man has forgotten'. Such strategies do seem to exist: The activities of fakirs do not seem to be limited to the special times or places of religious ceremony where trance or ecstasy or some form of hypnotism or analgesic might be invoked – they do it anywhere. For some years in the 1960s French holidaymakers on the Riviera diverted themselves from the torments of acquiring a sun tan at St Tropez by attending the world fakir championships. The 1963 renewal was won by Fakir Rayo, who had himself crucified upside down – nails through hands and feet – and maintained this indubitably fixed position for 3 hours, 20 minutes.

Dr Larbig invited an Indian fakir into his laboratory at the University of Tübingen in West Germany who claimed to be able to be buried alive, to lie on nails, to be crucified for hours. To demonstrate his authenticity to the laboratory staff, the fakir took four metal spikes and thrust them into his stomach, tongue and neck. There was no sign of blood. The team reported: 'From all overt behavioural indicators, there was no evidence that he experienced any pain whatsoever.'

The fakir's method of preparation was apparently to think himself into a trance-like state by concentrating on some point just above his eyebrows. His face was blank, his eyes staring, and the team said he sat more than half an hour without once blinking.

Fourteen gallant volunteers offered their services for Dr Larbig's experiments to try themselves against the fakir. They were taken to a dimly lit, electrically shielded, and sound-proof room, and placed in reclining chairs. Electrodes were attached to their ear lobes, their fingers and above the eye, but only for recording purposes: it was the ones attached to the leg which were to administer pain. The subjects were asked to prepare themselves in any way they knew to cope with pain. Then they were given a strong electric shock. And 40 more like it. When they were released, the victims were asked to assess how bad the pain had been. Pretty bad seemed to be the general view, though the fakir, still unblinking, appeared to have borne up best. But Dr Larbig's instruments had thrown up something more precise to justify the trials of the 15 sufferers.

The recordings of the brain waves of the fakir were quite different from those of the rest of the subjects. The slow brain-frequencies of the so-called theta band are normally associated with deep sleep. But the fakir showed them every time he felt pain; it was as though he could put part of his brain to sleep at will. The fakir showed, quite strikingly, slower and stronger theta waves when the pain came on: the print-outs were undeniable. The conductivity of the fakir's skin was also quite different from that of the others during the experiment. There was no question that the fakir had been able to bring about measurable changes in his brain and body – theta powers Dr Larbig called them – in order to reduce the pain he felt.

For all its rather gruesome aspect, Dr Larbig's experiment had lifted a corner of the mystery. The meditative techniques of the fakir seemed undoubtedly to produce physical changes in brain and body and thus control the feeling of pain, but there was no hint of how the fakir prevented the appearance of blood, and left only marks on his skin, not wounds, after the spikes and the knives were withdrawn. It has always been this ability of mystics to defy not only pain, but burns, wounds, and potentially fatal perils, that has gripped the imagination.

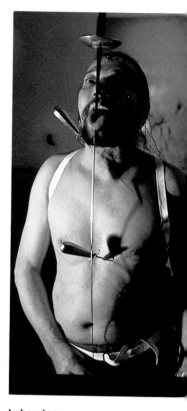

Laboratory demonstration by an Indian fakir at the University of Tübingen. He seemed able to produce measurable changes in his brain and body – theta powers – to reduce pain.

Above all, there is the firewalk. It challenges all credulity that men, women, sometimes even children, should venture on to the scalding stones of the fire pits and emerge unscathed and unscarred, immune from the fearful, even fatal, burns which all logic suggests should be the result, yet the firewalk is to be encountered all over the world.

The pits are prepared each May at Langadhas in northern Greece for the festival of St Constantine and St Catherine – hot enough in 1982 to give London mechanic George Mills severe third-degree burns when he tried to join in. Each April there is a ceremony at Pietermaritzburg in South Africa. In 1970 something went wrong and the firewalkers, local Hindus, were all badly burnt, but the ceremony persists. There are fire pits in Japan and the Philippines and Fiji, Navajo Indians walk through fire, and Polynesian Islanders stroll across huge pits of red-hot stones as though they were on a city boulevard.

Nearly a century ago westerners were trying to understand. In 1901 the American Professor S. P. Langley of the Smithsonian Institute, later to make his name as a pioneer aviator, was on a voyage in the Pacific islands. When the ship reached Tahiti, he turned his enquiring spirit towards seeing a firewalk and, particularly, to assessing how hot the fire really was. He had heard of Papa Ita 'who is said to be one of the last remnants of a certain order of the priesthood of Raiatea'. Through friends, Langley arranged for the priest to come over to the main island for a ceremony. 'He is the finest looking native that I have seen,' reported Langley, 'tall, dignified in bearing, with unusually intelligent features. He said that he walked over the hot stones without danger by virtue of spells and by the aid of a goddess who was formerly a native of the islands.'

Langley watched the preparation of the trench, about two feet deep, nine feet across and 21 feet long, with basalt stones piled on top of the logs which were used to set the fire. 'By the aid of Chief Engineer Richardson,' reported Langley 'who attended with a stoker and one of the quartermasters kindly detailed by Captain Lawless, the ship's master, I prepared for the rough but conclusive experiment presently described.' Chief Engineer Richardson was a sceptical man. He had already advised Langley that 'Native feet are not like European feet' and that he had seen natives stand

**Firewalking in Mauritius, 1881.**

on steam pipes on the ship, something no member of the crew could possibly have endured.

Langley was bent on investigation, but he was beguiled enough by the ceremony. 'The mise-en-scène was certainly noteworthy. The site, near the great ocean breaking on the barrier reefs, the excited crowd talking about the red-hot stones, the actual sight of the hierophant and his acolytes making the passage along the ridge where the occasional tongues of flame were seen at the centre, with all the attendant circumstances, made up a scene in no way lacking in interest. Papa Ita, flower-crowned and dressed with garlands, appeared with naked feet and a large bush of Ti leaves in his hand and, after going around the fire uttering what appeared to be commands to it, went back and, beating the stones nearest to him three times with the Ti leaves, advanced steadily but with obviously hurried step directly over the central ridge of the pile.'

The priest made four passes, followed by a number of disciples. Langley then set about his investigation. He levered out one of the stones from the middle of the pit, which almost everyone had stepped on. 'I had brought over the largest wooden bucket which the ship had, and which was half-filled with water.' The stone was dropped in. 'The water was thrown into such violent ebullition that a great deal of it boiled over and escaped weighing. The stone continued to boil the water for about 12 minutes when, the ebullition being nearly over, it was removed to the ship and the amount of evaporated water measured.' Langley took the stone and the statistics home to Washington. After determining the specific heat and specific gravity of the stone, he was able to conclude that the stone had been at about 1200 degrees Fahrenheit.

The fire pits were indeed hot and confirmed as such to the satisfaction of the turn-of-the-century scientific world, far too hot to be overcome by the callouses of native feet or the application of alum powder, as the theories of the day maintained. The firewalk continued to intrigue and to baffle Westerners.

In 1922 the French Bishop of Mysore in India, Monsignor Despatures, at the invitation of the local Maharajah attended a firewalk to be conducted by a Muslim mystic. The Muslim began by simply pushing a palace servant into the pit. 'For the first moment or two,' wrote the bishop, 'the Indian struggled to get out of the fire, then suddenly the look of terror on his face gave place to an astonished smile, and he proceeded to cross the trench lengthwise, beaming contentedly upon those who were standing round on either side of him.' There then followed what must be one of the most bizarre episodes in the history of a baffling phenomenon. The entire Maharajah's band marched into the flames three by three, carrying their instruments in their hands with the sheets of music still on top, while a new cartload of dried palm leaves was thrown in to freshen the fire. The bishop wrote: 'I noticed that the flames which rose to lick their faces, bellied out round the different parts of the instruments and only flickered round the sheets of music without setting them on fire. Two Englishmen, the head of the Maharajah's police force (a Catholic) and a civil engineer crossed without any sign of burning. When they came back into my neighbourhood, I asked them what they thought of it. "Well," they said "we felt we were in a furnace, but the fire did not burn us." ' The proceedings concluded with the Muslim suddenly falling in agony and begging for water. A Brahmin told the bishop: 'He has taken upon himself the burning of the fire.'

In the autumn of 1935, Harry Price organized the most high-powered investigation of firewalking ever made. In the unlikely setting of Mr Alex Dribbell's garden at The Halt, Woodmansterne Road, Carshalton, Surrey, and with the assistance of Mr Dribbell's gardener, Price prepared a fire pit. His subject was a young Indian, Kuda Bux, then newly arrived in London and 40 years later, in the 1970s, a famous draw as a magician at the Los Angeles Magic Castle. The supervising committee in Mr Dribbell's garden were members and associates of the University of London Council for Psychical Investigation, a distinguished lot, including four professors.

Price set out the questions he hoped to answer, and they remain to this day a succinct summary of the conundra. Is firewalking based on trickery? Can anyone do it? Do the performers prepare their feet? Can they convey their alleged immunity from burns to other persons? Do the walkers apply a paste of alum salt soap and soda, as has been alleged? Do they have to be in an ecstatic or exalted condition? Do they have to possess faith? Do they inject an anaesthetic into their feet? Do the ashes form an insulating layer on top of the fire and thus prevent burning? Does the performer have to hurry along the trench or can he stroll? Does he fast or otherwise prepare himself mentally or physically for the ordeal?

Harry Price may not have succeeded in answering many of the questions, but he certainly put on a bizarre show, recorded for posterity on 16mm film. There was a howling gale that day in September, with intermittent rain adding to the trials of Woodmansterne Road. Price defeated the elements with seven tons of oak logs, a ton of firewood, a load of charcoal, ten gallons of paraffin and 50 copies of *The Times*, which did sterling service as firelighters.

Kuda Bux elected, for no ascertainable reason, to turn up in a black frock coat and trousers. He immediately answered one of the questions by taking a snack: he did not need to fast. Professor Joad, a great star of the day on the wireless, was present, together with a BBC producer, R. S. Lambert. A London University physicist and three colleagues were the stokers, charged with measuring the temperature of the fire and getting up a good heat. Professor C. A. Pannett was the official doctor.

Kuda Bux's feet were examined, then carefully washed, dried, and had their temperature taken. A little test patch of elastoplast was applied to the sole of one foot. The wind was still whistling through Mr Dribbell's trees and the spectators were in overcoats and trilbies, but the pit itself was as near to Indian conditions as Price could make it. The body of the fire was at 1400 degrees Centigrade – beyond the melting point of steel. Even on the surface ash, Dr R. E. Gibbs's thermocouple recorded 430 degrees.

Harry Price and his University of London colleagues had every reason to take the utmost precautions with Kuda Bux, for he had given them a merry run-around when they had first met, six months before. Kuda Bux was a Kashmiri who had arrived in London under the stage name of Professor K. B. Duke; he had instantly captured the headlines with demonstrations of what he called 'eyeless sight'. Price and his friends had run a test in which

PEARSON'S WEEKLY

HE WILL WALK THROUGH FIRE

2ᴰ

Kuda Bux firewalking in a Carshalton garden before members of the University of London Council for Psychical Investigation in 1935.

they plugged Kuda Bux's eyes with dough, covered the dough with surgical bandages, taped them down and then put a black mask on him. Still he managed to copy written messages and, indeed, to read a book. Ruefully, Price recorded: 'Kuda Bux would not allow us to adopt measures that would absolutely preclude his seeing down the side of his nostrils. All we learnt that afternoon was how extremely difficult it is to blindfold a person, if ordinary methods of blindfolding only are used,' a discovery re-made by the television crew who in 1980 filmed magician James Randi driving, apparently blindfold, through the rush-hour traffic of Philadelphia.

But firewalking was different. As the University of London physicists confirmed that afternoon in Carshalton, the fire was very hot indeed. There was apprehension as well as excitement as the small but distinguished crowd gathered round the pit. Dr E. H. Hunt, who had seen firewalks in India, was worried that the conditions were exceptionally severe. He said: 'The trench is shallower than is customary and with the high wind increasing the surface combustion and blowing away all the ash, the heat is far more intense and is transmitted without any insulation.'

Kuda Bux went ahead. Walking steadily and deliberately he took four strides and covered the 11-foot length of the pit in 4.5 seconds. Shortly afterwards he did the walk again, this time in 4.3 seconds. Professor Pannett examined his feet and found them completely uninjured: 'By careful scrutiny could be seen here and there the whitened appearance of the skin which occurs when the very surface of the epithelium is scorched without blistering. There were no signs of hyperaemia or blistering. The patch of plaster was quite unharmed, except that the fluff of the cotton at the cut edge looked very slightly scorched. If this were so, these cotton fibres must have reached a temperature approaching 120 degrees Centigrade.' Kuda Bux's feet had actually got slightly cooler and were measured at 93 degrees Fahrenheit.

Two of the witnesses at Carshalton were so impressed by the feat they had seen that they decided to have a go themselves. Mr Digby Moynagh took two steps across a corner of the trench and retired with blisters. Then Mr Maurice Cheepen also took two short quick steps across a corner. His feet were examined by Professor Pannett who observed bad blistering and bleeding at three points. Learned accounts of the great experiment were published in *Nature* and *The Lancet*, the scientific and medical journals, and a report appeared in *The Times*, but Harry Price felt himself little nearer to understanding the mystery. He had seen two colleagues burnt – one quite badly – yet the Kashmiri was unscathed, despite walking four times as far. The only clue, he felt, might be a certain speed and flexibility in walking so that 'no one portion of the skin was in contact with the hot embers for as long as half a second': he had checked this against his slow-motion cine film. Otherwise, he was more baffled than ever.

He noted:

1. The ash was carefully removed before each walk, so it could not be an insulation.
2. Moisture on the feet appears to be a hindrance rather than a help since it may cause hot particles to adhere (this had been Digby Moynagh's experience).
3. The feet did not seem to be excessively calloused.
4. Kuda Bux did not fast or indulge in any other obvious preparation.
5. There were no special ointments on the feet – they had been washed and dried by the doctor.
6. Immunity from burning was clearly not, on this occasion at least, 'conveyed' to other people.

Charles R. Darling, however, one of the physicists in charge of the thermocoupling, was convinced that the experiment had provided the answer. 'Firewalking is really a gymnastic feat,' he declared: the foot is never in contact with the coals long enough to cause a burn. The physicists, having timed Kuda Bux's foot-contact with the fire as about half a second on each step, tried to press the disc of their thermocouple against the surface of the fire for half a second. 'Actually, owing to the difficulty of working near the fire, this period was always exceeded. But a number of trials showed a rise of 15 to 20 degrees C.' Not enough to cause a blister.

'The agile way that Kuda Bux walked across the fire compelled admiration and would be difficult to imitate without much training,' said Mr Darling. 'It was lack of training in this particular which prevented Mr Moynagh and Mr Cheepen from succeeding. Also both were much heavier men than Kuda Bux and this caused them to sink more deeply into the fire and increased the time of contact. The feat was merely another form of the fireside experiment of picking up a hot cinder and returning it to the fire, when the fingers are not burnt if the action is performed quickly.' It does not seem that Mr Darling was filled with sufficient certitude, however, to test his theories on himself.

Kuda Bux, Harry Price and most of his colleagues are dead: the Carshalton firewalk was almost 50 years ago. As far as a scientific explanation is concerned, we have now progressed a little further since those puzzled and painstaking endeavours by the National Laboratory of Psychical Research which were carried out on that unusual afternoon in Mr Dribbell's garden.

In 1982 the intrepid doctors and students of the medical faculty at Colombo University in Sri Lanka put on an exhibition designed to counter magic and superstition in that most supernatural land. It was necessarily wide-ranging. Vasectomies were on offer on the spot, with a 300-rupee grant thrown in; there were educational stalls explaining snake-bite treatment, venereal disease and family planning. But the star attraction, morning and evening, was the firewalk, in which the doctors walked confidently up and down the red-hot coals in their white coats, ostentatiously chewing pork and taking sips of alcohol, thus extinguishing any notion that spiritual purity might be armouring them against the fire.

None was burned and the astonished spectators were nonchalantly referred to the work of Dr Jearl Walker, professor of physics at the Cleveland State University in Ohio. They were perhaps more confident than their guru, who has now given up the practice. 'I have walked across hot coals about five times now, but really hurt myself once,' said Professor Walker, 'so now I've stopped.'

Jearl Walker had long been intrigued by firewalking and became convinced that it was made possible by what is known as the Leidenfrost effect. Johann Gottlieb Leidenfrost was a German doctor who wrote a tract in 1756 on the properties of water. One of the many things he had noticed was that if he let water drop on to a very hot spoon, the drops danced about and lasted longer before evaporating than if the spoon was cooler. The same happens on a hot stove or griddle.

Jearl Walker did some experiments and found that there was quite a sharp change at about 210 degrees Centigrade when drops of water, instead of evaporating into steam in ten seconds or less as they do at lower temperatures, would dance about and last for a minute or even longer. This effect lasted right up to temperatures of 500 degrees or more. He also took close-up photographs which showed that the drops were kept constantly clear of actual contact with the hot surface by a thin layer of vapour. This, he concluded, must be the secret of firewalking. The drops of sweat or water on the firewalkers' feet (and some do walk through a tray of water before re-entering the fire) would form a protective layer for long enough to allow the walker's feet to remain unharmed.

He thought there would also be a quenching effect from the sweat on the very top surface of the fire. The theory was fine, but Jearl Walker was no ordinary professor of physics: he decided to try it himself and set up a five-foot bed of hot coals in the back garden. 'I suddenly found it remarkably easy to believe in physics when it is on paper,' he said 'but remarkably hard to believe in it when the safety of one's own feet is at stake. As a matter of fact, walking on hot coals would be such a supreme test of one's true belief in what one had learned that I have suggested that graduate schools might substitute it for the PhD examination in physics. On one side of a pit of red-hot coals would be a line of fresh PhD candidates. On the other would be the physics professor with a handful of certificates. If a graduate student really believed in physics, he would stride across the coals without hesitation. If he had any serious doubts he would not be able to bring himself to do it.'

Jearl Walker could hardly hesitate. 'Clutching my faded copy of Halliday and Resnick's *Physics* in one hand, I strode over the five feet of hot coals. Apparently I am a true believer in physics. I have to report, however, that my feet did get a bit hot.' On a later demonstration he got burnt, which he put down to having dry feet. 'Oh well,' he said, 'I am almost a true believer.'

Walker's gallant ventures in the cause of science hardly answered all the questions, not least about the effects of weight and the extended strolls in which the Pacific firewalkers indulge. His belief, too, in the efficacy of water and sweat on the feet contradicted Harry Price's observations. It was left to the Germans to make a comprehensive assault on the subject.

When the elaborate ritual for the annual firewalk at Langadhas began in May 1980, there were additional burdens for three of the walkers. Taped to their heads were the electrodes for an electro-encephalograph brain scan, and attached to their bare feet were thermocouples for temperature readings. Measurements from both were relayed, via a back-pack transmitter, to an indefatigable German team from Tübingen.

The villagers of Langadhas have celebrated for centuries the Emperor Constantine's feat in saving relics from a burning church without himself being scorched. Early on 21 May each year the firewalkers of Langadhas meet in the private sanctuary. Already, they have prepared with days of fasting. The drums begin the heavy rhythm which will continue all through the day until the walk begins, at dusk. Candles are burning in front of the ikons in the sanctuary, focusing the attention of the worshippers until, as the German researchers noted, they seem to be in a hypnotic trance. Then the long dance begins, at first slowly but, as the hours pass by, with increasing fervour. Chickens, even young goats, are sacrificed as the trance deepens until, as the sun sets, the procession starts for the fire pit.

The German team had already assessed the fire. It was four yards across with about two inches depth of coals and a surface temperature of 500 degrees Celsius (932 degrees F.). Crouched over their tape recorders, the scientists spoke voice cues, marking the time that their wired-up test walkers were actually on the fire. A second channel recorded the radioed EEG brain and temperature readings from the back-pack.

Langadhas is almost unique, at least in the Western world. The walkers strolled on and off the fire for almost 20 minutes and showed no outer signs of pain nor burn marks on their feet. Two of the Germans, who gallantly donned the electronic hardware and ventured on the fire themselves, retired rapidly with third-degree burns. The scientists soon detected some surprising results. Although the temperature at the surface of the fire was measured at 500 degrees, the thermocouple on the soles of the walkers' feet gave a reading of 'only' 180 degrees (356 degrees F.), an anomaly for which they could offer no explanation. Also, in one of the walkers, there was a great increase in the theta activity in the brain when he walked on the fire.

This theta activity was a similar phenomenon to the effect they had noticed in their laboratory as their 'guinea-pig' fakir thrust spikes through his tongue, neck and stomach. They concluded that this was a 'partial cortical blockade' which in some way inhibited pain. But, though useful, they were forced to admit that it was by no means an essential mechanism, for their other two wired-up walkers showed no such increase in theta activity in the brain.

The scientists were obliged to fall back on the view that perhaps firewalking isn't really very dangerous – more a test of courage – and that the feet have a physiology which is actually quite well armoured against heat. Two sets of burned feet among their own team, however, were sufficient evidence that this may be rather a hazardous conclusion.

In our era of gurus, karma and meditation it is inevitable that transcendental explanations have taken over from the more mundane world of thermocouples and stop watches.

The Rev. Jon Mundy, a Methodist minister in Katonah in up-state New York, found himself joining in a firewalk at Swami Vishnu Devananda's summer *ashram* near Montreal in Canada in 1970. 'That morning I went up into the mountains to meditate. I needed an answer from the Holy Spirit. Then it came. I would do what everybody else was going to do. Before the walk it was just getting dark and the fire had this incredible glow. You could see the heat rising, it was that hot. We did what we call chaotic meditation, dancing, jumping and singing. I didn't feel like I'd gone into a trance. Then, seconds before we stepped onto the coals I felt like something had happened and just walked right across, probably no more than six steps. I wasn't burned at all. I remember I fell on the ground face forward and held there kicking my feet. It was the exhilaration of having done something so incredible.'

Another American, John Harmon McElroy, then a visiting lecturer at the University of Salamanca, walked the fire at San Pedro Manrique in Spain in 1969 – 15 or 20 feet across a bed of coals – and reported a similar elation. 'I found the experience so delightfully stimulating that I at once turned and stomped back through the bed a second time. It was exhilarating in a way that cannot be compared to any other experience I have ever had. It was as though the soul itself were being deliciously bathed in the fire. I felt tingling and glowing throughout my body and a quite filling sense of peace and well being and completeness. It was not an empty feeling but a full feeling.'

A procession of flagellating pilgrims from a 14th-century manuscript.

This is the language of Haight-Ashbury and Sergeant Pepper – a long journey from the academics of Carshalton, Ohio and Tübingen – but at least one distinguished surgeon and scientist has done a firewalk in public.

Dr Gerald Feigen, a handsome grey-haired surgeon, lives in a vast elegant apartment overlooking San Francisco Bay. Chief of a surgical service at Mount Zion Hospital, and author of numerous research papers, he is a fascinating polymath. Amateur painter and sculptor, skilful ventriloquist, travel writer and expert on design, he was a friend of the famous architect, Buckminster Fuller. It was Fuller who had set him on the road to the firewalk. Feigen had often visited Tahiti and Fuller expressed a great wish to see a firewalk for himself, so the two men arranged to meet on the island of Bora Bora to see the walk performed by a group from Raiatea.

It took three days to prepare the pit: hibiscus logs, with flat stones laid on top. On the evening of the third day the fire was ready and four Ti leaves were ceremonially placed at the corners of the pit. Dr Feigen was immediately beguiled. 'I noticed that there was an aura of something around. It was dark. There was an insistent wind; dark clouds in the sky. And the spell of tropical islands, you know, is always there. It's a marvellous feeling. Your stress mechanisms just let go. All of a sudden this group came out from the distance carrying burning torches and wearing the grass skirts which are the dress of both the men and the women. Then Tanatos – who was the priest – looked up at the sky and said, "Goddess of the Moon, favour us" – or some such thing – and the black clouds parted, and the moon came out, and you could see the bottom of the water, it was so bright.

'Well, that immediately cast its own hypnotic effect. There's a resistance to the supernatural which we scientific-type people have. But when a man can open up the clouds . . . Then he said, "Goddess of the Wind, favour us," and that insistent rushing wind just stopped, right off, as he said it. He uttered some incantations. Then this young couple came out and walked across the fire. As they walked I noticed some things in my mind – mainly that they were walking pretty darned fast; and also that they were stamping, walking with their feet flat. They came across and seemed none the worse for wear. I found myself in a state of what you might call "auto-hypnosis". I got myself believing that it was possible to do it – because if they did it, and they came across, and they got the man to part the skies . . .

'Of course, I realized later that he was quite a meteorologist. I had no preparation on my feet, and there's nothing that you do beforehand to toughen yourself up. There are so many legends about firewalking. There is a mechanism physiologically called the formation of endorphine. Well, it's possible that in this hypnotic state you could produce endorphine. Anyway, when they had processed three or four couples, this old man turned and said "Would any of you like to join us?" He didn't say it as a dare, or a challenge, he just said it.

'Fuller turned to me and said he had to get an honorary degree at Yale and he just thought he'd better not do it. And I thought he'd better not also, because he was getting on in years by then. Myself, I was in a state of intense excitement, yet perfect calm. I knew I'd be able to do it because they did it, and it was quite possible to do it, and at that particular point whatever pain mechanisms come into play to prohibit pain must have gotten into play. I don't know how, but I know I was willing to surrender to the involvement.

'So I took my shoes and socks off and I walked over perfectly confident. I didn't have a feeling of fear. When we started out I noticed that I felt cool from my feet up to my knees; from my knees up I felt hot. So there was some cutting off of the normal skin sensitivity. And we moved very rapidly, because I felt if I'd stopped and tripped – goodbye. Not just a burn here and there, but I'd really be fried. And I noticed that it was possible if you looked ahead, to pick your rocks like when you're crossing a stream. So I crossed over this thirty feet, and when I got to the other end I turned to Fuller and said, "Bring me some water and I'll turn it into wine."

'I don't believe there are any more tricks. You don't need to have some kind of a mysterious chemical that you rub on your feet, or go into any kind of training. All you have to do is believe and surrender.'

**Brahmin firewalkers in India in 1908. Firepits take days to prepare and today temperatures of over 900°F have been recorded.**

# 9

# Water, Water, Everywhere

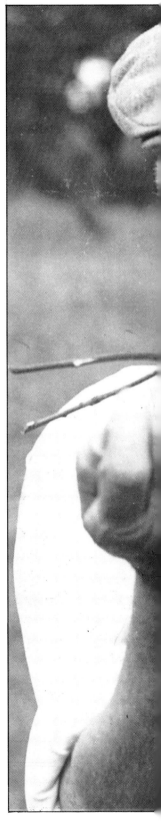

ONE FINE WEEKEND IN 1952, the burghers of Rheindahlen in West Germany, strolling in the Hardt Forest immaculately dressed as usual in Sunday suits, were confronted by an extraordinary sight. Crossing the Schwalm River and wending his way through the trees was a solitary horseman. The bridle lay abandoned on the horse's neck and the rider seemed to be concentrating entirely on the forked stick he was holding in both hands. From time to time the stick would twist, turn, dance, as if it had a life of its own. Enquiries soon revealed that the stolid onlookers were witnessing a mounted version of the *Wünschelrutengänger* or wishing-rod-walker, and that the practitioner was a full colonel in the British Army. They were also seeing perhaps the most spectacularly successful exercise in water divining ever known.

Colonel Harry Grattan, CBE, Royal Engineers, is a soldier in the modern mould. A highly qualified member of the Institute of Engineers in London, and a Second World War veteran of the tough river crossings of the post D-Day campaigns, he had, by 1952, been handed the job of building a new Headquarters for the British Army in Germany at Mönchen Gladbach, between the Dutch border and the great cities of the German Ruhr.

It was a major project. Mönchen Gladbach, tucked away amidst the firs and poplars of the Hardt Forest, does today house the HQ of the British Rhine Army, the HQ of Nato's Northern Army Group, the central command of the 2nd Allied Tactical Air Force, and the HQ of RAF Germany. Colonel Grattan knew he was planning for at least 9000 people who, among other things, would need three-quarters of a million gallons of water per day. And water was a problem. The three local waterworks at Rheindahlen, Uvekoven and Waldniel would have needed expensive new equipment to supply the base. In any case their water was alkaline and very hard. Furthermore, even in those days before the depredations of the Baader-Meinhof gang, the British Army was inclined to prefer the security of its

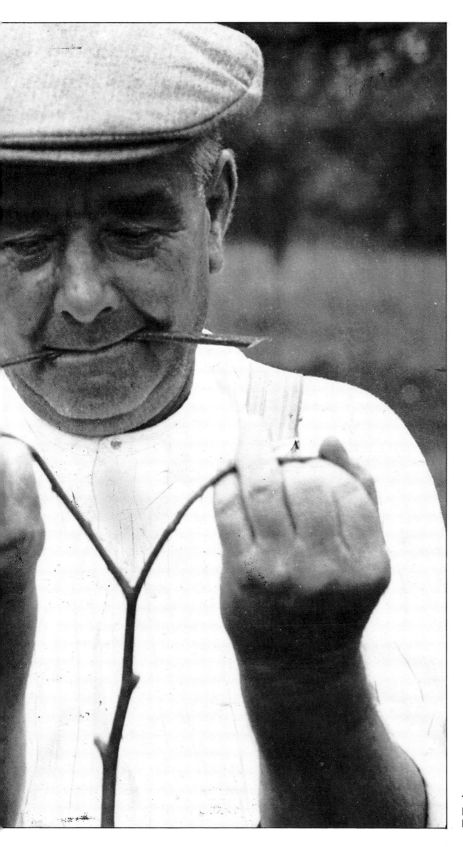

The late S. J. Searles of North Cray, Kent, a well known water diviner.

Colonel Harry Grattan and (opposite) the map showing the outline of the water-bearing 'sandwich' he dowsed at Mönchen Gladbach, on which the Rhine Army HQ was built.

own supplies, and they certainly did not relish what, even then, would have been water rates of £20,000 a year.

Colonel Grattan knew that a family living in a hunting lodge on an estate in the middle of the Hardtwald site drew their own softer and much more pleasant water from a private well. He determined to try to tap this source. Trial bores, on geologists' advice, produced only a little water at a depth of 23 feet and then nothing until the test was stopped at 120 feet. 'I was very busy with other planning,' the colonel recalls, 'but on the following Sunday afternoon I found time to prospect for the first time with a rod. All engineers distrust water divining. I, as Chief Engineer, was not prepared to place uncorroborated reliance on it. But when it became evident that in my private capacity as a dowser I was able to help myself in developing and using our own water, I was ready to take full advantage of my gift.'

As soon as the colonel began quartering the site he felt a reaction. 'Everywhere to the west of our borings there was a steady pull on the rod. So we decided on two trial bores. The results were spectacular.'

The trials showed that the ground was mainly solid and impervious black and brown clay, but between 73 and 96 feet down there was a 'sandwich' of gravel which threw up a pure, soft and slightly acid water of excellent quality: there was such good pressure that the water rose spontaneously more than 40 feet up the bore. The colonel thought this must mean an artesian source far away in the hills along the Dutch border. The German authorities, responsible for the actual site construction, were sceptical of such supernatural surveying. They were convinced that the water would peter out beyond the nearby River Schwalm and therefore that the supply would soon dry up. Colonel Grattan had to engineer a direct order from his superior General Sugden in order to pursue his exploration, and did so on horseback, divining rod in hand, setting off west towards the hills.

'First I discovered that the behaviour of the rod is in no degree lessened by being mounted on horseback and, secondly, I observed that the strong and even pull of it, as I left my boundary and crossed the Schwalm, continued undiminished. The indication of underground water appeared to continue unabated as far to the west as I could ride that Sunday evening.'

As his researches continued, the colonel discovered that he could even dowse while driving a motor car. Gradually, in motorized, equestrian and pedestrian expeditions, he began to sketch the boundaries of his 'sandwich' of pure soft water. To the north, in Waldniel, he found the rod stood still for just a single pace before it reacted again – apparently to the harder water feeding the public water works only a few hundred yards away. The line to the west was even more disconcerting. It took in Merbeck and Klinkum and ran south so firmly that it seemed certain to take in the existing German waterworks at Uvekoven. It was a nervous moment.

'It would have spoilt everything,' says the colonel, 'because I knew their water was entirely different. But as I traced the line nearer and nearer towards Uvekoven, it suddenly jinked eastwards and missed the water-works by a bare 300 yards. It was unbelievable.' But test bores confirmed the colonel's map. One, throwing up fine pure water, was within 400 yards of the Uvekoven water works with its alkaline, hard water. Another was about half a mile from the Waldniel works.

The colonel had divined more than 30 square miles of water-bearing

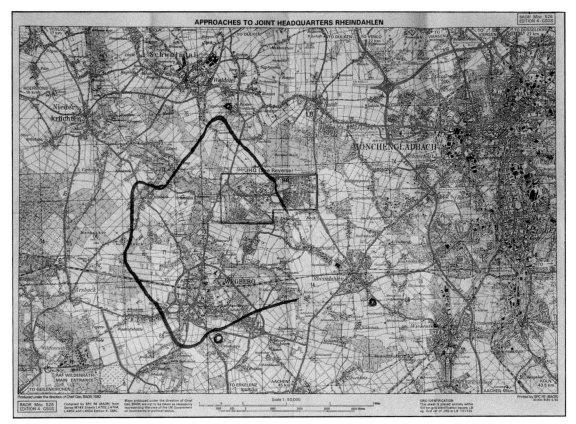

'sandwich' against all local engineering advice, and in a patch entirely surrounded by inferior hard alkaline water feeding the German waterworks. On that basis the private waterworks of the British Rhine Army were constructed. Thirty years later they are still providing a million gallons a day to the 10,000 population of Mönchen Gladbach at a saving running into millions of pounds. The colonel, still with the gift and living in retirement at South Cary, Somerset, was able to return in 1983 to the base and inspect what is still the most impressive tribute, in its detail and its precision, to the dowser's art.

Yet Colonel Grattan and Mönchen Gladbach are a rarity among a fraternity plagued by the wildest claims, the most improbable ventures, and the most spurious practitioners.

The Vicomte Henry de France, himself one of the most respected chroniclers of divining in Europe, reports that his friend Joseph Treyve, who was manager of a horticultural centre near Moulins and a renowned water diviner, used to prepare for a day's wild boar hunting by pulling out a large scale map of the area and swinging a pendulum over the woods and thickets in order to be informed where the boar were skulking that day. One afternoon, when one of his workmen failed to show up, Treyve got out a street map of Moulins and ascertained, via the pendulum, which café was harbouring his tippling employee. The man was speedily returned to his labours. Map dowsing can apparently be a truly long-distance affair. An English vicar, the Rev. H. W. Lea Wilson, reported finding water for his brother 5000 miles away in Uganda simply by dowsing over maps in the rectory study. Villagers in Kasner in India and in Sri Lanka have also benefited from his advice.

Dowsing is remarkably widespread. A survey by Ray Hyman and Evon Vogt suggested that there were at least 2500 practising dowsers in the United States, and they found a wonderful array of instruments. Besides forked twigs from peach, willow, hazel, elm, cherry, persimmon and a host of other trees, there were barbed wire, baling wire, pennies on a wire, quicksilver in bottles on a string, horse whips, shovels, keys suspended from the Bible, pitchforks, and pendulums.

There have been dowsers, not only seekers of water, but especially men looking for metals, since the earliest recorded times. Even Moses has been claimed as a colleague by enthusiasts, since he produced water by striking a rock with a rod. Agricola, writing in *De Re Metallica* 400 years ago, included a description of how the 'aquilegus' or diviner worked. The forked sticks were held, one branch in each hand and palm upwards, so that there was a degree of tension. The stick dipping or pulling towards the ground marked the place where water was to be found.

An 18th-century book, *Mineralogia Cornubiensis*, included an illustration. A pair of elegantly ruffled hands hold two L-shaped rods pointing almost upright. By the late 19th century mechanization had reached the dowsing world. There was Fred H. Brown's Electro Terreohmeter and Messrs Mansfield of Liverpool, England were offering their Patent Automatic Water Finder. By 1976 enthusiasts could buy for £3.50, Mrs Sylvia Simnett's four-part Omni Detector kit. This must have been unrivalled value for money: not only could it apparently find water – journalist Jonathan Sale of the London *Guardian* was converted into a water diviner in ten minutes flat, and his wife with him – but the Omni Detector also could 'determine the sex of eggs, find lost watches, pens and golf balls, trace missing persons or animals, find the right foods for slimming, and test water for pollution'. Sales were brisk. But then 1976 was a year of drought in Britain, making market conditions especially favourable.

In the same year the Inner London Education Authority was running Teach Yourself Water Divining classes at its Kensington Institute which were so oversubscribed that a second course had to be organized. For the truly dedicated there was a three-day residential course at the Moor Park Adult Residential College.

Watching a dowser at work can be a startling experience. The rod is apparently held quite lightly but firmly, with the palms upward. There is rarely any ceremonial or mumbo jumbo. The dowser just begins to walk over the ground to be searched. Then suddenly the rod may start to leap about as though some unseen hand is trying to wrestle it away, only to return to quiescence as soon as the dowser seems to get out of range. Then, as the dowser comes closer again to the sensitive spot, the rod may start to bend slowly downwards, with the dowser apparently making every effort to keep it in place but failing to resist what seems to be an inexorable force.

In a demonstration near Helston, for Yorkshire Television in 1979, Cornish tin miner Frank Richards of Wendron seemed to be almost thrown to the ground by the force acting on the rod he was holding while searching for a lode. Within a year Richards was extracting commercial quantities of tin from a seam on the spot he had identified.

There have been experiments which have seemed to suggest that dowsers have some special sensitivity to electro or geomagnetic fields. A Dutch Professor of Geology Solco Tromp reported that dowsers could detect when a galvanometer was switched on or off and a French professor at the Ecole Normale in Paris, Yves Rocard, and Dr Zaboj Harvalik, once of the University of Arkansas, both reported similar results, but none of their work has been successfully duplicated.

In recent years, the dowsing rod has been bent to the service of seemingly every quest – mystical, mercenary, magical and mundane. The huge Swiss pharmaceutical firm, Hoffman-LaRoche, have claimed to site their new factories round the world on the advice of two dowsers on their staff, Dr Peter Treadwell, director of one of their Swiss plants, and Dr Rudolph Rupp, a senior engineer. Their best efforts so far have been at Thana near Bombay, in Indonesia and the Philippines, and at the new site of Village-Neuf in Alsace. The US Marines training at Camp Lejeune in North Carolina for service in Vietnam were given courses in dowsing for mines. The South Vietnamese Navy were already ahead of them, with a certain Captain Vo Sum apparently able to detect opium by dowsing. He could also, so the tale goes, find missing ships. Before the war was over, Captain Vo Sum's acolytes, shorn perhaps of other props of hope, were pendulum-dowsing their way back to their comrades through unknown jungle and predicting by dowsing the direction of those unnerving night attacks in which the Communists specialized.

The French have led the world in medical dowsing, in which the magical rod not only finds the seat of any and every affliction in man and beast, but also cures. A series of French priests armed with ball and string as well as crucifix have evangelized for dowsing, from Father Jurion, with his crystal ball and chain, diagnosing and prescribing astounding cures for cancer, to Abbé Bouly, who ascribed his award of the Legion of Honour to his work

**Dowsing for metal in 16th-century Germany.**

The Abbé Lambert, who dowsed successfully in Kensington Gardens and Hyde Park. *Right:* Drilling to a dowser's instructions on Lord Glenconner's property at the Cannes Country Club; water appeared, as promised.

dowsing for microbes in French hospitals. Missing persons, lost objects, are regularly recovered, thanks, it is said, to dowsing. In New Zealand they dowse for ghosts.

The Abbé Gabriel Lambert came to London between the wars for a demonstration with Harry Price. He used a gaily-coloured striped bobbin, pear-shaped and hung on a silk thread. Price, acting for his National Laboratory of Psychical Research, took the Abbé into Kensington Gardens and Hyde Park to demonstrate his powers in a search for underground streams. Price reported: 'The Abbé would purposely swing the bobbin laterally, and when we came over the hidden stream, the bobbin would make a spasmodic movement, change its course and begin spinning furiously, describing a larger and larger circle the longer we stood over the source of activity. When we reached the bank of the subterranean river the bobbin would stop dead – just as if it had been hit by a stone.

'The cessation of the spinning was even more spectacular than the commencement. We found many hidden springs and a fairly broad river running into Knightsbridge. When we came to a nappe (a pool of still water) the bobbin would make quite a different movement. The Abbé said that he could tell the depth of the hidden supplies, their approximate volume, and directional characteristics. He could also tell whether the current was rapid or sluggish.'

Price prepared a map of the streams which the Abbé had claimed to locate and had the discoveries 'confirmed by a Park official'. The Abbé had his dowsing faculties well under control: 'He states that if he is looking for a nappe he will pass a dozen running springs without becoming aware of the fact. He will likewise be unconscious of a flowing river if he is looking for minerals or a metallic lode. When we crossed the Serpentine by means of the bridge, his bobbin did not respond. To provide the other "pole" when using his bobbin, he carries in his free hand a small bottle of pure water, if looking for drinking water, or a piece of ore similar to the metallic lode he is trying to find.'

Harry Price was himself a satisfied customer. The engineers who were employed to sink a well at his house in Pulborough in Sussex searched fruitlessly for two weeks before calling in an old dowser who found an ample supply of water in the course of an afternoon.

There seems to be nothing under the earth or on it, according to the devotees, which cannot be found with a hazel twig or a bent coathanger, a pendulum or merely the bare outstretched hands of a properly sensitive person. But the main commercial thrust of modern dowsing has been the bid to find the elusive buried riches of the earth – ores, minerals and, above all, oil. Today dowsers ask up to $1000 a day for their arcane advice – and seem to find takers among the real-life contemporaries of Ewing Oil.

For everyone in the business remembers 1943 and the West Edmond field. West Edmond lies in a geologically unpromising part of central Oklahoma State, but the high prices and heavy demand of the war years encouraged speculation. The Fox Brewing Company of Chicago, keen to switch to another intoxicating industry, took a chance on a wildcatter named Ace Gutowski. A local farmer J. W. Young had convinced Gutowski that oil lay beneath West Edmond and had produced his evidence – a goatskin-covered bottle hanging from a watch chain which, said Farmer Young, infallibly swung from north to south when over oil. And there was no mistaking the fact that the goatskin did swing between the two poles when Mr Young dangled it over West Edmond. So Gutowski, with the Fox Brewing Company's money, drilled a hole – and promptly discovered the largest oilfield found in Oklahoma since the golden days of the 1920s.

Ace Gutowski and the scene of his success at West Edmond, Oklahoma, the largest oilfield discovered in the state since the 1920s.

Grateful beneficiaries of the dowser's instincts are dotted all across the United States. Up north in Illinois, the bemused school board of Edwards County Senior High School find themselves sitting on a sudden fortune, gushing over them at the rate of $500 a day, and still rising – all because dowser Clayton McDowell came by. Principal Bob Wallace says: 'It was like a gift from God. State aid for our school's been cut, even federal aid. Books were getting worn out. Vocational programs such as building trades and nursing were cut. We had a referendum last spring for more money, but it was voted down. Then this happens.

'Some years ago a couple of guys drilled at the bottom end of our land – two or three wells – but they were dry holes. So we were really surprised when Clayton McDowell came along and wanted to drill.'

McDowell has helped to transform Edwards County. His dowsing style is as laconic as his speech. When he can bear to tear himself away from his stud of 170 trotting horses, on the edge of West Salem, Illinois, he sets out to dawdle the highways of the county in his pale blue Cadillac. As the mood takes him, he lolls back in his seat and picks up the nylon dowsing rods. Wife Marje is left to grab the steering wheel. If the pull comes strongly enough, they turn around and try to mark the limits of the 'hot' territory. Then Clayton sets about buying a drilling lease from the landowner. In 1983 he sank 33 production wells in the state – the small, unattended

rocker wells which are emptied daily, like a milk round, by the oil companies. All but three are producing.

'I don't walk about in the fields,' says McDowell. 'I got my leg shot off by a drunk once and the artificial one gets stuck in the mud. Got pulled off one time. So now I work from the car.

'I really don't know what makes it work. Some people it works for, and some people it doesn't. But it seems like it works for me pretty good.'

And for Edwards County Senior High School, with the flow already at 110 barrels a day. As Bob Wallace says: 'As an academic I find it hard to believe, but it's sure gonna make a hell of a difference to my school.'

One of the most celebrated of contemporary oil dowsers is Paul C. Brown, now 80 years old. He has worked recently for Golden Sun International and the M and M Oil and Gas Corporation of Inglewood, California. Small, weather-beaten, slow-talking, he claims to have earned his living as a full-time professional oil dowser since 1954. Brown produces a curriculum vitae which shows him having worked for Getty Oil, Standard Oil, Rothschild Oil, Supreme Oil and Gas, with a string of claimed successes stretching from the Dominguez Hills strike at Long Beach, California, to the Red River field in Vernon, Texas.

Brown denounces geologists as no better than medicine men doing a rain dance. His own abilities, he says, are 'sort of like a spiritual motivation. Having discovered it, you can develop it like learning to walk, a slow, difficult process. It takes time and practice.' But once it's there, it would seem, it can provide a living for nigh on 30 years.

The claims of dowsers have inevitably beguiled the military. The Royal School of Military Engineering at Chatham in England has an exhaustive library of divining literature and a regular feature of its courses has been demonstrations for sceptics by possessors of the gift. Former Royal Engineer Bill Male, who now appropriately looks after the water supplies which Colonel Grattan found at Mönchen Gladbach, says: 'When I was at Chatham there were always a few people with the gift. And there was absolutely no doubt that it worked. We used to organize the most convincing tests to show the doubters.' But when the school tried a statistical approach they could produce no evidence that diviners trying to locate water running in a pipe under one of their lawns could do any better than chance. So, in 1970, the British Ministry of Defence's Military Engineering Experimental Establishment decided to conduct a most elaborate examination to see if dowsers could help to save the lives of their troops by detecting buried mines. The Establishment did not stint. Nearly 400 acres with seven miles of roads and tracks were commandeered and 20 defused mines were buried. Seven convinced dowsers were then pressed into service. On the principle of beginning with the tough one, the military researchers began with map dowsing.

As Dr R. A. Foulkes, acting as observer, reported in *Nature*: 'The map plus a sample mine was sent to each experimenter because it was reasonable to suppose he should know what he was looking for.' Whether the receipt of an unsolicited parcel bomb upset the dowsers or not, the fact was, said Dr Foulkes 'that the map diviners could not even match the accuracy of volunteers taking random guesses at the location of the mines'. The officers

of the Experimental Establishment then went on to test more direct methods. A large area of heath and heather was bulldozed level and four hundred separate squares marked out.

It was an ambitious project. The soldiers wanted to find out if the dowsers could distinguish between five different classes of buried objects: metallic mines, plastic mines, concrete blocks, chunks of wood or just nothing but plain earth. 'It was felt that twenty-foot centres would be far enough apart,' goes the official report 'in order to "eradicate" the influence of one object on another and all the dowsers agreed with this condition.' The dowsers were taken away for morning tea and a small army of troops was set to work in the interests of science. 'Holes were dug at the centres of every square and different gangs of men buried each class of object so that no-one could know the localities of all four hundred. The only master location plan was locked in a safe throughout the experiment.'

By the time battle officially commenced, the squad of dowsers had accreted to platoon strength – 22 in all. There were metal rods, wooden rods, hazel twigs, even a nylon rod, and one dowser used a plumb line. All day the 22 weaved to and fro across the heath, some taking hours to plot the mines, others making rapid and peremptory marks as their rods reacted with impressive violence. Sadly, by nightfall, the Ministry of Defence had reaped little reward for their investment in research. One man missed 142 of the 160 mines. Another found all but 13 of them, but only at the cost of digging up 332 of the 400 squares.

Perhaps the most intriguing dowsing trial of all took place in Australia in 1980, under the eye of the Amazing Randi – with $50,000 at stake, $10,000 of it James Randi's own money, in his accustomed habit of backing his own perspicacity in matters of fraud.

Australia, with its great tracts of dry bush land and its low rainfall has always been willing to pay well for men who could find water: diviners have flourished for a century or more. New South Wales businessman Dick Smith invited Randi to adjudicate this latest test.

By the time Randi flew in, the extra $40,000 had been subscribed to make up the prize for a successful dowser. On the appointed day eleven

**At the convention of the American Society of Dowsers in Danville, Vermont, 1983. Each September the town is inundated by hundreds of dowsers, each with a different method.**

dowsers turned up at the chosen arena – a field at North Ryde outside Sydney. They were all ages, and a fine evocation of outback Australia. 'I reckon this is going to be the easiest pay day of my life,' said one old timer, James Beattie. Jackie Cochlan, who had come 300 miles for the trial, said: 'I've done nothing else but dowsing for 30 years. I've raised a family on it.'

Randi's preparations were as scrupulous as he could make them. There were to be two principal tests, one to find a nugget of gold placed in one of ten boxes, the other to find water flowing through one of ten pipes. The rate of chance success was thus 10% in each case. The 11 contestants watched as the jousting ground was prepared. Each was given a trial run over a pipe where they knew water was flowing, to ensure conditions were satisfactory. Then each dowser was asked to state what he thought would be his success rate. All predicted at least 80%, some were expecting 100%. It was agreed that 80% would constitute proof and therefore win the prize.

So the contest began. The implements varied from a conventional hazel twig to forked wire, twin metal rods bent at the end and one yard-long steel rod with a pig's tail curl in the middle. The search for the gold nugget was dispiritingly clear-cut. In 35 tries, the dowsers only picked the right box four times – scarcely better than chance. So the contestants turned to the water trial. Ten pipes had been laid nine inches below the surface, and connected to a main supply. The water was to be turned to one pipe only – randomly chosen – for each trial. Each dowser was allowed five trials, and no restriction was put on the time or method used. But most of the men

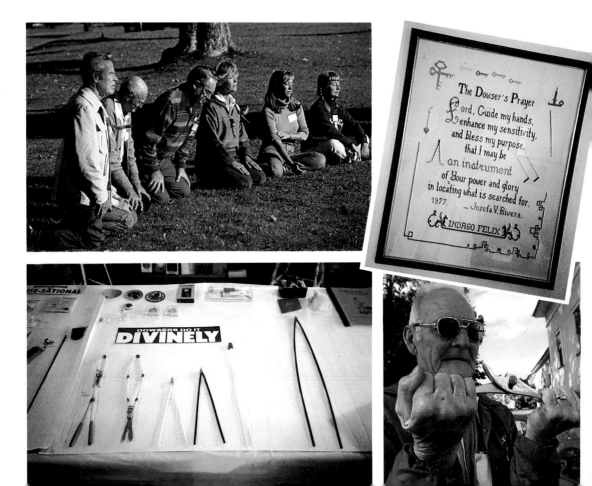

were quick and confident in their conclusions as the rods and pendulums seemed to pull and dance decisively at some particular point.

Afterwards the 11 convened in a local hall for the results to be reported by the scrutineer, a local vicar. To judge from the small talk, the problem was dividing up the $50,000 among so many winners. But as the results were read out hope turned to disbelief as it became apparent that no one had got anywhere near the 80% accuracy they had forecast. Disconsolate figures, clutching tubes of Foster's lager, watched the 'easiest pay day' disappear. Overall, announced the referee, combining the results of all the searches, the accuracy rate had been 12%, not 80%.

Randi ostentatiously folded up the $50,000 cheque and left. The dowsers went off to the bar, already speculating about what adverse situation had stymied the tests – perhaps it was the walkie-talkie radios or the television crews. They had already gone back to the townships of the outback when an extraordinary fact emerged from the analysis of the results. Taking only the search for water, and ignoring the search for the gold nugget, the diviners had scored 22% success – more than twice as good as mere chance would suggest. Not good enough to part The Amazing Randi from his money. But good enough . . .?

Randi's dowsers were all practical men, farmers and bushmen, to whom the dowsing power, which they believed themselves to possess, was merely a fortunate and natural extension of the arts of survival in the Australian outback – mysterious perhaps, but not mystical. But in Britain and the United States the official dowsing organizations have drifted far from the mainstreams of water dowsing into the stronger currents and whirlpools of the outright paranormal.

It takes considerable dedication to find your way to the Fall convention of the American Society of Dowsers in Danville, Vermont. Air Vermont will get you as far as Burlington Airport. From there a bus wends its way through the classic Vermont woodlands in all their autumnal glories, seventy-five miles to Danville. The bus calls at Montpelier to pick up the few hardy souls who have ventured up by train – Amtrak stops once a day – at 5.21 in the morning!

But Danville itself is worth it – the 'lost' America of the 1940s – neat white houses clustered round a village green, a post office, school and the Protestant and Catholic churches dominating the town. For a week, each September, it is taken over by hundreds of dowsers. Some can be seen at any time of the day, dowsing abstractedly with twig and pendulum along the village green, in and out of people's gardens, practising right up to the door of the Masonic Hall canteen.

But for most the principal enticement of the convention is the exotic array of lectures and seminars: Sig Lonegren on 'Spiritual Dowsing'; Hans Oppersdorf on 'Dowsing for Wildlife'; Anne Williams on 'Pendulum Dowsing and Alternative Health Care'; Richard Wright on 'The Dowser, the Mystic and the Physicist'. For though, as the warning in the office says, 'Opinions expressed in workshops and other convention activities do not necessarily represent the policies or philosophy of the American Society of Dowsers', there is no doubt that it is the wilder shores of dowsing which dominate the conversations at the chicken barbecue and the vegetarian suppers: can murderers and their victims be found by dowsing? Can the pendulum find – even, with the help of acupuncture, cure – disease and sickness? Can map dowsers find water, oil, lost property from thousands of miles away, merely by oscillating the little pendulum over a chart? The magazine advertisements admit to no doubts. $49.50, including postage, will secure for you the cheaper nickel version (copper is $60) of the Cameron Aurameter which, apart from the journeyman tasks of locating underground water by map or in the field, will also 'measure auras surrounding life forms, telepathic beams and rays emitted by organic or inorganic forms or substances'.

The British Society of Dowsers, too, though ballasted with baronets, military men and engineers on its council, is prone to veer into these uncharted waters.

In 1982 its official journal carried a report from a former South African police officer who was continuing from retirement to bring offenders to book. He had helped an old lady in the Transvaal who was having her sheep stolen. With the aid of the pendulum he was able to tell her that it was her servant who was the culprit. 'The police took the Bantu male to his hut and found a skin on the roof', just as Lieutenant Loubser (retd) had described. Then there was the lady in Valhalla, Pretoria, who had lost some jewellery. Lieutenant Loubser was again able to assist: 'By addressing the pendulum, I got answers indicating that the rings were in her bedroom in one of the wardrobe drawers. According to the answers I received, the rings were in the centre one of three drawers.'

At about the same time the British West Midlands Dowsers were working over an Iron Age Hill fort, and Worthing Dowsers, having been flooded out by a downpour while trying to dowse the force lines in Shipley Church, Sussex, were listening to Jack Temple talk about healing with the pendulum.

This plunge into mysticism has distanced dowsing enthusiasts from any serious contact with the contemporary scientific world. But there has been one serious piece of scientific work on water dowsing which had the most intriguing results.

Duane G. Chadwick is on the faculty of the Utah State University Water Research Laboratory in Logan, Utah. 'Few people could have approached the subject of dowsing with more skepticism than me,' he wrote, 'but having been challenged on the subject on occasions, some preliminary thinking was finally engaged in, in an effort to see if there was some scientific basis for the dowsing reaction.'

Chadwick and his colleague Larry Jensen started from the known observations of geologists that underground water can cause 'perturbations' in the Earth's magnetic field. Could dowsers be sensitive to these perturbations? Dowsing twigs would certainly act as amplifiers of any small muscular reaction. Indeed, Chadwick and Jensen worked out that a conventional forked dowsing rod might amplify a small muscle movement by up to 300 times.

So, in a series of experiments in an apple orchard and in North Logan City Park, they set about testing the idea that dowsing reactions might coincide with the spots where some changes occurred in the Earth's

Duane G. Chadwick of the Utah State University Water Research Laboratory. 150 people were recruited to walk the test dowsing course.

magnetic field – changes which were known to be sometimes caused by the presence of water. More than 150 people were recruited to walk the test course. Few of them were dowsers; most were just students or university staff. The sites were as free as possible of suggestive inclines, green spots, fences, or other obstructions which might have influenced the walkers. They were given a pair of L-shaped rods made out of clothes-hanger wire, and told to hold them out roughly horizontal. If they felt any kind of reaction, they were to stop and put down a small block of wood.

The sun was shining and the temperature was in the eighties when the North Logan City Park test was done, and its results confirmed the surprising first observation from the apple orchard trial – almost everyone had a dowsing reaction, all but one out of 48 triallists. Indeed they dropped an average of 11.3 blocks each. The location of each 'drop' was carefully noted and the triallists sent home. Then Chadwick and Jensen went over the course with devices called cesium vapor magnetometers, which they mounted on a wooden sled. One magnetometer was mounted eight inches above the ground and another at a height of 40 inches. The differential reading showed the fluctuation of the magnetic field along the track which the dowsers had trodden.

The two researchers then plotted the two sets of results on a graph – first the magnetometer readings showing the peaks and troughs in the strength of the Earth's magnetic field along the test course, and then the dots showing the places where the triallists had dropped their wooden blocks when they felt a dowsing reaction. The outcome was startling. The dowsing reactions bunched quite unmistakably at the points where there was also a peak in the magnetic field read-out.

Unfortunately the grant from the Office of Water Research did not run to any test bores; so Chadwick and Jensen went on to other things, leaving behind, in a dozen pages of closely worked calculus, the simple piece of work which could provide some common ground on which the warring battalions of sceptics and believers might one day meet.

# 10

# Is There Anyone There?

OF THE 49 DEATHS by drowning reported in Britain during the first weekend of August 1933, none was to prove more uncanny in its consequences than that of Edgar Vandy. Vandy, a 38-year-old inventor and engineer, died in a swimming pool at Masketts Manor Farm, a country estate in Sussex which he was visiting for the day. Sunday, 6 August marked the peak of a record heatwave that year and when Vandy and his companion, Nelson Charters, discovered there was a swimming pool in a wood near the house, they decided to have a swim.

The pool was fed by an underground stream but was lined with concrete at the bottom and edged with crazy paving. It was four feet deep at the shallow end, sloping gradually down to seven feet. The two men changed in some bushes at the side, Vandy struggling into a swimsuit he had borrowed from Charters's sister, who worked as a secretary on the estate. What followed was described by Nelson Charters to the inquest on Edgar Vandy's death, its drama undiminished by the terse report in the local *Sussex Gazette*.

'The deceased entered the water two or three minutes before witness, who did not actually see him enter, as his view was obscured by some shrubs. When witness first saw deceased in the water his arms were outstretched as if he had just broken the water after diving. He began splashing in the water, and witness realized something was wrong. Witness jumped in immediately. By the time he reached him deceased was beginning to sink. Witness seized hold of deceased but could not keep his grip, and deceased sank. Witness then went for assistance.'

At the end of the brief hearing the Coroner, Dr E. F. Hoare, returned a verdict of 'misadventure', but Edgar's distraught brothers, George and Harold, were not satisfied. They believed that crucial questions about the tragedy had not been answered; above all, the doctor who had examined the body and conducted the post-mortem had not established precisely how

*Opposite:* **Spiritualism at its most spectacular. In a séance at Ephrata, Pennsylvania, in 1953, medium Ethel Post Parrish materializes her 'spirit guide' 'Silver Belle'.** *Left to right, top to bottom:* **The pictures, taken at one-minute intervals in infra-red light, show 'Silver Belle' growing from a cloud of 'ectoplasm'.**

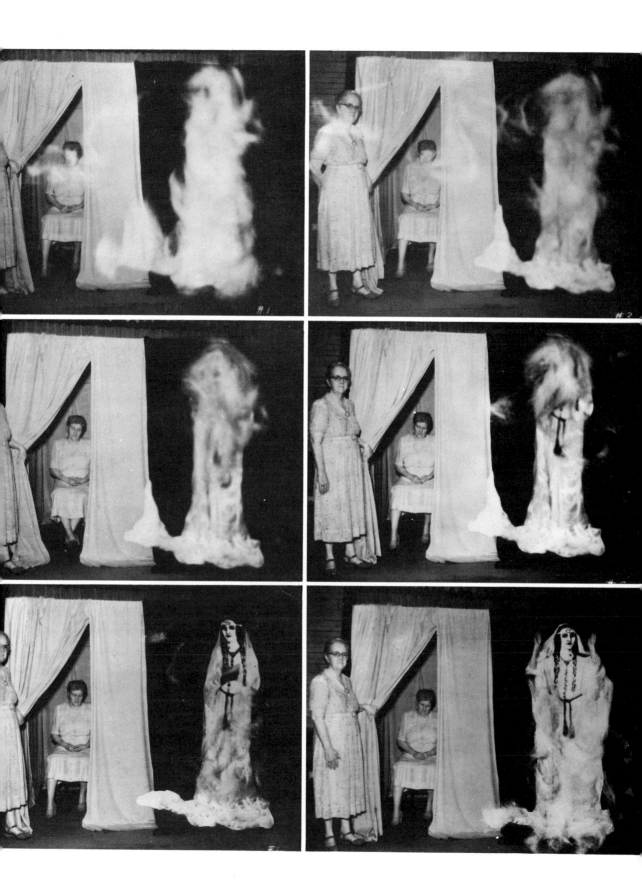

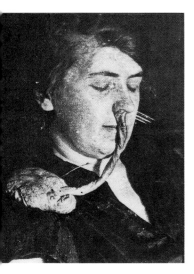

Margery Crandon, a celebrated American medium, supposedly producing ectoplasm. She was exposed in a famous 1930s scandal, see p. 205.

Edgar Vandy had come to drown: he had merely recorded a couple of slight abrasions and suggested that Vandy had struck his jaw and knocked himself out while diving into the pool.

The brothers felt, too, that no one had adequately explained why the doctor and the police had not reached the scene until more than an hour after the accident. Since conventional methods of investigation had failed them, Harold and George Vandy turned to the most unorthodox: they decided to seek the truth from the dead man himself, through people who claimed to be able to communicate the experiences of the dead to the living – spiritualist mediums.

Spiritualists believe that the human personality survives bodily death and passes into another existence from which the dead can communicate with the people they have left. But direct contact is impossible: messages can be sent only through a gifted intermediary known as a medium or sensitive.

There are two types of mediumship: 'physical' and 'mental'. 'Mental mediums' use their minds and bodies as channels through which the dead can speak. Traditionally consultations, or 'séances', are held in a darkened room: the atmosphere is designed to encourage the spirits to make contact; often there is sweet music and the sitters hold hands in shadowy communion. The medium closes his or her eyes and goes into a trance; breathing is laboured, the face strangely contorted. Suddenly an unearthly voice breaks the expectant silence. The dead are in touch.

A sitting with a 'physical medium' is often a far more spectacular affair. In the heyday of spiritualism – the late 19th and early 20th centuries – sensitives boasted extraordinary specialities. Some produced screeds of automatic writing, claiming their pens were guided by the dead; others used a device called an ouija board which, at the spirit's direction, picked out pronouncements letter by letter. At some séances, a metal cone known as a 'trumpet' flew around, passing on whispered messages; or loud raps would beat out the answers to questions put by the bereaved. As proof that the spirits were present, invisible hands played musical instruments or left their imprints in lumps of wax; tables flew about the room and could not be held down; small objects known as 'apports' – flowers, keepsakes or fruit – appeared, apparently from the spirit world.

Some much-sought-after mediums apparently produced a mysterious substance called 'ectoplasm' from their bodies. The exact properties of ectoplasm were hotly disputed and seemed to vary from medium to medium. For example, one called Madame d'Espérance gave forth 'a kind of white and vaporous mass, quasi luminous, like the steam from a locomotive', while the ectoplasm that oozed from the mouth of Frau Maria Vollhardt of Berlin was a rubbery fluid in which some observers noticed the marks of her teeth. From ectoplasm, if conditions were right, an emissary from 'The Beyond' materialized amidst the awestruck company.

Mediumship today tends to be less theatrical than it was at the beginning of this century. Few mediums now claim to be able to produce materialized spirits, although sitters at the séances of Rita Goold of Leicester have been presented with the apparent reappearance of dead people such as the Scottish medium Helen Duncan who died in 1956 and Raymond, the son of Sir Oliver Lodge, killed in 1915 while fighting in the First World War.

Usually, however, a modern séance is much more low-key. Visitors to the imposing headquarters of the Spiritualist Association of Great Britain in London's Belgrave Square book appointments for a consultation with one of the resident mediums just as they would at a doctor's surgery. The séance is likely to be conducted in good light and without the medium going into a deep trance. On other occasions, a medium will hold a mass séance in a large hall, standing on a spotlit platform, plucking names out of the air and sometimes appearing to hold a conversation with unseen spirits.

Mediums have usually been successful in giving comfort to the bereaved. But providing incontrovertible proof that the dead can speak to the living has always been a far more difficult problem. Indeed, it is the crucial one.

Most mediums are paid for their services, and for some of them the temptation to cheat has been overwhelming. The dimly-lit conditions apparently favoured by the spirits have enabled unscrupulous 'physical mediums' to execute 'feats' which are no more than crude conjuring tricks. Many a 'mental medium', too, has exploited the gullibility of the sitters to lucrative effect, seizing on clues unwittingly provided in conversation, or 'fishing' for useful information which can be 'revealed' later. So 'physical mediums' have often gone to great lengths to demonstrate that séance phenomena could not have been produced by trickery: they have been bound hand and foot, held by the sitters and subjected to the most intimate searches. 'Mental mediums' strive to reveal facts that could have come only from the deceased person, the true voice from the dead.

George Vandy had had dealings with mediums before; he had consulted one after the death of a sister, and he was also a member of the Society for Psychical Research. He therefore took discreet precautions against the known hazards of such sittings. Each séance was arranged by the brothers under an assumed name, so that the medium would have no opportunity to discover any facts about them through normal channels of enquiry. They were careful to give no clue to the reason for their visits and always took with them a skilled shorthand writer, so that there would be an accurate record of every word that was uttered. So it was that 18 days after Edgar Vandy's lifeless body had been recovered from the swimming pool in Sussex, George Vandy, disguised as 'Mr J. Felton', visited Hyde Park Mansions in north London, the home of a medium called Miss Frances Campbell. With him, to act as note-taker, was Nelson Charters, who had been present at Edgar's death. According to the transcript, the first revelation about Edgar Vandy came a few minutes into the sitting:

'*Medium*: "You have a brother in the spirit world who passed over as the result of an accident."
*G.V.*: "Yes, that is so."
*Medium*: "He is extremely anxious to communicate and is trying to give a little proof. He is deeply attached to you and expresses gratitude to you because of the effort you have made. He is quite different from you. He keeps brushing his hair back like this [passing her hand over her hair from back to front]."
*G.V.*: "I don't recognize that."
*Medium*: "He keeps doing it."'

['G.V. afterwards remembered it was a regular habit of Edgar's when thinking, and he could not explain forgetting it.']

As the sittings progressed – they were held over four months and involved four separate mediums – a succession of convincing and verifiable details emerged about Edgar Vandy and the manner in which he had died.

Miss Campbell, for example, revealed that he had a scar on his face, that the name of one of his brothers began with the letter 'H', that he played the violin and that he owned 'a sort of comic instrument' (it was a one-stringed fiddle). He had met his death 'in an unusual way': 'He had some blow to the head. His head was jerked back so violently that he thought at first his neck was broken. There were some bruises. He had no one with him at the time. He had about five seconds' knowledge before he went. He shows me water. Was there water in connection with his death?' Moments later, the medium provided further, more precise, details to an astonished George Vandy: 'It's something to do with his death, his tongue. He shows me his arms and legs. He was dressed in a short swimming suit . . .'

['*Note by G.V.*: His tongue was bitten through due, we believe, to his tongue being between his teeth at the time his chin struck the edge of the pool. I did not know this fact at the time of the sitting, but it was known to Charters. Edgar had no intention of bathing when he went on this visit and he did not even know there was a bathing pool on the estate, so he took no bathing costume with him. One was lent to him, and it was rather on the small side and somewhat tight.']

Three even more bizarre yet convincing revelations came up during the sitting. The first was the incident of the tennis racquet:

'*Medium*: . . . "Now he's showing me a tennis racquet. He is holding it up like this [holding her two hands diagonally], and that's strange, because he didn't play tennis. He doesn't look like a fellow who would play tennis."
    *G.V.*: "I don't understand the racquet. He didn't play tennis."
    *Medium*: "Make a note of it and check it up."'

['*Note by G.V.*: The reference to the tennis racquet was obscure to me, for I knew that Edgar did not play tennis or possess a racquet. My sister supplied the clue when I mentioned the incident to her. It appears that a few weeks previously she had a spare exposure on a spool and she used it to take a photograph of Edgar in the garden. It was a bright sunny day and he was dressed in tennis shirt, trousers and shoes. My sister, to complete the picture, fetched her racquet and asked him to pose with it . . .']

The second revelation was the medium's assertion that there was a cigarette case hidden in a chest of drawers in Edgar's bedroom. Despite the fact that he knew Edgar did not smoke, George Vandy checked the statement:

'. . . The evening after the sitting my brother Harold and I went to the chest of drawers, the position of which in the room is correctly given. Edgar's

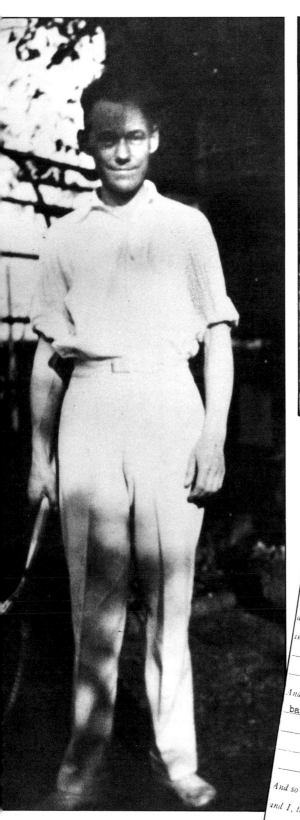

EDGAR VANDY

as to h is        death; and I, the said EDWARD FITZWILLIAM HOARE,

do say:—

That the said—        EDGAR VANDY

day of —— August ——————————————— on the —— 6th

in the Parish aforesaid——————— at ——— Musketts Farm

Died

And that the Cause of Death was— Drowning in a swimming pool whilst

bathing, and so dying by MISADVENTURE

And so do further say that death was due to— Drowning

and I, the said EDWARD FITZWILLIAM HOARE do further say that the said

Edgar Vandy

—— male person of the age of — 38 ye

and an Eng

drawer contained his underclothing, all carefully folded as explained by the medium, and placed methodically. We did not find a cigarette case, but in a corner at the bottom we found a new aluminium soap box. This when held in the hand, as shown by the medium, looks exactly like a metal cigarette case. The area is that of an average cigarette case, from which it only differs in its outward appearance by its thickness . . .'

Weirdest of all was the matter of Edgar's hat:

'*Medium*: "Your other brother makes short journeys in his work. I get the letter 'H'. [Note: Correct – his name is Harold . . .] He is wearing something belonging to your brother who has passed over."
*G.V.*: "I don't think that is right. What is it?"
*Medium*: "He's persistent about it. Check it up." '

['*Note by G.V.*: One morning after Edgar's death Harold took one of Edgar's hats by mistake. He did not return it but left it at the office with no intention of wearing it. On the day of this sitting his own hat was uncomfortable, so in the afternoon, almost involuntarily, he took Edgar's hat off the peg in his office and wore it. He was wearing it at the time the sitting took place. I knew nothing of this until I discussed the incident with Harold after the sitting.']

Before the sittings, both brothers had been sceptical about the possibility of communicating with the dead but, as the sessions went on into the autumn of 1933, more and more facts about Edgar Vandy emerged to challenge their convictions. One medium said that the last book Edgar had been reading before his death was about travel (it was *Scott's Last Expedition*), and produced the names of a brother, a sister, two of his cousins and a friend. Another revealed that the dead man had had a mole under his right arm, the whereabouts of a missing diary (it was in his microscope box), Edgar's likeness to the aviator, Lindbergh, and even his Christian name.

The other, striking, aspect of the sittings was the amount of detail the mediums were able to give about the invention Edgar Vandy had been working on at the time of his death. He called it the 'Lectroline Drawing Machine'. George Vandy later described it: 'It would take too long to go into technical details, but briefly it drew the original lettering and decorative work for printing by lithography and other methods of printing, more quickly and accurately than is possible by hand.' Laboriously, but convincingly, throughout the séances, the mediums managed to convey a picture of the machine, many details of which had been kept secret during its inventor's lifetime to protect patents. Even the fact that someone known as 'Mac' had helped to sort out a technical problem did not escape one medium's inner eye.

But the question that George and Harold Vandy had set out to answer was never resolved: the exact cause of Edgar Vandy's death remained a mystery. There were vague hints that he might, indeed, have struck his head while diving, but little more. A sense of frustration pervades the transcripts: it is as though, in communicating through the mediums, Edgar Vandy had been able to leave his calling-card, but no real message.

If fraud can be discounted – and 50 years on there is no reason to doubt

*Far left, top to bottom;* **Katie, Leah and Margaretta Fox. Leah Fox's parlour in New York** (*above*), **where séances were held and** (*left*) **a replica of the Fox homestead at Hydesville. A stone by the entrance reminds visitors that it was 'the birthplace of modern spiritualism'.**

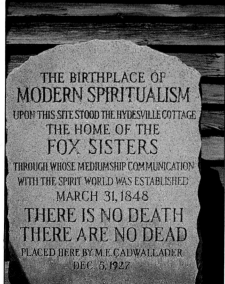

THE BIRTHPLACE OF
MODERN SPIRITUALISM
UPON THIS SITE STOOD THE HYDESVILLE COTTAGE
THE HOME OF THE
FOX SISTERS
THROUGH WHOSE MEDIUMSHIP COMMUNICATION
WITH THE SPIRIT WORLD WAS ESTABLISHED
MARCH 31, 1848
THERE IS NO DEATH
THERE ARE NO DEAD
PLACED HERE BY M.E. CADWALLADER
DEC. 5, 1927

the good faith of the people involved – the Edgar Vandy case seems one of the most striking of all the systematic attempts to communicate with the dead.

Spiritualism has a chequered history which began in 1848. In a poor, wooden house at Hydesville in New York State lived J. D. Fox, a farmer, his wife Margaret and their two daughters, Margaretta, 15, and Katie, 11. Soon after they had moved into the house, the family reported weird rappings which kept them awake at night. Gradually, the Foxes discovered that they could communicate with the unseen rapper and discovered from their 'conversations' that they were in touch with the spirit of a pedlar who had been lured to the house and murdered, his body afterwards having been buried in the cellar.

News of the strange manifestations spread rapidly. 'Hundreds came and heard and retired, some astonished, others having their curiosities much excited, but none satisfied,' wrote one of the earliest witnesses, the Rev. Lemuel Clark. 'At length the excitement became so general and so great, and the throng at the house so large and so constant, that the family were compelled, for want of an opportunity to do their necessary work, to break up and leave the house.'

Within months what had, at first, been a local curiosity became a world-wide sensation. In darkened rooms all over America, the dead rapped out messages to the awe-struck faithful. As one commentator put it, 'It seemed as though the spirit world, having at last hit upon a means of communicating with ours, could not get enough of it.' The transformation of the craze into a religion was as inevitable as it was rapid.

But the clouds of witnesses revealed through mediums were soon matched by darker clouds of fraud and doubt. The Fox sisters came under suspicion early on, and much energy and ingenuity were expended by sceptics in 'explaining' how the raps were produced. In 1850 John W. Hurn declared the girls were cracking the joints of their big toes; Dr Charles Lee of Buffalo maintained they were snapping their knee-joints – 'kneeology', he called it; in 1851, Mrs Culver, a relative of the Foxes, claimed Kate had shown her how to produce the sounds by tapping her big toe. Much later, after countless public demonstrations attended by the faithful, Margaretta, who had fallen on hard times, confessed fraud, apparently settling matters:

'My sister Katie was the first to observe that by swishing her fingers she could produce certain noises with her knuckles and joints, and that the same effect could be made with her toes. Finding that we could make raps with our feet – first with one foot and then both – we practised until we could do this easily when the room was dark.'

The deception, she told *New York World* readers, had left her no peace of mind. 'I have seen so much miserable deception! Every morning of my life I have it before me. When I wake up I brood over it. That is why I am willing to state that spiritualism is a fraud of the worst description . . . I want to see the day when it is entirely done away with. After my sister Katie and I expose it I hope spiritualism will be given a death blow.'

By then, though, it was far too late, and Margaretta's sensational confession failed to stem the tide of spiritualism. 'Tea and table-tipping' were all the rage. In Britain, Queen Victoria had shown considerable interest, while in the Channel Islands the French author, Victor Hugo, claimed to have contacted not only his dead daughter, Léopoldine, but also those more rarified entities 'the Spirit of the Tomb' and 'the Spirit of Criticism'.

Amongst scientists, controversy was unrestrained; at the Royal Society, Michael Faraday constructed an elaborate apparatus to prove table-turning was caused, not 'by diabolical or supernatural agency' but by the sitters unconsciously (or deliberately) pushing the surface with their hands.

Thomas Henry Huxley, the biologist and philosopher, was scornful of the banality of the spirits' pronouncements: '. . . supposing the phenomena to be genuine,' he wrote, 'they do not interest me. If anybody would endow me with the faculty of listening to the chatter of old women and curates in the nearest cathedral town, I should decline the privilege, having better things to do. And if the folk in the spiritual world do not talk more wisely and sensibly than their friends report them to do, I put them in the same category. The only good that I can see in a demonstration of the truth of "Spiritualism" is to furnish an additional argument against suicide. Better live a crossing-sweeper than die and be made to talk twaddle by a "medium" hired at a guinea a séance.' Others, however, like the physicist Sir William Crookes, after intensive investigations embraced the subject (and, it was said, at least one comely medium) with enthusiasm.

Spiritualism's most formidable, passionate and vociferous critic was not in fact a scientist but the legendary stage magician and escapologist, Harry Houdini. He believed he was uniquely qualified to carry out the crusade. 'The fact that they are *scientists* does not endow them with an especial gift for detecting the particular sort of fraud used by mediums, nor does it bar them from being deceived, especially when they are fortified in their belief by grief, for the various books and records of the subject are replete with deceptions practised on noted scientists who have essayed to investigate prominent mediums. It is perfectly rational to suppose that I may be deceived once or twice by an illusion, but if my mind, which has been so keenly trained for years to invent mysterious effects, can be deceived, how much more susceptible must the ordinary observer be.'

Houdini was a reluctant but zealous campaigner against the spiritualists: reluctant because he would genuinely have liked to believe in communication with spirits of the dead, zealous because he was outraged by the exploitation of the grief and gullibility of his fellow men. 'We have prohibition of alchohol, we have prohibition of drugs, but we have no law to prevent these human leeches from sucking every bit of reason and common sense from their victims. It ought to be stopped, it must be stopped . . .' (Later, in Britain and America, Houdini's views were recognized and laws were passed to ban fraudulent mediums from operating; the New York Police Department for many years maintained a 'Séance Squad' which used to infiltrate and 'bust' dubious sittings.)

Houdini's experience as a magician allowed him not only to suggest how a medium might be producing effects, but to demonstrate many ways of doing so. For example, the kind of raps made by the Fox sisters: 'One of the simplest expedients is for the medium to slightly moisten the fingers and slide them very gently on the top of the table. A little experimenting soon shows the amount of pressure necessary to produce the desired amount of

HOUDINI

Exposes the tricks used by the

Boston Medium "Margery"

to win the $2500 prize offered by the Scientific American.

Also a complete exposure of

ARGAMASILLA

The famous Spaniard who baffled noted Scientists of Europe
and America, with his claim to

X-RAY VISION

PRICE, ONE DOLLAR

sound . . .' Alternatively, the rapper could use 'Heath-Robinson' machinery. 'One of these consists of a small hollow metal tube in which a long, heavy burlap needle is arranged to move up and down like a piston, and attached to it to operate it a stout black thread. The tube is fastened to the inner side of a trouser leg. The free end of the thread is brought out through a seam and an inconspicuous little hook attached. After being seated at the séance table the medium attaches the little hook to the opposite trouser leg and draws on it until the needle point comes through the cloth. He then watches an opportunity to press on to the point of the needle a cork to which has been attached a piece of lead. This accomplished, all he has to do is to place the knee in the proper relation to the table, and by moving the other back and forth the piston is made to work up and down, causing the leaded cork to rap out all sorts of messages.'

Bizarre, perhaps, but there was often a lot of money at stake. Fortunes might depend upon the word of the spirits, who demonstrated a gratifying tendency to wish to reward the mediums who had put them in touch with their relatives.

Several court cases in Britain had brought this problem to public attention, amongst them what became known as the 'Great Planchette Case' of 1903. A young man named Henry Sheppard Hart Cavendish won an action against a couple, Charles and Madeline Strutt, and their solicitor. Cavendish had inherited property worth £230,000 on his 21st birthday. Before Mr Justice Byrne in the High Court of Justice, Cavendish claimed that he had given the Strutts almost total control over his financial affairs on the advice of the spirit of his dead mother and a trio of Archangels, Gabriel, Uriel and Michael. The spirits had communicated through a 'planchette', which was described by one court reporter as 'a little heart-shaped piece of wood with two wheels at the broad end and a hole for a pencil at the point. Parties to the séance place their fingers on the instrument and wait for the pencil, beneath which a paper is placed, to trace a message.'

Houdini also built up a dossier on the lengths to which fraudulent mediums would go to obtain knowledge of their unsuspecting sitters. These included tabulating newspaper death notices, indexing the births, marriage and engagement columns, hunting amongst court records of mortgages and property, bribing lift-boys for household tittle-tattle and employing pickpockets to rifle sitters' possessions. Some would buy letters sent for pulping – 'one useful letter, out of a ton of rubbish, being enough to pay them a great profit'. Disgruntled employees were milked for information, clerks were 'planted' in hotels to open, read and re-seal guests' letters, telephone conversations were transcribed, eavesdroppers supplied 'lowdown' from the saloons of steamers, from funeral teas and Turkish baths.

Though the shabby secrets of unscrupulous mediums withered beneath his scrutiny, Houdini still hoped against hope for proof of the survival of the spirit. Above all, he hoped to communicate with his mother, to whom he had been deeply attached. Thus, in 1922, he eagerly seized upon an invitation from Sir Arthur Conan Doyle to attend a séance in the Ambassador Hotel in Atlantic City at which Lady Doyle, as medium, would bring him the long-awaited message:

'I was *willing* to believe, even wanted to believe. It was weird to me and with a beating heart I waited, hoping that I might feel once more the presence of my beloved Mother ... I especially wanted to speak to my Mother because that day, June 17, 1922 was her birthday. I was determined to embrace Spiritualism if there was any evidence strong enough to drown the doubts that have crowded my brain for the past thirty years.'

But, despite his fervent hopes, Houdini rejected utterly the rather vague message that purported to come from his mother, because 'although my sainted mother had been in America for almost fifty years, she could not

'The Great Planchette Case' in session in 1903. Plaintiff Henry Sheppart Hart Cavendish (*centre*) holds the 'planchette' which 'told' him to hand over control of his financial affairs.

**Houdini and Sir Arthur Conan Doyle. Houdini exposed many spiritualistic frauds, but Doyle and his wife (*right*) were believers and the movement's most influential champions.**

speak, read nor write English.' He found Conan Doyle's protestation that 'a Spirit becomes more educated the longer it is departed and that my blessed Mother had been able to master the English language in Heaven' to be quite ludicrous. Houdini's investigations led inexorably to the wistful conclusion: 'after years of ardent research and endeavour I delare that nothing has been revealed to convince me that intercommunication has been established between the Spirits of the departed and those still in the flesh.'

Other sceptics were just as active in the search for truth, and many a medium was exposed as a shabby fraud when one of the sitters suddenly turned up the lights in mid-séance or lunged at allegedly materialized spirits. At such times ectoplasm, that mysterious substance said to emanate from the spirit-world, invariably turned out to be butter-muslin, the instruments that played celestial music were found ensconced mundanely beneath the mediums' voluminous skirts, trumpets used to relay voices from 'The Beyond' were found twirling on sticks or lengths of cat-gut, and even catalogues of useful 'props' like 'spirit hands' or plaques daubed with luminous paint – all obtainable by mail-order – fell into the hands of the non-believers. Indeed, from an early stage, fraud amongst mediums was so rife that the psychical researcher Harry Price remarked sharply to Conan Doyle, 'the history of Spiritualism is one long trail of fraud, folly and credulity.'

LUNCHEON

GIVEN BY SPIRITUALISTS IN HONOUR OF

SIR ARTHUR CONAN DOYLE AND LADY DOYLE

ON THE EVE OF THEIR DEPARTURE FOR SOUTH AFRICA.

The founders of Britain's Society for Psychical Research began systematic investigations into the claims of spiritualists and few of even the best-known mediums escaped the taint of trickery. Eusapia Palladino, for example, was often caught out. She was an Italian, famed for the physical phenomena she claimed to be able to produce, including images of spirit faces in wet clay, sudden elongations of her body and the ability to make tables perform in a manner little short of acrobatic. On one famous occasion in 1910, when Eusapia was in mid-performance, two investigators, swathed in black to avoid detection, crept under the table and found the agile Neapolitan trying to levitate it with her foot. Inevitably, her supporters maintained she resorted to deception so as not to disappoint her clients only when the spirits were having difficulty in getting through.

There was another scandal in 1932, concerning a celebrated American medium, 'Margery'. Fingerprints she claimed had been left in wax by her dead brother Walter, on one of his visits from the spirit-world, turned out to have come from her dentist who had attended many of her séances and was, unfortunately for 'Margery', very much alive. The revelations of 'Margery's' trickery were all the more sensational because, despite her pseudonym, she was known to be the wife of the respected Boston surgeon, Dr Le Roi Goddard Crandon.

Occasionally, séance-shenanigans reached the courts. The Scotswoman Helen Duncan who, in her time, was a famous materialization medium, was twice convicted of fraud. The first case, brought in 1933, came about after a sitter by the name of Miss Maule had grabbed the apparently materialized spirit of a little girl, producing a tell-tale sound of ripping cloth. Sure enough, when the lights went up, Mrs Duncan was discovered busily trying to stuff a torn white undervest up her dress. Undeterred by the £10 fine imposed by the Sheriff, Mrs Duncan continued her activities but, in 1944, in a headline-catching trial at London's Old Bailey, she was sentenced to nine months' imprisonment under the Witchcraft Act. The events leading up to her arrest had had more than a touch of the Keystone Cops about them, especially when a whole posse of policemen descended on the séance room at 'The Master Temple Psychic Centre' above a shop in Portsmouth to search for the cloth that two eye-witnesses believed had been used to form the body of a materialized spirit.

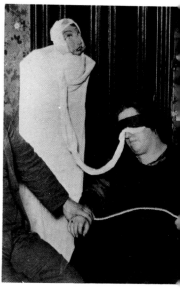

Helen Duncan, the famous materialization medium, who in 1944 was sentenced for fraud under the Witchcraft Act.

Many psychical researchers found 'mental mediums' far more impressive, since they eschewed lurid theatricals. The best-known of the early 'mental mediums' was Mrs Leonora Piper who, like 'Margery', came from Boston. During her trances she was able to reveal facts about her sitters which she could not, apparently, have acquired by normal means, and detectives employed to tail her during the investigation of her claims reported that she took no special steps to find out about her sitters. Further proof of her powers was furnished by another sleuth. He had been hired by Sir Oliver Lodge, after Mrs Piper had revealed obscure details of the lives of Lodge's uncles. The man tried to gather similar information through normal detective-work and his conspicuous failure to do so sealed Mrs Piper's reputation.

Her abilities were endorsed by the most eminent psychical researchers of the day but, in retrospect, her record is less than convincing: her most stringent test was also her most abject failure.

**Mrs Leonora Piper, a 'mental medium' and** (*right*) **Margery Crandon, a 'materialization medium', with a remarkable 'hand' supposedly emerging from her body. The 'hand' was later shaken by sitters at the séance.**

In 1896 she was consulted over the death of a young American, Dean Bridgman Conner. Conner had gone to Mexico to work in a circus in 1894. A few weeks later, his family in Vermont learned that he had died. One night, Conner's father had a dream in which his son appeared and announced that he was not dead after all but was alive and held captive in Mexico. This increased suspicions Conner's family and friends already held about his death: the story told them by the Consul-General in Mexico had been misleading – no one had seen the dead body, there was talk of missing jewellery.

Mrs Piper and her 'controls' agreed that Conner had been abducted. He was, they said, imprisoned in a hospital in southern Mexico. As a result, three separate searches were made, directed at long distance by Mrs Piper. Detailed instructions flew by telegram between Boston and Mexico. They all proved worthless. Finally, an enterprising journalist from *The Boston Globe* established that Conner had, indeed, died in the circumstances originally reported, and that throughout the wild goose chases the body of Dean Bridgman Conner had lain in grave 559 in Mexico City's American cemetery. 'The whole thing,' said the weary journalist at the end of the trail, 'was a fabric of nonsense erected on a dream.'

The reputation of the most famous 'physical medium' of the Victorian era has been less easily called into question, although determined sceptics have claimed some success in doing so. Daniel Home was an American who, through his Scottish ancestry, claimed his father was an illegitimate son of the tenth Earl of Home. Pale, fair-haired and debilitated by TB, he cut a romantic figure on his arrival in Europe in 1855, and the powers he demonstrated in the salons of the aristocracy made him a social sensation. Though the spirits apparently spoke through him, it is by the extraordinary events he claimed they caused in his presence that he must be judged.

Amongst his more routine accomplishments was the ability to make tables sail about the room, complete with knick-knacks and objets d'art. Once a table with a flowerpot on it amazed onlookers by appearing 'suspended in the air, where it remained some minutes, and then as suddenly sailed back again to the library, leaving us sticking between the tea-table and a sofa, and only able to hurry after it to see it depositing itself in the middle of the room in a most easy manner'. At another séance, Home apparently made an Erard grand action piano fly through the air, along with the Countess Orsini who was playing it at the time. 'Everybody would be delighted to disbelieve in Home – but they can't. They hate him and believe the facts,' one of his greatest admirers, the poet Elizabeth Barratt Browning, told her sister.

Reports that Home could elongate his body at will enhanced his reputation, and his ability to hold red-hot coals sealed it. Home's friend Lord Adare witnessed a fire-handling feat on 30 November 1868:

'Home, entranced, went back to the fire, and with his hands stirred the embers into a flame; then kneeling down, he placed his face right among the burning coals, moving it about as though bathing it in water. Then, getting up, he held his finger for some time in the flame of the candle. Presently he took the same lump of coal he had previously handled and came over to us, blowing upon it to make it brighter. He then walked slowly round the table and said, "I want to see which of you will be the best subject . . ." Mr Jencken held out his hand, saying, "Put it in mine." Home said, "No, touch it and see." He touched it with the tip of his finger and burnt himself.

'Home then held it within four or five inches of Mr Sarl's and Mr Hart's hands, and they could not endure the heat. He came to me and said, "Now, if you are not afraid, hold out your hand." I did so and having made two rapid passes over my hand, he placed the coal in it. I must have held it for half a minute, long enough to have burned my hand fearfully; the coal felt scarcely warm . . .'

In all, Home gave at least 1500 séances. Perhaps the most notable feature of them, apart from the extraordinary demonstrations themselves, was that they were conducted, not in the eerie semi-darkness insisted upon by other mediums, but in full light. 'Where there is darkness, there is the possibility of imposture,' he used to say. Moreover, he seemed able to produce evidence of his strange powers in any setting, and he never took money for his services, preferring to be paid in kind; as a result, he dined at the best tables of Europe, slept in the brocaded four-posters of the aristocracy and passed his days in enthralled and elegant company in the palaces of royalty.

Home was never detected in trickery, but this is not to say that his character was never attacked. The poet Robert Browning, for one, could not stand him, denouncing him as a 'dungball' in his vitriolic poem 'Mr Sludge the Medium'. Diligent searches by more recent sceptics among old conjuring books and mediums' secret manuals have yielded many techniques which Home could have used to astound his audiences. For example, several formulae for protecting skin from burning coals have been known for years, including a weird but effective brew which includes camphor, mercury and storax. Home could have applied it to his face and hands before brandishing the red-hot cinder in front of Lord Adare, although this does not explain how Adare himself was able to clasp it.

But the main target for sceptical researchers has been what Home's supporters claimed as his most remarkable feat ever. On Sunday, 13 December 1868, in the presence of three eye-witnesses Home appeared to float out of a window on the third floor of Ashley House in London's Belgravia, 85 feet above street level. He then flew back through another window.

That, at least, is what seems to have happened, but the accounts given later by the three young men who were there – Captain Charles Wynne, his cousin Lord Adare, and the Master of Lindsay – are riddled with inconsistencies; they disagree on matters as fundamental as the lighting conditions and even on which floor of the building they were. Amongst the more plausible theories advanced to explain the apparently astonishing feat are that Home had somehow managed to hypnotize his young and impressionable companions, or that he had Lord Adare in his power because the two men were having a homosexual relationship. Other researchers have tried to establish how Home could have achieved his effect by normal means.

The veteran psychical researcher, G. W. Lambert, for example, found an old photograph of Victoria Street taken at the same period as the levitation. It shows so much equipment lying around to be used for the construction of the underground railway that Home could have used some of it to engineer his flight, without anyone really noticing. Lambert says: 'It would have been easy for D. D. H. to enlist the help of one or two labourers to bring along, after work one night, some lengths of dirty rope, which no one would have missed. Given access to the roof of the house over the two windows facing Victoria Street to be used for the 'levitation', a loop could have been made fast, and a double rope let down to the level of the two windows on the third floor. With the help of such a contrivance, slung from above, D. D. H. could have travelled safely in the dark from one window to the next, and by next day all trace of the device could have been removed.'

Not content with armchair theorizing, the late Archie Jarman scoured Belgravia in search of Ashley House. He finally found it, not in Victoria Street but in nearby Ashley Place. The building had become offices, but Jarman identified the rooms as belonging to a firm of architects and surveyors: 'I rather bashfully told of Home's aerial flight to a Mr Perry, a senior member, and was relieved that he did not think me quite mad. Instead he was very interested. I asked if two of his rooms were connected by folding doors. He said, "Yes, come and see them." We walked to the western end of the offices and, between two, were the folding doors. I had arrived.'

Outside each window was a balcony, and just below was a stone ledge about five inches wide. The following Saturday, Jarman shinned up a ladder, in the hope of walking along the ledge; but he realized at once that the angle at which it jutted from the wall made it impossible. Back on the ground once more, Jarman scanned the building with binoculars, and finally found what he was looking for: above some of the windows were steel pivot-bolts, which had obviously once been used for 'perambulator' blinds. The pivot-bolts were roughly halfway down the window, and a rope could easily have been slung between them. Home, Jarman realized, could easily have used such a rope to hold on to while walking along the narrow ledge.

So was the Ashley House event a real levitation or a skilfully executed and carefully prepared fraud? Jarman points out that it is curious that Home should have forbidden his friends to look out of the windows when the sight of him flying from one to the other would have provided unchallengeable proof of paranormal powers. Sadly, this is a case where time will not tell: the

**Accounts of Daniel Home's ability to levitate made him the talk of London society in the 1860s. Archie Jarman (*below*) investigated the claims and worked out how Home might have deluded his admirers.**

opportunity to question the witnesses to the remarkable event has long gone, and Ashley House itself has been demolished since Jarman's visit. Only strong suspicions remain.

Even the appalling slaughter of the First World War, in which as many as 60,000 soldiers died in a single day, and the resulting boom in spiritualism as desperate relatives sought to make contact with their lost loved-ones, failed to provide the definitive proof of survival after death that both the spiritualists and the psychical researchers hoped to find.

Another generation of investigators had emerged by then to evaluate the mediums and their elusive powers, including Dr Samuel Soal. His scientific approach to the subject appeared to be just what was needed to dispel the aura of fraud and nonsense which had surrounded spiritualism for so long. Yet, as we have seen, on re-examination his work raises a question that, hitherto, had seldom been posed: could some *researchers* have cheated?

Like many others, Soal had suffered the loss of a close relative in the Great War, and it was in the hope of contacting his brother Frank, who had been killed in France in September 1918, that he began to make regular visits to a sparsely-furnished room at the top of the British College of Psychic Science in London's Holland Park. There, in the dim light of a shaded bulb, and with the window tightly shuttered, he consulted a medium called Mrs Blanche Cooper. Her method of communication was a well-tried one, since she was able to call up different voices which spoke to the sitter through a speaking-trumpet. The medium did not go into a trance and, Soal reported, 'While the voice is not speaking she keeps up a continuous humming noise with her lips, and this humming ceases when the voice comes into play. Throughout the period of my own experiments the medium seemed unable to sustain the voice for more than a minute or two at a time, and the information was given for the most part in rapid snatches, punctuated by periods of silence lasting from a minute up to a

Dr S. G. Soal, the
ESP experimenter,
and the medium,
Mrs Blanche Cooper.

quarter of an hour.' The voice seemed unable to speak if a musical box was not playing, and Soal had to wind it up at intervals with his left hand, while Mrs Cooper clasped his right. A pair of 'spirit guides' featured in the conversations: 'Nada' who spoke in 'a rapid girlish whisper' and 'Afid' who had a 'gruff and sepulchral' voice and usually 'arrived' to herald the end of each séance.

Soal's brother Frank, on the other hand, was pretty talkative. At the first sitting most of the answers given could have been the result of canny guesswork by the medium, but thereafter he provided a delighted Samuel Soal with a gratifyingly detailed account of episodes in their childhood: the 'dear old place' where they used to live; the field where they played; the hut in a hedgerow where they had built a brick fireplace. Odd incidents cropped up which Mrs Cooper could not have known about and would almost certainly never have discovered, even had she been devious enough to make inquiries about her sitter's childhood.

Frank reminded his brother of an afternoon in August 1914 when they had freewheeled home from a bicycle trip; he used the word 'starbobs' for starlings in an account of how he and a friend had tried to smoke the birds out of the thatch of a barn – 'I would hazard an opinion that "starbobs" is about the last word that a fraudulent medium would be expected to get by enquiries in the district,' wrote his fascinated brother. Frank also told of his friendship with a local priest, Father M'Kenna; revealed that Samuel had once given him an induction coil for Christmas and that the River Crouch could be seen from the top of a tall elm tree in which he had built an 'eyrie'. Then there was the incident of the medal: after Frank had described how he had buried a medal in the hut, Soal and his brother Charles visited the site and dug up a strange lead disc from the earth in the place Frank had described. Although Frank failed a test set for him by offering only one half-correct answer to three questions about his life, the number of accurate facts given through the medium appeared astonishingly high.

But the Blanche Cooper sittings may not be all they seem, for Soal's later writings and behaviour indicate that his investigation was by no means a model of psychical research. At almost every stage there is evidence that suggests calculated deception.

The first pointer to this is that the real conditions prevailing at the séances were never clearly established in Soal's published report. The truth of the matter is that the 'voices' were almost inaudible and very hard to follow, despite the fact that they came through a trumpet against which Soal put his ear. There is independent testimony for this; in 1922 the distinguished psychical researcher, E. J. Dingwall, sat with Mrs Cooper and reported that, 'Scarcely a word could be heard as the music [from the musical box] drowned what little noise the voices made.'

There are constant references to the problem in Soal's own notes; at sitting No. 23, for example, he says, 'The voices were more indistinct than usual' and No. 24 was, apparently, 'A very poor sitting. All the voices were extremely indistinct and listening was a great mental strain.' It was not until many years after the séances that Soal publicly acknowledged this crucial factor, when in a letter to *Psychic Science* in 1938 about Mrs Cooper's mediumship, he noted: 'There is no doubt that it required immense

Luiz Antonio Gasparetto claims his paintings, made at enormous speed, are the works of famous painters.

patience to listen continuously to these whispering and often inarticulate voices.' Thus, it may have been that Mrs Cooper was merely making inarticulate noises in the hope that Soal would interpret them according to his own thoughts, memories and preoccupations.

Soal was certainly an odd fish, and two aspects of his personality which were not revealed to readers of the Blanche Cooper transcripts are relevant to an assessment of the cases. Far from being an objective scientific observer of the psychic scene, he was himself an automatic writer and had even attended classes in the subject. Under the pseudonym of 'Mr V' he contributed to a volume of scripts alleged to have been dictated from beyond the grave by Oscar Wilde. He was also prone to muttering under his breath and, in the 1938 letter, suggested this as a possible explanation for the incident of the buried medal: '. . . This particular case might be explained on the basis of involuntary whispering. It may be that in the year 1910, I had actually noticed my brother Frank poking a leaden disc into the earthy floor of the hut by means of a stick. Such a trivial incident may have passed completely from my conscious memory.'

A combination of talking to himself and automatic writing would certainly go a long way towards providing a normal explanation of how transcripts of the sittings came to contain so many verifiable facts about Frank, and it is significant that many details came to light only after Soal had ascertained them. It is quite possible, too, that Soal was unaware he had been writing automatically, since one observer of him at work elsewhere noted that 'He wrote in a state of semi-coma.'

All the same, for a man of science, his treatment of evidence seems to have been cavalier. There are signs, for example, that he re-worded his notes, and yet still presented them as accurate copies of the jottings he had made in his green notebook during the sittings. Take sitting No. 23 of 30 January 1922. The published text says: '. . . The voices were rather indistinct.' Yet two other versions, in Soal's handwriting, say different things, one that 'The voices were more indistinct than usual,' and the other 'The "voices" at this sitting were very indistinct.' Small details, perhaps, but the discrepancy raises the question of what the original notes said, and why these do not seem to have been available for later inspection.

At best, there are too many holes in the evidence for the Cooper sittings to be taken as providing any evidence for survival or even for ESP between sitter and medium; at worst, the whole episode can be seen as a successful attempt to provide an enigma which would establish Soal firmly in the vanguard of psychical research.

To the relief, no doubt, of many mediums, psychical researchers today take a less feverish interest in spiritualism, and the days are long past when mediums were feted in high society or when passions rose to such a pitch that gangs employed by rival 'sensitives' came to blows in the séance room. Nevertheless there are surprising modern cases where people claim to be in contact with the dead.

Rosemary Brown from south London, a woman without formal musical training, has produced musical scores of some merit which, she says, have been 'dictated' to her by dead composers such as Beethoven, Liszt and Chopin. The works seem to be communicated at such speed – as fast as

Mrs Brown can write down the notes – that it is difficult for onlookers to believe that there can be any creative contribution from Mrs Brown herself. Yet such cases are notoriously hard to analyze, and musicologists who have studied the scores have been disinclined to recognize in them the authentic voices of the great composers, believing instead that they are merely spontaneous pastiches produced by a sincere and naturally gifted musician.

Stella Horrocks of Bradford, Yorkshire, claims to be in touch with the spirits of some of the world's greatest authors and politicians – more than 50 of them. She proudly shows visitors to her terraced house the notebooks in which she believes she has taken down the latest works of Jane Austen, Virginia Woolf, Noël Coward and many others. Perhaps the most spectacular of all 'psychic artists', however, is a Brazilian, Luiz Antonio Gasparetto, who dashes off pictures in the style of famous painters, at breathtaking speed – which he claims are their latest works. Sometimes he does two at once, with one sheet of paper the right way up and the other upside down! In 1978 he astonished viewers of BBC's *Nationwide* programme by producing 21 skilfully executed pictures in just 75 minutes.

Researchers are still arguing about the phenomenon of 'Drop-in' communicators. These are the apparent spirits of dead people who crop up unexpectedly in séances and whose life-histories and very existence have never been consciously known to either the medium or the sitters. The communicators usually prove impossible to trace, but when it can be done, an explanation for their 'presence' can often be found. One notable case highlights the intriguing problems they pose.

In the early 1970s a group of six psychical researchers held regular meetings to explore the phenomenon of table-tilting. None of them was a spiritualist. The sessions were held in complete darkness while a tape

Rosemary Brown and some of the compositions which she claims have been 'dictated' to her by dead composers.

recorder played music by Mozart or Strauss. The sitters sat round a specially built table which had three legs, two of them hinged to a hardboard base which allowed the table to rock in one direction but not in any other. The sitters would ask questions and the table would rock in reply – one tilt for 'No', two for 'Doubtful' and three for 'Yes'. More detailed messages could be laboriously built up by reciting the alphabet while the table rocked. Each tilt signified a letter, and the last one reached before the table stopped moving formed part of the next word.

In August 1973 a message was spelt out which purported to come from a woman called Grace from Hackney in north London. She had recently died. Grace gave her exact address in life and sent her love to her son Colin. In later sittings, Grace provided further information, including the precise time and date of her death.

On the off chance, one of the group went to the address Grace had given and, to his amazement, met a young man called Colin who turned out to be Grace's son and was able to confirm the details given at the table-tilting session. But a check through national and north London local newspapers revealed Grace's obituary, which contained all the details that had been verified, except for the fact that her house had been in Hackney. Since the paper which had printed the obituary was *The Hackney Gazette and North London Advertiser*, there was a strong possibility that someone at the table had made an informed guess. So was this a case of 'cryptomnesia' – the power of the mind to recall things of which there is no conscious memory? Had one of the sitters glanced at the obituary in the paper and then trotted out the facts at the séance without ever remembering having read the original article? It seems probable; this is known to have happened in similar cases. But which of the six people involved could have read the article remains a mystery – and also what prompted him to choose it from all the other material buried in the recesses of his mind.

It is not always possible to find easy solutions to the problems posed by 'Drop-in' communicators, however. A well-authenticated series of sittings begun in the 1940s by a local government official and his wife from Cambridgeshire yielded a number of cases for which no conventional sources such as newspaper obituaries can be found.

For example, one of the war-time communicators said he was the Rev. Duncan Stevens of Hinckley Road, Nottingham and that he had been a curate at Frinton in Essex before joining up. In the RAF he had flown in a Blenheim and had crashed over water about ten months before August 1942. While a check revealed that several of the facts given by the Stevens-communicator appeared to be wrong, the ones given above were absolutely correct and Dr Alan Gauld, who investigated the sittings, could find no obituary of Stevens which the sitters would have been likely to have read. Furthermore, none of the people who took part in the séances had any connection whatsoever with Nottingham or Frinton, and although one of them was the widow of an RAF man, her husband turned out never to have been stationed at the same base as Stevens.

Hypotheses to explain such strikingly accurate communications have not, to date, proved very satisfactory. If this really was a case of a dead airman contacting the living, why did he get some facts right and others hopelessly wrong – such as the county in which he had been stationed when he flew his last sortie? One theory is that some mediums may possess a faculty for 'Super-ESP' which enables them mentally to rummage through files and records. But this falters too; why should they get the facts wrong? Whether the explanation for 'Drop-in' communicators is mundane or supernatural, the questions the phenomenon raises take us deep into the uncharted depths of the human mind.

The most bizarre of all the new evidence said to point to the survival of the dead is undoubtedly the 'Electronic Voice Phenomenon'. It was discovered in 1959 by the Swedish musician and film producer Friedrich Jürgenson. One evening, in the summer of that year, Jürgenson recorded the songs of the birds in the countryside around his villa at Mölnbo. Later, when he played back the tape, he was astonished to discover a faint male voice on it, talking in Norwegian about birdsong. As he played and re-played the tape, his incredulity grew; the tape had been blank before the recording session and he had certainly heard no one speaking Norwegian in the remote spot where he had taped the birds.

This was merely the first of many messages Jürgenson was to detect on tapes and soon, on another spool, he recognized the voice of his dead mother. Intrigued, he continued his researches and found that he could pick up the strange voices on the radio by twiddling the tuner switch and recording on a cue given to him by a helpful 'spirit guide' called Lena.

Before long, another investigator had entered the field, the Latvian-born philosopher and psychologist, Dr Konstantin Raudive. Before his death in 1974 Raudive recorded more than 100,000 of the mysterious messages which, thanks to his diligence and his advocacy of them as evidence of survival, came to be known as 'Raudive Voices'. A notable feature of 'Raudive Voices' is that they are usually claimed to speak in a mixture of languages – often several in the same sentence.

With Raudive's use of tape recorders, microphones, diodes and a device known as the 'Goniometer', communication with the dead had obviously moved firmly into the 20th century, and as reports of the phenomenon

'Electronic Voice Phenomenon' pioneer Friedrich Jürgenson (left) was awarded the Commander's Cross of the Order of St Gregory the Great by Pope Paul VI, not for his work on 'spirit voices' but for making a documentary film about the Vatican. Dr Konstantin Raudive (below) continued Jürgenson's work on EVP with recording instruments like this 'Goniometer'.

spread throughout Europe they came to the attention of a young Cambridge University science graduate, David J. Ellis.

With the aid of a studentship in psychical research, Ellis decided to assess Raudive's claims that he was in contact with, amongst others, his mother, various dead relatives and friends, statesmen like Winston Churchill and John F. Kennedy, and even Adolf Hitler. After more than three years and many visits to researchers, including Raudive himself, Ellis came to the reluctant conclusion that there was 'no reason to postulate anything but natural causes: indistinct fragments of radio transmissions, mechanical noises and unnoticed remarks, aided by imaginative guesswork and wishful thinking, to explain the voice phenomenon'.

Ellis found that Raudive, who was no expert in technology, had not realized that the radios and other devices he had used were capable of picking up fragmentary and distorted broadcasts, however they were tuned. Moreover, Raudive's interpretation of many of the alleged communications was suspect. Thus, he interpreted a series of phrases as follows:

*'Glaube du Cedin.'* (Believe you, Cedin.)
*'Romani Nimowald Zamuchils.'* (Romani Nimowald is exhausted/tormented to death.)
*Ich folgu you tonight.'* (I follow you tonight.)

Very mysterious, but other listeners found a more mundane and convincing interpretation: what they heard was a trailer for a pop show on Radio Luxembourg called 'Jensen's Dimensions' starring the Canadian disc-jockey Kid Jensen. It actually ran as follows: 'Hello, this is Kid Jensen reminding you about 'Dimensions' later on tonight on 208: soft Rock, hard Rock, Jazz and Blues. It's all for you, tonight, at one o'clock.'

In general, Ellis found Raudive's interpretations of the voices too subjective and it was significant that the languages spoken by the strange communicators were ones he knew. It was worrying, too, that the voices with apparently the most important messages to impart were also the faintest. And even the clearest of recordings produced markedly varied interpretations from unbiased helpers who took part in listening tests. Other sounds appeared to derive from uncontrolled utterances on the part of the experimenters or people in the vicinity of the tape recorder.

Ellis summed up: 'As a "phenomenon" it is interesting that so many otherwise intelligent people have become convinced as to its paranormal nature . . . Possibly the undoubted sincerity and persuasive manner of its main protagonists, combined with the mystique which even the simplest instrumentation has for the layman – especially when backed by "experts" who say that normal reception of the voices is impossible – have been reinforced by the thrill of discovering these faint sounds on one's own recordings and interpreting them into apparently relevant phrases . . . Perhaps all these factors acting in concert have contrived to give this modern version of "The Story of the Emperor's New Clothes" the status that it has.'

Raudive was undeterred by Ellis's strictures, and just before his death embarked upon an extraordinary new venture, the analysis of chirps made by a budgerigar called Putzi which, Raudive had been led to believe, might have been relaying messages from its dead owner, a teenage girl, to her parents. This episode was viewed with some hilarity, even by Raudive's disciples and co-workers, but many of them have continued their research into the Electronic Voice Phenomenon, undeterred by the sceptics.

More orthodox investigations continue, notably into the nature of the mind of the medium and the mechanics of the trance state. This is a field in which there are far more questions than there are answers, partly because there is no machinery for measuring 'mind'. Is mediumship a form of mental illness? Are they hallucinating or exhibiting secondary personalities? Are 'sensitives' more in need of treatment than investigation, as one critic bluntly put it?

The answers may come as researchers probe further. Doctors at London's Institute of Psychiatry have come up with one intriguing clue to the wellspring of mediumship. Some mediums show impaired functioning of the right temporal lobe of the brain, consistent with an injury to the head. It is possible that this finding may eventually point to a specific area of the brain which controls mediumistic behaviour.

The eternally teasing question concerns whether there is life after death and, if there is, whether the dead are attempting to communicate with us, the living. Some investigators have entered into pacts with friends, promising to communicate after their death. Others have left codes breakable only with a key to be provided from beyond the grave.

The eminent American psychical researcher J. Gaither Pratt, when he died in 1979, left a combination lock and promised to 'return' with the combination. So far, despite the efforts of helpful mediums, the lock has remained tightly fastened. To the eager investigators, how depressing must be the silence of those who, in life, were most dedicated to unravelling the problem of survival.

Despite this, spiritualism still flourishes throughout the world. In Britain, there are spiritualist churches in most large towns from Bognor to Dundee. The Spiritualist Association of Great Britain organizes well-subscribed classes for trainee mediums. In the United States in 1981 the National Spiritualist Association of Churches announced a campaign to bring spiritualism to the masses in the form of 'Satellite Séances', when, according to the NSAC's hand-out, 'an actual Spiritualist séance will be telecast weekly across the Western Hemisphere'. America also boasts whole communities devoted to the cause. Some, like Cassadega in Florida, are open throughout the year. Resident mediums, who advertise their powers on discreet signs, are available to hold séances for the comfort of bereaved visitors. Others, like Lily Dale in New York State, offer similar services but for the summer season only.

Occasionally, allegations of fraud still surface to ruffle the placid waters of the psychic pond. Two of the most notable scandals of recent years concerned Camp Chesterfield, a psychic community in Indiana. The first broke in July 1960 when two researchers, Tom O'Neill, editor of a magazine called *Psychic Observer*, and Dr Andrija Puharich, were allowed to film some séances. They took the latest in cinematic equipment into the séance room – an image-enhancer and infra-red lights to help them penetrate the darkness. Both the film-makers and the camp authorities had

Draped in a bedsheet, self-confessed phony medium Lamar Keene (*top left and right*) **shows how in the dim red light of the séance room he would appear as a 'spirit guide'.** *Centre and below:* **The 'Cathedral of the Woods' at Camp Chesterfield. Tom O'Neill's exposé of some filmed séances at Camp Chesterfield, in the Psychic Observer in 1960, caused a scandal.**

FRAUD UNCOVERED AT CHESTERFIELD SPIRITUALIST CAMP

INFRA-RED MOTION PICTURES REVEAL THIS GREAT DECEPTION

*Shocking—Amazing—But True!*

By The Editor

undertaken the experiment in the hope of convincing sceptics of the validity of spiritualism, but the developed films showed, literally, a different and shocking picture: where misty spirit-forms and ectoplasm had materialized in front of the sitters, the celluloid showed the familiar figures and faces of some of the camp's best-known incumbents swathed in chiffon and gauze.

The second exposé came in 1976 with the publication of *The Psychic Mafia*, the memoirs of a self-confessed phony medium, M. Lamar Keene. One of the most notable of his revelations about the strategems employed by the mediums to impress their clients and winkle money out of them was the camp's extraordinary secret filing-system:

'... There were billet-sized cards and papers, from every service or public séance ever held at Chesterfield. The files were arranged alphabetically by geographic location – cities, states, countries. Each contained the name of the person and the question asked. There must have been tens of thousands of individual index cards.

'The files also included personal objects, keepsakes, clipped to individual cards. These were "apports" to be returned to the sitter the next time he visited the camp. Think how impressed that farmer from Pumpkin Creek, Michigan, would be when during his second visit to Chesterfield he received from the spirits the very tie-clip he had not seen for he couldn't remember how long.' How little had changed since Houdini's warnings of half a century before.

In the wake of such scandals, and the countless others that have preceded them over the years since the Fox sisters first claimed to be in touch with the spirits, the remark by one observer that 'Spiritualism is the music hall of psychic phenomena' may seem to be something of an understatement. The prevalence of fraud and the frequency with which sincere believers have been taken in tend to cast doubt upon the most apparently impregnable evidence for survival.

Even the case of Edgar Vandy does not escape suspicion. Despite the elaborate precautions taken by the brothers of the drowned inventor, could not their request for the names of suitable mediums have given unscrupulous people the cue to inquire into their family circumstances and even set up surveillance of their day-to-day behaviour? Could a friend or relation have provided details in the hope of alleviating grief? Certainly, a century of careful and sceptical research has yielded practically nothing in the way of proof that the living can communicate with the dead, or that the human spirit survives the decay of the flesh; but the harvest of insights into the credulity of mankind and into the yearning for a continuing existence has been rich indeed.

'I do not feel the smallest doubt now that we survive death,' wrote Frederick Myers to a friend in 1890, 'and I am pretty confident that the whole scientific world will have accepted this before AD 2000.'

Sadly, it is far more likely that Omar Khayyam was right, when he said, long before tables tipped and spirits rapped:

> Strange is it not? that of the myriads who
> Before us pass'd the door of Darkness through
> Not one returns to tell us of the Road
> Which to discover we must travel too.

# 11

# Life Before Life

UNDERLYING THE SEARCH for the strange powers of the human mind is the most fundamental quest of all – is death the end? Shall we live again? Have we, indeed, lived before? Hinduism and Buddhism, the two greatest religions of the East, claiming the allegiance of hundreds of millions, are founded on a belief in reincarnation – a conviction that we reappear on earth in a chain of linked existences. Death is merely a prelude to a new life.

Yet, despite the Christian creed of 'resurrection of the body', it has never been assumed in Western cultures that the dead return to live on this earth: 'life everlasting' was only to be expected in some heavenly abode beyond space and time – certainly not back in Balham or the Bronx. Today, however, surveys in the United States suggest that four out of every ten people believe in earthly reincarnation. In Britain, one in six of those who completed a questionnaire in *The Times* claimed to have had 'an experience which convinced you that you must have had a previous life or lives'. And a growing number of research workers are claiming to produce evidence – if not proof – of what those previous existences were, often with astonishing precision and with details of life centuries ago which, it seems, could not possibly have been acquired by normal means. Most of this evidence is produced by hypnotizing people and then 'taking them back' through childhood, through birth, and then through to their previous incarnation.

To see one of these 'regressions' is traumatic. Mike O'Mara is a distinguished American publishing executive in London – sane enough to have commissioned the book of *Arthur C. Clarke's Mysterious World*! To watch him handle a business crisis on a day when a lawsuit threatened to cripple one of his projects was to lose all doubts about his coolness and competence. Yet to see him under hypnosis and being pushed back to his 'past life', is to witness an unnerving transformation. His head lolls, his speech is slurred and foul, his accent is bog-Irish; to all intents and purposes he is transformed into an ignorant Celtic drunk:

*Opposite:* **A. J. Stewart, convinced that she was and is James IV of Scotland, portrayed** (*inset*) **in life, and at Flodden.**

**Mike O'Mara** (*left*) **who regressed under hypnosis to become a 19th-century Dubliner.**

**Mike O'Mara** (*left*) **who regressed under hypnosis to become a 19th-century Dubliner.**

'Poteen? I don't like it. People who drink that stuff, they got hair comin' outa their feet, an' they don't wear shoes, an' it's just as well, they couldn't afford them anyway.'

Slowly, in the fits and starts of inebriate mumbling, a specific character emerges to fit the personality. He is Stephen Garrett, living in the Dublin of the 1890s, falling into the hands of the police.

'I think I might have been a bit obvious. Stealing from stalls at the side of the road.' The hypnotist asks what uniform the police wore. 'I think a grey hat.' Was it tall or flat? 'I think two kinds. But they had big belts. Held their fat guts in.' It turns out there were two different police uniforms for Dublin and beyond. O'Mara, still in the character of the sot, Stephen Garrett, describes the shops and the docks of 19th-century Dublin, being knocked over by a cart, taken to some institution, being strapped down, flogged, drugged.

Gradually, convincing incidents of a down-and-out's life in Dublin at the end of the 19th century emerge, conveyed in what, if it were to be acting, would be a consummate performance.

In his normal waking life Mike O'Mara evinces no knowledge of all the wealth of detail of Irish life a century ago which he reproduces so colourfully.

Whatever happens in these hypnotic regressions the subjects can appear to be actually living the part, even to the point of personal peril. When the first post-war ventures into past-life regression were being tried by hypnotists in Britain, they had some nasty shocks.

Henry Blythe, a West Country hypnotist who practised both privately and on the halls, discovered he had a subject, Naomi Henry from Exeter, who could reproduce the life of an Irish woman, Mary Cohen from Cork.

'What year is this?'

'1790.'

'Whereabouts in Cork do you live?'

'On a farm.'

'What is the name of the farm?'

'Greengates.'

'What is the name of the nearest village?'

'Grener.'

Carefully, in a number of sessions, Blythe took Naomi Henry through the various stages of a life which had apparently been spent milking the cows, marrying a violent husband and losing her children. Blythe suggested she was getting older, decade by decade, until she was 70.

'How much longer have you to live?'

'A woman said not long.'

'Have you any pain?'

'No, that is all gone.'

'Has the priest been to see you?'

Silence.

Blythe had by now interested the London *Daily Express* in the case, and there was a shorthand writer present. Still there was silence from Naomi Henry, whether in her Mary Cohen role, or as herself. Blythe describes what followed.

'I was watching her closely, my fingers on the pulse of her left wrist. There was still no reply from Naomi, and suddenly I felt her pulse die away: her breathing stopped, every trace of colour left her face. She appeared to be dead. I bent closer to try and discover a trace of breath, but there was nothing. The atmosphere in the room was tense. I could feel the fear in my wife and the shorthand writer. Hurriedly, I spoke urgently, whispering into Naomi's ear: "You are quite safe, I am with you. You are safe, safe, safe." Slowly, her pulse began to beat again, her breathing resumed, some colour returned to her face. I estimate that about five seconds had elapsed. I heard a gasp of relief from the witnesses.'

The incident was enough to deter the *Daily Express* from dabbling in such waters; they abandoned their investigation. Blythe, with some hesitation, continued his sessions with Naomi Henry, and even extracted another 'life' from her as Clarice Hellier, a Bristol girl at the turn of the century.

Hypnotist Arnall Bloxham extracted 11 former lives out of Ann Ockenden, a Midlands schoolteacher – nine of them as a man.

Anyone who has seen a professional hypnotist's stage show, such as the presentations throughout England for many years past by Martin St James, will not be surprised by uninhibited and fantastic performances under hypnosis. St James's victims respond spectacularly: ordinary coalminers at Batley Variety Club declaiming a pro-Tory political speech for 20 minutes on end without pause or repetition; housewives desperately tearing off their clothes, convinced they are on fire, until Martin St James intervenes in time to save their modesty; feats of unusual strength are commonplace; and there emerge hidden talents as singers and dancers.

The credibility of the 'past lives' of hypnotic regression subjects turns on the wealth of detail which they provide and which apparently they could not possibly have known by normal means.

Naomi Henry from Exeter, who nearly died under hypnosis in the character she was inhabiting, an 18th-century Irish woman.

In the autumn of 1952, Colorado businessman Morey Bernstein, who was also an amateur hypnotist, started a series of sessions which were to result in one of the most celebrated cases. His subject was Virginia Tighe, a 29-year-old who hailed from Madison, Wisconsin. In the course of six regressions, Virginia Tighe became Bridey Murphy, an Irish woman living in the first half of the last century. (Ireland seems to have a special place in the history of past life recall!)

The recorded tapes are impressive. The girl from Wisconsin is transformed into Bridget Kathleen Murphy, born 20 December 1798. She lives with her father, a Protestant barrister, in a secluded house outside Cork. She marries the son of another barrister – a Catholic, so there have to be two weddings. They move to Belfast and live in a cottage in Dooley Road. Bridey dies, it seems, in 1864. But it is the local detail which has marked out this case. Virginia Tighe had never been outside the United States. Yet, as Bridey Murphy she was able to name some family grocers, Farr and Carrigan, who had existed at the time. An 1801 map of Cork showed an area called the Meadows with a few houses round it, as Bridey had described. She referred to coins such as the tuppence, which seem only to have been used at the time of Bridey's 'life', used authentic words such as 'linen' for handkerchief, 'ditching' for burying. There is a theory that she had absorbed it all from a television film. But although American newspapermen also managed to find relatives and friends of Virginia Tighe of Irish extraction who might have given her the local colour and conveyed the beguiling accent, 30 years of investigation have not uncovered a conclusive, mundane explanation of Bridey Murphy as she emerged from Virginia Tighe during 1952 and 1953, in a sitting-room in Pueblo, Colorado, before witnesses including a sceptical, indeed hostile, husband.

Mrs Yvette Jones, of Warley, near Birmingham in England recently described being regressed by a hypnotist back to a life as a three-year-old child in the 17th century.

'I seemed to be floating in a long dark tunnel, then found myself in a small paved courtyard,' she recalled. The hypnotist said, "What is your name?" "Mary –" I answered. There was a long pause, then "– Johnson." "Where are you?" "In my father's garden in London." "What does your father do?" "He is a cloth merchant." "In what part of London do you live?" The word "Eastcheap" came to me, but for some reason I felt unable to say so. "Who is on the throne?" "King Charles," I replied. "Which King Charles, Mary?" I was silent. There was only one King Charles and he was married to Henrietta Maria.

'"What are you wearing, Mary?" I became animated. "Oh, a pretty green velvet dress and green velvet slippers," I said proudly. I was always well dressed because of my father's trade. "My father calls me 'My little Lady Greensleeves.'"

'"What year is it?" I wanted to say 1643 but, again, felt tongue-tied. "Are there any soldiers in the streets?" I began to tremble, suddenly afraid. "There are many soldiers, they frighten me – they carry guns and pikes." I had a mental picture of hard-faced men my father called Puritans.

'"What religion are you, Mary?" "We are Catholic," I said – they

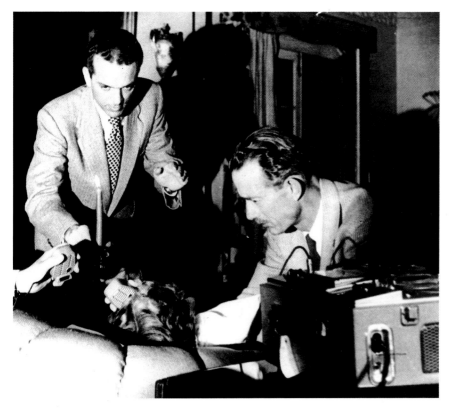

Virginia Tighe and (*left*) a recorded hypnosis session with Morey Bernstein, during which she 'became' Bridey Murphy in the 19th-century.

told me later I'd pronounced it in the 17th-century way – "Catholeek".

'The hypnotist then told me to come forward to the last day of my life. "How old are you now?" "I am four," I said. Immediately my mouth was very dry and I was conscious of extreme thirst and high fever. "What's the matter with you, Mary?" "Plague," was the only word I could utter, as my tongue stuck to the roof of my mouth. "Have you any spots or boils on your body?" "Yes," I said, and indicated a swelling under my right armpit.

'"How long have you been ill?" "Three days," I replied. "Are they giving you medicine to make you feel better?" "Just cold water." I tossed restlessly in my chair, hot and thirsty.

'"I want you to come now to the very last moment of your life, Mary." My head lolled to one side and once again, I found myself in the inky blackness of the tunnel which had no ending.

'After I was "restored" to the 20th century, I felt strange for a while. Throughout the session I had been aware of street noises. My 17th-century self was real enough, yet I knew I was still living in the present.'

The dialogues between hypnotist and subject in the special circumstances of regression parallel what appears to be a by-no-means-uncommon spontaneous experience in normal life – when a person feels that he has not only been, impossibly, in a particular place before, but has actually taken part in events there: he feels he has lived the scene in a past life.

An Indian Army major, A. D. McDonough, from Worthing in Sussex, told of an incident on the North West Frontier, near Attock:

'I reached a ridge which overlooked a precipitous drop into a densely wooded valley, shaped much like a horseshoe.

'Suddenly, I found myself down in the valley, amid a large number of ancient Greek soldiers. The whole scene was a busy encampment. In the centre of the valley were three altars. But what attracted me most was a group of men at the head of the valley, looking up at something. I went over and found that it was a newly-cut inscription in Greek on the dressed surface of the rock, commemorating the death of one of Alexander the Great's generals. Now I never studied Greek, but I was able to read the inscription clearly and understand it. There was a tense atmosphere of sorrow in the vicinity.

'A sudden blank and I was back in my place on the ridge, still gazing into the valley with a vivid recollection of what I had seen.

'I determined, however, to explore that valley, and did so with the help of Indian coolies, for the whole place was densely covered in rank vegetation and jungle growth, and full of large fallen boulders. I headed for the place where the rock-cut inscription was, and after much labour in clearing rank vegetation, I exposed what was once a dressed surface, and on a part of it were traces of incised Greek letters, but the greater portion of the inscription had disintegrated and fallen off.

'Still, there was ample evidence to convince me that this was the rock-cut inscription I had seen.'

Major McDonough concluded that he had been at the spot where Alexander the Great's army had camped before fording the Indus River into India, in 329 BC.

Another soldier, Alex Ainscough of Wallasey, Cheshire, related an experience during the retreat of 1918 in northern France:

'We were billeted at Quevilly, in the suburbs of Rouen. I knew nothing of Rouen.' Ainscough went into the city to get some of his favourite tobacco from the British army canteen. He then had half-an-hour to spare.

'I decided to investigate the street and the old turnings off it. It was a warm evening, and my decision had hardly passed through my brain when a strange chill struck me. I seemed suddenly to become familiar with my surroundings. I was marching with seven other men at the head of a column. We were all clad in black chainmail, and we were all tall. In front rode three men on horseback, also clad in black mail. We were going to see the burning of Joan of Arc. Here comes the strange part of my experience. I followed the street and eventually came to the outside of some kind of market, and on the pavement were marks cut into the stones.

'A tablet above stated that Joan of Arc had been burned on the spot.'

But not everyone who feels themselves transported in time manages a brush with history's high dramas. Mrs W. Barnard of Kenton, Middlesex, in England, was motoring in Ontario, Canada. 'As we approached Smith's Falls, I started to describe the town. My husband knew I had never been in Canada before, so he was surprised when I described a part of the main street, a grocer's shop, name of Desjardins, on one corner opposite a Royal Bank of Canada branch on the other corner. Our surprise was complete when we drove up the main street and saw the bank on one corner, and a grocer's shop on the other, exactly as I had said, except that the name on the grocer's shop was not Desjardins. 'My husband stopped the car and went into the grocer's shop. There he was informed that the last owner's name was Desjardins – 30 years ago.'

Sometimes, an experience of 'reliving the past' can be so overwhelming that it transforms a life. A BBC playwright, Ada Stewart, was in Scotland in August 1967, planning to visit the Flodden Field battle site in which James IV of Scotland was killed by the English army under the Earl of Surrey.

She had already taken a great interest in James, who had been something of an Arthurian figure among the more blackguard monarchs of the age. That night she was struck by a vision of the Flodden battle. She was on her back – 'staring up at what seemed like a tunnel of staves and blades, and beyond them, hands and merciless faces of men intent on killing me.

'My left arm I raised to cover my head, to ward off the blows. All the hate of the world was concentrated on me at that moment, and nobody was stopping it. I howled, a howl of pure animal terror as the blades thrust down upon me.' From that moment, A. J. Stewart was convinced that she actually had been James IV in a previous life, indeed that she *was* James IV.

She began to dress in all-black costume with white cuffs and ruffles. Her writing and speech assumed an antique style. She wrote an autobiography of James 'presented by A. J. Stewart', explaining some of the enigmas of the king, such as why he built the world's then biggest warship (apparently it was to attack London). She adopts, in the most matter of-fact way, King James's supposed point of view in many aspects of daily life.

When she saw Van der Goes' picture of King James III and the future James IV she said, 'Oh, no. That's not the way it was originally. It was just my father and St Andrew. I had myself painted in later, as an act of penance, kneeling behind him. That is me in my coronation robes over my funeral black, with my poor lank hair in need of washing. If I remember correctly, there was a vine painted where I now kneel, because my mother was at that time pregnant.' This is one piece of autobiographical King James which has been shown to be wrong, courtesy of the Courtauld Institute's Stephen Rees-Jones, plus X-ray and infra-red photography.

But it is the hypnotic regressions, rather than waking experiences, which compel the most serious investigation. Their vividness, the undoubted authenticity of the records (now many thousands of them on tape and film); the almost impossibly obscure information thrown up during such experiences – all these have compelled many people to take them as evidence amounting to proof of life after death and reincarnation on this Earth.

But the human mind is perhaps stranger than even these enthusiasts allow. A Finnish psychiatrist, Dr Reima Kampman, who worked up at Oulu, a port at the top of the Gulf of Bothnia on the edge of Lapland, determined to make a detailed study of the phenomenon of producing other personalities under hypnosis. He used a group of teenage secondary school students, all of them as mentally healthy as he could find. More than 30 were able to summon up, under hypnosis, multiple personalities. One 13-year-old conjured up no fewer than eight secondary personalities.

The first one was Bessina who lived in Babylon some 2,500 years ago. She was succeeded by some 'water-like' intermediate state, then came Ving Len in Nanking, China, around the year 100. The next one was Gunhild,

Dr Reima Kampman and 'The Cuckoo Song'. Under his hypnosis a young Finnish girl sang this music which she had once briefly seen.

the wife of a fisherman, who was born in Storviken, Norway, in 846. Then there was Dorothy, the daughter of an English innkeeper, born near Norwich in the village of Laughton in 1139. She was followed by Genevienne de Bonde in Paris at the end of the 17th century. Then came Emily Sunderland, an English lady and the wife of a member of the House of Lords, in 1743. After her came a Swedish peasant girl, Judith Martinson, born in the 1800s. Then Karolina Prokovjeff, the daughter of a Russian officer. She died from tuberculosis in Leningrad after the revolution.

Across the whole gallery of personalities, extending over thousands of years, the girl produced an astonishing amount of detail and description of everyday life. But it was the medieval English personality 'Dorothy' which was the most startling. 'Dorothy' gave what Kampman described as 'amazingly explicit' accounts of life in 12th-century England, where her father had been an innkeeper: place names were accurate, distances were given in miles, contemporary events were reported correctly. At one point 'Dorothy' sang a song which she called the 'Summer Song'. Kampman was fascinated: why did 'Dorothy' here suddenly change from Finnish into a strange language that reminded him of English? Did the song really date back to the 12th century? Professor Ole Reuter was called in. He quickly identified the language as Middle English. Even the words were recognisable. This was 'The Cuckoo Song', a canon song treasured by the British Museum as an extreme rarity.

The feat seemed impossible of rational explanation in a 13-year-old Finnish secondary school girl who had hardly learnt any English at all in her normal life. It was not until nearly seven years later that the girl, now making a name for herself as a singer, was re-hypnotized by Kampman in the course of a follow-up investigation. An astonishing story unfolded.

Kampman took the girl, now 19 years old, carefully and slowly back to the point where she might have come across 'Summer Song'. She recalled once going to the library and borrowing a pile of books, including *The Hound of the Baskervilles*. But she had to kill time until her bus came. Idly she had glanced at a book called *The Story of Music* and riffled through the papers.

Kampman's transcript reflects his astonished pursuit of the girl's hypnotic memory:

> '"Is there an English song or something very old?"
> "It was just there."
> "Have another look at it."
> "I cannot read that. I've had English at school, but I cannot read that."
> "But are there words?"
> "Yes."
> "And notes?"
> "Yeah, there."
> "Whereabouts at the library is that book?"
> "I don't know. It was here on the table. I just started to look and I thought I'll look at some magazines, but the book was here. I'll have a look at it."
> "Is it in Finnish?"
> "Yeah."
> "What is the story of it?"
> "*The Story of Music*. So it says, yeah."
> "Who has written it?"
> "Benjamin Britten. And Imogen Holst. I wonder [laughs] if that is a man or a woman."'

It took little time to establish that Britten and Holst had indeed produced a book called *The Story of Music*, containing 'The Cuckoo song'.

The source of 'Dorothy's' song was confirmed – as was the astounding reach of the girl's memory. In one unthinking glance she had, it seemed, absorbed a whole song in an obscure language – modernized medieval English, as it turned out – and reproduced it under hypnosis.

This is an extraordinary demonstration of the mind's capacity, under hypnosis, to reach unbelievably fleeting memories and impressions. Nearly 80 years ago members of the British Society for Psychical Research were investigating a woman who took on the persona of a medieval lady called Blanche Poynings. The investigators were spellbound:

'As presented to us, she was a lady of very distinct character, a great gossip, taken up exclusively with herself and her circle of friends and acquaintances, which was a very distinguished one. She was a great friend of Maud, Countess of Salisbury, and much of her talk was about that lady and her husband, the Earl. The Countess, she said, had been married three times, and she gave the names of her former husbands – Aubrey, and Sir Alan de Buxhall. She gave the names of the Countess's children by the Earl, and of her stepson, Alan de Buxhall, her own maiden name, Frances, and the names of the Earl of Salisbury's brothers.

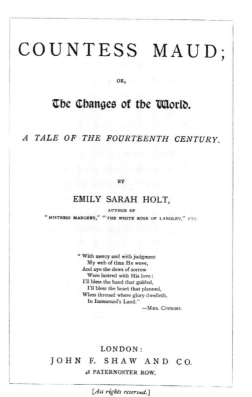

COUNTESS MAUD;

OR,

The Changes of the World.

*A TALE OF THE FOURTEENTH CENTURY.*

BY

EMILY SARAH HOLT,

AUTHOR OF

"MISTRESS MARGERY," "THE WHITE ROSE OF LANGLEY," ETC.

" With mercy and with judgment
My web of time He wove,
And aye the dews of sorrow
Were lustred with His love:
I'll bless the hand that guided,
I'll bless the heart that planned,
When throned where glory dwelleth,
In Immanuel's Land."
—MRS. COUSINS.

LONDON:
JOHN F. SHAW AND CO.
48 PATERNOSTER ROW.

**Under hypnosis in a medieval persona, the story of Emily Holt's book was retold as fact by a reader.**

She described with much vigour how the Earl, who was a Lollard, threw the images out of his chapel, and especially an image of Saint Catherine. This image, when they were removing it, fell on one of the men and made his nose bleed. She described the three kinds of bread – simmel, wastel and cotchet – eaten by different classes, and gave some account of her way of life. Her favourite dish was lampreys stewed in oil. On the saga went, in immense detail, until the investigator, G. Lowes Dickinson, had the idea of asking his subject: 'How can we confirm what you are telling us?'

'Read his will.'

'Whose will?'

'Wilshere's.'

'Where is it?'

'Museum. On a parchment.'

'How can we get at it?'

'Ask E. Holt.'

'Where is he?'

'Dead. There is a book. Mrs Holt.'

'Do you know where she lives?'

'No. Wrote a book. *Countess Maud* by Emily Holt.'

When woken out of hypnosis, the woman could recall nothing whatsoever of the book except the title and the fact that she had read it. But when G. Lowes Dickinson tracked down the volume he 'discovered in it every person and every fact (with one or two trifling exceptions) which had been referred to in the supposed life of Blanche Poynings'.

Reincarnation was therefore ruled out, but the mind's astounding powers of recall in the state of suggestibility known as hypnosis had been demonstrated in a most impressive fashion.

This recall faculty has already attracted the attention of police forces around the world. The Israeli Police Scientific Interrogation Unit has been using hypnotism since 1973, and reports a significant improvement in memory recall in 24 out of their first 40 cases.

Their most spectacular success followed a hideous terrorist attack when a bus was blown up in northern Israel: a number of passengers were killed and injured. The *Journal* of the Forensic Science Society carried a report from the police investigating the crime saying that they had been able to discover nothing of significance through routine questioning of the driver. So the man was hypnotized. He was then able to recall the smallest details of the long journey, in which many passengers had joined and left the bus.

'He remembered that at a certain bus stop a dark-skinned youth entered the bus, carrying a parcel. When the driver handed him his change he noticed a cold sweat on the young man's palm. Therefore, during hypnosis, he pointed out the youth as being a likely suspect. Although the driver faced the youth for only the short period of time needed to sell him a ticket, he was able to reconstruct an identikit portrait.' With the help of the picture a man was arrested, and confessed to the crime.

The New York Police have a permanent hypnotism unit consisting of a personable lady detective, Millie Markham, and Police Officer John Gaspar. A survey of the crime squads for whom they have hypnotized witnesses found that 70% of their colleagues felt the information obtained was helpful – and 91% felt it was accurate.

Early in 1982 two women in Manhattan saw a man shot dead in front of them; he had come to their aid when they were being mugged. Under hypnosis one of the women was able to provide a minutely-detailed description of the gunman, right down to the type of spectacle frames he was wearing.

'When we go into the hypnosis room, the only thing we have,' said Millie Markham, 'is the time, date, place of occurrence, subject's name and what information the detective on the case is looking for. Let's say he might want a licence plate number or a description of a person. We don't ask questions like, "Do you see the man there? Is he tall and skinny?" We say "What are you looking at? Describe this to me." You don't say "Describe the man to me," because you don't know if it's a man or a woman. Our questions are very open and no element of suggestion comes into them.' The squad has now achieved the acceptance of hypnotically-produced evidence as admissible in court.

The phenomenal reaches of memory are astonishing. Professor Erika Fromm, of the University of Chicago, was regressing a 26-year-old patient for demonstration purposes during a psychology class. Suddenly, when she got Don back to 'three years old' under hypnosis, he astonished her by breaking into fluent Japanese. 'The students in my class crowded around, gaping. He talked on and on in Japanese for 15 to 20 minutes. When

Hypnosis is successfully used by the New York Police Department to help in identification.

231

I progressed him to age seven, he spontaneously reverted to English.'

It emerged that during the Second World War, Don had been interned as a two-year-old with his family in California. Japanese had been the language of the camp, but he had spoken none after his release at the age of four and was aware of knowing only three or four words.

Back in 1902 a Scottish doctor, Henry Freeborn, had been treating a 70-year-old patient with pneumonia. In delirium she suddenly broke into Hindustani, apparently conversing with her *ayah* and asking to be taken to the bazaar to buy sweets. It was more than 66 years since she had left India, where she had been born and had been looked after by a native servant. She was not aware of ever having been able to speak the language.

In a comment on the case in *The Lancet* of June 1902, Dr C. A. Mercier wrote: 'It is to be noted that it was not the forgotten language alone whose memory was so strangely revived. Her whole personality was transported back. She spoke to friends and relatives of her girlhood and asked that she might be taken to the bazaar.' Coleridge, Mr Mercier recalled, described a case in which an illiterate maid-servant, when delirious, had recited for hours in Greek and Hebrew, apparently acquired from a parson for whom she had worked years before and who had been in the habit of reading Greek and Hebrew books aloud to himself in her hearing.

This power of the mind to recall things of which there is no conscious memory – cryptomnesia – may be the key to many 'past lives' produced in hypnotic regression.

Memories can be etched on the mind, it would seem, in the most fleeting moment. An American doctor, Harold Rosen from Johns Hopkins Hospital in Baltimore, described how one of his patients under hypnosis started writing in a weird script. It was eventually identified as Oscan, an obscure, pre-Latin language, used only in western Italy up to the beginning of the Christian era. It was principally known through a 2500-year-old lead scroll known as the Curse of Vibia.

Rosen eventually established that the curse had been reproduced on one page of a book being used by someone sitting next to his patient in a library years before. One glance had apparently sufficed to engrave it indelibly on the man's mind, without his knowing.

There is a theory current among some parapsychologists that memories of past lives may be transmitted in the genes from parent to child, in the same way as the DNA pattern carries all the necessary information for the entire lifetime's bodily development.

Dr Ian Stevenson, who is one of the leaders of reincarnation research, rejects the gene theory. He says: 'A person can transmit to his descendants, by genetic pathways, only memories of events occurring to him before the conception of his children. It follows that scenes of an ancestor's death could not figure among the events transmitted by genetic memory. Yet approximately two-thirds of the children whose cases I have studied claim to remember the death in the previous life remembered.'

Stevenson is also dismissive of regression: 'Although widely exploited by lay hypnotists and even by a few psychologists who should know better, hypnotic regression to 'previous lives' (with rare exceptions) generates only fantasies. This is why I prefer to study the apparent memories of very young children: these occur spontaneously, and the children's minds have not already been filled with normally acquired information.'

Stevenson has indeed devoted much of the past 20 years to investigating children who claim to have lived as somebody else in a previous life, mainly in India, the Far East, Alaska and Nigeria. There are obvious pitfalls in this approach: studying reincarnation in societies to whom it is a tenet of faith may be thought to load the dice a little; making inquiries through an interpreter must add to the hazards; also, children who conjure up an invisible friend are familiar in almost every family, no matter where they live. Sometimes these childish familiars stay around for years. They are usually superior in every way to the mere mortals in the family and particularly to the child itself.

H. Fielding Hall, who collected together his fascinating researches in Burma in a book, *The Soul of a People*, became irretrievably enmeshed in the religious outlook and expectations of Buddhism. Nevertheless he records some beguiling tales: a little girl showing extraordinary ability as a puppeteer, while claiming to have been a travelling marionette man named Maung Mon: a boy with deeply marked hands who said they were scars inflicted on him in a former life by dacoit bandits. Ian Stevenson has succeeded in raising such stories, much beloved by the Oriental press, out of the realm of anecdote on to a slightly firmer plane.

One of his prime cases concerns Bishen Chand, the son of a railway clerk in Bareilly, in Uttar Pradesh, northern India. A local lawyer, K. K. N. Sahay, had taken an interest in Bishen Chand before any attempt had been made to check the 'previous life identity' which the four-year-old Bishen Chand described. Sahay wrote it all down.

Bishen Chand had started asking about a place called Pilibhit, some 30 miles away, almost before he could utter any other words. Then he said he was the dead nephew of a man named Har Narain, of Mohalla Ganj in Pilibhit. He had lived next door to Sunder Lal, who had a green gate, a sword and a gun, and who held parties with dancing girls in his courtyard. He had studied up to class six and knew Urdu, Hindi and English.

Sahay determined to take Bishen Chand to Pilibhit to check the story. It is by no means clear that the pilgrimage was conducted on scientific principles, acceptable to the learned Western societies for psychical research, but it must have been a high day in Pilibhit.

First, Sunder Lal and the green gate were spotted. Then the house of the 'previous life' uncle, Har Narain:

'The boy recognized the building and the place where they used to drink wine, eat *rohu* fish, and hear the songs of *nautch* girls.' Out tottered a relative from the 'previous life', Babu Brij Mohan Lal, clutching a faded photograph. By now a sizeable crowd had gathered to oversee the next test. Could Bishen Chand spot himself and his 'previous life' uncle in the picture? Sahay must have held his breath. But all was well. 'Here is Har Narain and here I' pronounced the boy, pointing to the photograph of a boy on a chair. 'This was most remarkable,' wrote Sahay, 'and immediately established his identity as Laxmi Narain, nephew of Babu Har Narain.'

By now the one-time Laxmi Narain had been joined by two 'previous life' schoolfellows, so the caravanserai moved on to the old Government High

School, Pilibhit, and he correctly identified various classrooms. The classmates sneakily asked him to name his teacher. But by now, like the audience in some television game show, the crowd were shouting out the answers – it had been fat old Moin-ud-din of Shajehanpur.

'Previous life' Laxmi had clearly been something of a rake and the crowd, turning, demanded to know the name of his favourite prostitute. 'Padma,' said Bishen Chand, which the people certified as correct.

Then came the bizarre moment, frequently found in Indian reincarnation cases, and which outdoes even the improbable plots of Indian cinema – the boy was taken to meet his 'previous life' mother, still in this life. 'She put the following test questions,' recorded lawyer Sahay, 'and became convinced that he is the reincarnation of her late lamented son.' Laxmi Narain had died of fever at the age of 32.

Q. Did you fly kites?
A. Yes.
Q. With whom did you contest [in kite flying]?
A. I contested with every kite that came in my range, but particularly I contested with Sunder Lal.
Q. Did you throw away my *achar* [pickle]?
A. I did throw away the *achar*, but how was it possible to eat worms? You wanted me to eat worms, hence I threw your *achar* away.

Note: (by K. K. N. Sahay): The mother says that once her pickles got rotten and she had worms in her jars. She threw the worms out, but kept the pickles in the sun. Laxmi Narain threw them away, much to her annoyance.

Q. Did you ever enter into the service?
A. Yes, I served for some time in the Oudh Railway.
Q. Who was your servant?
A. My servant was Maikua, a black, short-statured Kahar. He was my favourite *Khansama* [cook].
Q. You used to sleep on a bamboo *charpoy* with no bleeding? [This question was put by B. Balbir Singh of Killa, Bareilly.)
A. You never saw my bed. I had a good bed with an ornamental plank towards the head side and had a *qalin* [thick cover] on it, and I kept two pillows under the head and two under my feet.
Q. What did I teach at Pilibhit? [This question was put by Sita Ram, now a teacher of the Government School, Bareilly, formerly a teacher at Pilibhit.]
A. You taught Hindi.

Thus was the four-year-old Bishen Chand accepted as the reincarnation of the dead Laxmi Narain, though it hardly seems to have been to his advantage. He ended up an excise tax collector in the town of Rampur.

Another celebrated Indian case also left its heroine, Shanti Devi, languishing in obscure government service in New Delhi, still pining for the 'previous life family' she had re-found and was then obliged to abandon.

Shanti Devi, born in Delhi in 1926, started speaking of her 'husband and children' almost as soon as she could talk. She gave her husband's name as Kedernath, her own as Ludgi. They had lived in Muttra, hundreds of miles from Delhi, in a large, yellow-stuccoed house. 'I died giving birth to another child,' Shanti Devi told the family doctor. 'Our sons are still there in Muttra with their father.'

Eventually, the family decided to send a letter to the name and address that Shanti repeatedly mentioned in Muttra. Again, it must have been a disorienting moment for the widower Kedarnath in Muttra when he opened the missive from Delhi. A visit was arranged and Shanti succeeded in finding the house where her 'previous life husband' had lived. Again there was a meeting with the 'previous life mother' and, most usefully of all, the identification of the spot where some jewellery had been buried in the back garden. But, inevitably, Shanti had to turn her back on her 'previous life family' and return in her incarnation as a nine-year-old girl to Delhi, and to a spinsterly career in government service.

In Sri Lanka there have even been twin reincarnations. In 1982 two three-year-old girls, Shiromi and Shivanthi Hettierachchi from the southern port of Galle, claimed to be reincarnations of two boys who had died in the briefly bloody and dramatic Marxist insurrection of 1971. Shiromi claimed that as Robert, a local boy who certainly did die in the revolt, she had leaped to her death from a rock at the nearby bay of Unawatuna. Shivanthi remembers being shot and killed as a boy called Johnny. The families of the dead youths claimed the details were accurate to an extent that would have been impossible for two three-year-olds to fabricate.

In the 24 years since Professor Ian Stevenson first published some of his evidence he has gathered stories, still mainly from the East, of infants with birthmarks that accord with knife and bullet wounds from their 'previous lives', unexplained phobias to water or aircraft, predilections for strange food, or surprising, untaught skills such as thatching – all of them, according to the children, founded on events in a previous incarnation.

One case in the West, however, does display some of the curious features of Stevenson's more remarkable Eastern reports. It was founded in tragedy.

Two little English girls, Joanna and Jacqueline Pollock, aged 11 and six, were walking home from Sunday church at Hexham in Northumberland, in May 1957, when a car mounted the pavement and crushed them against a wall. They were both killed.

Their father, John Pollock, though a Roman Catholic convert, had been a convinced reincarnationist for years. He seems to have believed that the accident was a judgement on him for his views, and also that the girls would be restored to him in a new incarnation. Less than a year later his wife Florence became pregnant; John Pollock immediately told her she would have twins, that they would be the way of restoring the dead girls to them.

Against predictions by gynaecologists, twin girls were indeed born in October 1958. John Pollock immediately noticed a thin white line on the brow of the second-born twin. The dead Jacqueline had carried an identical scar after a fall from her bike at the age of two. The same baby also carried a thumb-print birthmark on her left hip: so had the dead Jacqueline.

Florence Pollock did not share her husband's views and apparently held him to a promise not to discuss them with the children until they were into their teens. Nevertheless, she could not deny the steady sequence of events

Jennifer and Gillian Pollock, the twins supposedly the reincarnation of their dead twin sisters, with Dr Hememndra Banerjee from the University of Rajasthan who came from India to research their case. *Below:* Dr Ian Stevenson.

Queen Isabella of Spain, alias Elizabeth Long of Los Angeles, is carried in suitable state into the city's annual Reincarnation Ball.

which seemed to confirm her husband's conviction. The family moved from Hexham within four months of the twins' birth. At the age of three the girls returned for the first time, and immediately seemed at home. 'We used to live there,' they said as they passed the Pollocks' former house. 'The swings and slides are over there,' – even though the playing field was still out of sight. 'The school's just round the corner,' they said, before they were within view of the school that the dead girls had attended.

The twins were not allowed to play with toys which had belonged to their dead sisters, but one day their parents relented. Jennifer immediately named two dolls. 'That's your Mary and this is my Suzanne' – the same names the dead girls had bestowed. One day in the yard of their new house at Whitley Bay, Northumberland, John Pollock found the two girls screaming with fright. 'The car. It's coming at us.' A car outside in the road had turned and was facing straight at them, though safely enough on the other side of the wall. By the time they were six, the phenomena had ceased and at 13 the girls remembered nothing when they were told the story by their father. Appearing on Tyne Tees Television in 1981, John Pollock had lost none of his certainty. He simply said: 'We were fortunate to be chosen for a most wonderful revelation of the truth: that we can hope for another life on this earth.'

Like so many of the 'truths' which have been hijacked from Asia to Manhattan and Munich, Kensington and California, this one has been absorbed into show business. Should we live again, perhaps it is our proper fate to receive that beguiling invitation card – 'Come as you were' – and land up at the Los Angeles Reincarnation Ball, the annual gathering of Atlanteans, Pilgrim Fathers, various versions of Richard III, and Isabella of Spain, attended by four beautifully-muscled bearers – all convinced of their place in the past.

# Epilogue
## ARTHUR C CLARKE

So – WHAT DOES THIS ALL PROVE? Probably very little, because we can hardly decide, in one book and thirteen half-hours of television, questions which some of the best minds in history have been debating furiously for hundreds of years. The most we can hope to achieve is to make the credulous more sceptical, and the sceptical more open-minded.

So it might be a good idea, as a sort of calibration exercise, to look at two of the 'strange powers' which human beings, without question or controversy, undoubtedly do possess. Perhaps they may even seem commonplace to you; but to me they are almost beyond belief – because I possess scarcely a trace of them myself.

If there had been only one such case, I doubt if I would have taken seriously a report of a man walking a rope stretched over Niagara Falls, repeating the exploit while pushing a wheel-barrow containing another man, and then stopping to cook and eat a meal a hundred feet above the roaring waters. Emulating Jefferson, I would rather have believed that a hundred Yankee reporters were lying.

But this (and much more) is what Blondin did a century ago – bringing his career to what I consider a spectacular close by dying peacefully in bed at the age of seventy-three, only a year after his farewell tightrope performance in Ireland. Many others have repeated his exploits and even surpassed them – like the gentleman who recently walked between the twin towers of the World Trade Center.

I find such feats amazing because I could not remotely emulate them, even if my life depended upon it; that is why they appear 'strange' to me. However, though remarkable, they are not in any way mysterious; indeed, they make excellent biological sense. An ability to walk along high, narrow branches must have been of the utmost value to our remote ancestors. Those who did not possess it left few descendants; Blondin et al trace their lineage back to those who did.

But now consider my second example, which is far more mysterious – because it makes no evolutionary sense at all. It is a truly fantastic skill of virtually no survival value, and little practical use in the past, present or foreseeable future.

Here is an extract from J. R. Newman's fascinating quartet of volumes, *The World of Mathematics*, describing the behaviour of ten-year-old Henry Safford in 1846, when presented with a little problem in mental arithmetic:

'Multiply in your head,' [ordered the compassionate Dr Adams] '365,365,365,365,365,365 by 365,365,365,365,365,365.' Henry flew round the room like a top, pulled his pantaloons over the tops of his boots, bit his hands, rolled his eyes in their sockets, sometimes smiling and talking, and then seeming to be in an agony, until, in not more than one minute, said he: 133,491,850,208,566,925,016,658,299,941,583,255!'

Newman adds that an electronic computer might do the job a little faster but it wouldn't be as much fun to watch. He is now wrong on both counts – today's machines would not be a 'little' faster – they would do this calculation in less than a blink of an eye. And Dr Newman didn't live to see the advent of video games.

Here is an even more amazing example, taken from my friend Dr Jeremy Bernstein's book *The Analytical Engine*. It describes the exploits of the Dutchman William Klein, who until his retirement in 1976 was a mathematician at CERN (the European Nuclear Research Centre). He set a speed record – duly noted in the *Guinness Book of Records* – on 27 August 1976 for mentally calculating the perfect seventy-third root of a five hundred digit number. It took him two minutes and forty-three seconds. But in April of 1979 he got this down to two minutes and nine seconds . . .

To me, the ability even to grasp mentally – let alone extract the seventy-third root of – a five hundred digit number is totally incredible. Just to see what it looks like, here *is* a five hundred digit number, chosen to make things easy for the printer (not to mention myself):

12345678901234567890123456789012345678901234567890123456789012345678
90123456789009876543210987654321098765432109876543210987654321098765
43210987654321098765432112345678901234567890123456789012345678901234
56789012345678901234567890123456789009876543210987654321098765432109
87654321098765432109876543210987654321098765432112345678901234567890
12345678901234567890123456789012345678901234567890123456789012345678
90098765432109876543210987654321098765432109876543210987654321098765
43210987654321123456789012345678901234567890123456789012345678901234
567890123456789012345678901234567890

The seventy-third root of this monstrosity is approximately 6868629, which is about the limit of my attention span for numbers.

How could such a fantastic power as Mr Klein's ever have evolved in the human brain? The apes seem to manage very well in the jungle with remarkably little mathematics. Even in modern society, these feats of mental calculation are useful only as parlour tricks and circus acts, because electronic computers have made them completely unnecessary.

Certainly, something very odd seems to be going on here. I am tempted to link it with the astonishing ability of small boys to unscramble Rubik's fiendish cube (which did not even exist before 1979) despite its 43252 00327 44898 56000 combinations.[1]

Whatever the explanation of their origin, these feats of calculation show that the brain has the power to store – and retrieve with complete accuracy – huge blocks of information.[2]

This is precisely what seems to have occurred in cases of pseudo-reincarnation, and knowing exactly *what* has happened here makes them none the less wonderful. The achievements of 'Dorothy' and 'Don' described in Chapter 11 seem to me almost as marvellous, and as improbable, as genuine reincarnation.

I suspect that the explanation of some (but not all) ghosts or apparitions will also be found in the information-processing powers of the human mind, particularly in the circuits between the brain and eye. It is a cliché that seeing is believing; but it is equally true that believing is often seeing.

Anyone who has studied those cases of UFOs *whose explanations have been discovered beyond any possible doubt* will be astonished (and perhaps chagrined) at the mind's almost unlimited powers of self-deception. The inability of eye-witnesses to describe accurately even commonplace phenomena, especially when some emotional stress is involved, has long been recognized – and indeed exploited, particularly in the courtroom. When honest observers can disagree completely on the details of a traffic accident, should we be surprised that a re-entering spacecraft a hundred miles away could be interpreted as a Flying Saucer landing in the next field – as has indeed happened? Or that a random pattern of objects glimpsed under poor lighting conditions (at night, on the borders of sleep . . .) could be mistaken for a dead friend?

But simple misinterpretation could not possibly explain some of the dramatic cases described in Chapter 5. I would like to make a suggestion which, I am sure, is not original, though I do not recall seeing it in print. To reverse Niels Bohr's famous comment on a colleague's theory, it may even be crazy enough to be true.

Everyone knows that the eye is a camera.[3] A convex lens produces an image – upside down, in case you hadn't noticed – on the retina, a curved screen of sensitive cells at the back of the eyeball, which acts as a kind of infinitely re-usable colour film. Now for the crazy idea.

Many homes now possess slide projectors – the modern version of the

---

[1] My acknowledgement to Cubemeister David Singmaster's *Notes on Rubik's 'Magic Cube'*. He points out that a computer generating a million patterns a second would take 1,400,000 years to show them all. The record time for solving the cube is now less than half a minute. I never succeeded in several months of desultory twisting.

---

[2] And even more astonishing, purely *random* information, lacking any pattern or structure. The specialist will find some almost incredible examples of this in a book published in 1971: Bela Julesz – *Foundations of Cyclopean Perception* (a best-selling title, if ever I saw one . . .).

---

[3] Incidentally, a very poor one – the great physiologist Helmholtz said that he'd demand his money back if an instrument-maker did such a lousy job for him. This does not alter the fact that the eye is a miracle of *biological* engineering. Consider the problems involved, in growing a camera out of jelly . . .

Victorians' beloved 'magic lantern' – usually employed to bore friends and relatives with holiday snaps. Now a slide projector is simply a camera run backwards; you put the picture inside it, add a light source, and the lens returns the image to the outside world.

*What if the eye can do something similar?*

The analogy would not, of course, be exact, for there is no light source at the back of the retina; the image would be a mental one, in the 'mind's-eye' of the beholder. After all, something remotely similar must occur when we recall a past or distant scene to memory, but I am suggesting a much more precise and detailed process, occuring only under rare conditions.

But this would not explain apparitions observed by more than one person; if this line of reasoning is correct, then the eye would have to behave *exactly* like a slide projector, literally throwing an image upon a screen in the outside world.

Such an idea is so obviously absurd that I would not have dared to mention it – except for the fact that something quite similar can indeed occur with our second most important sense organ, the ear.

Just as the eye is a camera, so the ear is a microphone. And a microphone, like a camera, can work in both directions. It can receive sounds – and it can also create them. In some of the early telephones, the same instrument was used both as mouthpiece and earpiece.

There is a well-known hearing defect (which I suffer from myself occasionally, confound it!) called 'tinnitus' or more descriptively 'ringing in the ears' (in my case, it's a hissing). Now, this is usually subjective – that is, it can be heard only by the victim; one might argue that it exists only in his brain. As far as the sufferer is concerned, it makes no difference one way or the other; tinnitus can be 'real' enough to prevent sleep and even drive its maddened victim to suicide.

However, there are also rare cases where the sounds in the ear are *not* subjective; they can also be heard, faintly, by another listener. So the ear can indeed act both as microphone and speaker – though hardly a *loud*speaker.

I cannot help wondering if anyone has ever learned the trick of talking through his ears, and gladly present the concept to any author (or secret agent) rash enough to make use of it. In any event, this curious pheno-menon seems quite sufficient to account for most cases of auditory hallucinations; whether my suggested visual equivalent also exists is a matter for the future to decide.

It has been known for a long time that many animals possess senses which we do not share, except perhaps in a vestigial form. Some insects can see into the ultraviolet, so that flowers which may be monochrome to us are vividly coloured to them. The pit-viper can detect long-wave infra-red (heat) waves, and can thus locate small animals in the dark because they are hotter than their surroundings. Being able to 'see' heat is a gift that would be quite useful to humans, as it would prevent many accidents. To us, unfortunately, water looks exactly the same whether it is ice-cold or boiling. But to the pit-viper, the difference would be perfectly obvious from yards away.

The ability of bats and dolphins to locate objects by their built-in sonar is less surprising, because we do share this gift to some slight extent; for centuries, blind people have tapped sticks in order to generate the abrupt sounds that are most suitable for obstacle detection.

Perhaps there are other senses which we have not yet recognized, or which only a few exceptional people have developed. Some individuals seem to have a homing instinct, so that they are never lost even in strange surroundings. And then there are the dowsers, whose successes – and failures – were recounted in Chapter 9. The evidence for water-divining, if one considers examples like that of Colonel Grattan, would be good enough to convince any impartial jury. Yet almost every time a scientific demonstration is arranged, the performance of the dowsers is pathetic – nothing better than mere chance. Their débâcle does nothing to reduce their supreme self-confidence and their conviction that they really *can* find water, or gold, or oil – for they can always point to fully authenticated cases where this has actually happened. Perhaps the circumstances of the test were too artificial, too remote from the real world, etc., etc . . .

Perhaps; but the answer may lie in the fact that dowsers, like racing tipsters, conveniently forget their failures and proclaim only their successes. Those successes may be no more than allowed by the laws of chance – and those laws are very subtle indeed.

Given enough time, even the most incredible coincidences will occur; we can all give examples of this from everyday life. Here is my favourite.

In December 1969 I flew into Paris to address a UNESCO conference. The aircraft doors had just been opened and I was shuffling down the cabin when I noticed a Berlitz guide book lying on one of the seats. Instantly the thought flashed through my mind: 'I wonder what's happened to Charlie Berlitz? I haven't seen him for years.' (This, incidentally, was long before he'd struck gold in the Bermuda Triangle.) I took another three or four steps, and a voice behind me said: 'Hello, Arthur.' Guess who . . .

This incident still astonishes me – yet it shouldn't. In the course of a busy lifetime, many similar events *must* occur, purely by coincidence. Nevertheless, they give one an odd sensation somewhere at the top of the spine, and tend to induce a semi-mystical belief that there's a lot going on in the universe that We . . . Don't . . . Understand.

Arthur Koestler wrote a whole book on this subject – *The Roots of Coincidence*. And although J. B. S. Haldane was referring to the peculiarities of twentieth century physics, he summed up the feeling perfectly in his famous remark: 'The Universe is not only queerer than we imagine – it is queerer than we *can* imagine.'

It is hard for the non-mathematical layman to realize that even the most amazing examples of dowsing, telepathy or precognition could be due to nothing more than chance – which, it has been said, does not merely permit coincidences, but *compels* them to happen. A success like Colonel Grattan's could be exactly counterbalanced by a hundred failures that no one ever hears about. The trouble with this explanation is that no one will believe it; even in the cases when it is true, it would be virtually impossible to prove. As far as dowsing is concerned, everyone would be much happier if some physical mechanism could be discovered to account for it (everyone, that is, except the dowsers – because they would then be quickly put out of business by a handful of microchips).

Let me give an analogy. If human beings possessed absolutely no sense of smell, the performance of a bloodhound or a hunting dog would be as mysterious as dowsing is today. However, in this case we can understand what is happening, despite the limitations which G. K. Chesterton's canine poet so sarcastically, if ungrammatically, pointed out:

> Even the smell of roses
> Is not what *they* supposes –
> And goodness only knowses
> The noselessness of Man!

Can a genuine dowser 'scent' water in some way, just as a dog follows a spoor which we cannot detect? Such a capability would have such great survival value that, if it were possible at all, Darwinian selection would certainly have tended to preserve and enhance it.

There have been attempts to explain dowsing by an unusual sensitivity to very weak magnetic fields, and there is some evidence that the performance of homing pigeons is at least partly based on such an ability. (In this case, recognition of star fields and geographical features also appears to play a role.) The experiment with the cesium magnetometers described in Chapter 9 certainly gives credence to this theory.

However, until quite recently no one had been able to locate an organ of magnetic sensitivity – the biological equivalent of the compass – in any animal. Now a breakthrough has occurred.

Quite unexpectedly, the movement of certain bacteria has been found to be controlled by magnetic fields. The effect is unmistakable – even dramatic. If the magnet is reversed, so is the direction in which the bacteria swim. Why single-celled creatures should devote some of their rather limited mental faculties to achieving this feat is still obscure. But it has started biologists searching, and they have already made some striking discoveries. Microscopic assemblies of magnetic material – iron particles – have been found in certain organisms, and even in some higher animals. The idea of built-in compasses is no longer absurd.

Even so, it seems unlikely that dowsing (if it really occurs!) depends on the sensing of magnetic anomalies, because in most of the cases involved they are extremely minute – or even non-existent. We may have to look still more deeply into the structure of the physical world for the answer.

Some fifty years ago, in an American science-fiction magazine, I came across a verse which has stuck in my memory ever since (the author's name, unfortunately, did not).

> A being who hears me tapping,
> The five-sensed cane of mind
> Amid such greater glories
> That I am worse than blind . . .

As philosophers at least back as far as Plato have suspected, this does indeed describe the human situation. However, thanks to all the instruments of modern science (microscopes, telescopes, radiation detectors, gas chromatographs, magnetometers, electroscopes – to mention only a few of the best-known ones) we can now glimpse some of those 'greater glories', if only at second hand.

How many more yet remain to be discovered, no one can guess. We may – as the Victorian scientists rashly and prematurely believed – be nearing the end of the quest.

It is much more likely that we have barely begun.

And now I am going to risk going out on a limb (which will doubtless be sawn through very promptly) and give my own personal ratings of the validity, or otherwise, of the subjects discussed in this book. You may amuse yourself at the same harmless game, but please don't take it too seriously. Even if you agree with me now, you may not do so later – and vice versa. I fully expect to change my mind in future editions, perhaps after receiving feedback from the television series.

The scale runs from complete confidence to complete disbelief, with zero meaning that I can't (or won't) make up my mind one way or the other. To be more specific:

+5  Certainly true.
+4  Highly probable.
+3  50:50 chance of being true.
+2  Possible – worth investigating.
+1  Barely possible – not worth investigating.

Zero – Don't know.

−1  Very unlikely.
−2  Almost certainly untrue.
−3  Untrue beyond all reasonable doubt.
−4  Certainly untrue.

You'll notice that my scale is asymmetric, because although the ratings start at +5 they only go to −4. This is an inevitable consequence of the laws of logic. One can prove that a phenomenon *does* occur, but it is impossible to prove that it doesn't – as Randi and his fellow sceptics are continually demonstrating, with increasing exasperation. Human judgement must stop at −3; only God can go to −4.

Anyway – here it is. And if half my readers think I'm a stubborn sceptic, and the other half consider me a credulous dupe, I'll feel I've done a pretty good job.

| | | |
|---|---|---|
| 1. | Maledictions | +4 |
| 2. | Poltergeists | +2 |
| 3. | Precognition | +1 |
| 4. | PK | 0 |
| 5. | Apparitions | +4 |
| 6. | Telepathy | +2 |
| 7. | Stigmata | +4 |
| 8. | Firewalking | +5 |
| 9. | Dowsing | +2 |
| 10. | Survival after death | −2 |
| 11. | Reincarnation | −2 |

Over to you, gentle reader – and viewer . . .

# Acknowledgements

The pervasive evidence of Strange Powers at work in our own day and age is to be found in many countries and in the most varied cultures and traditions.

But tracking down the sober – even clinical – details has only been achieved with the help of many people, whether it be Gerry Witcher of United Press International, finding the death certificate of a hex victim in the registry in Oklahoma City or John Rourke of Kirstenbosch Botanical Garden in Cape Town, combing the natural history surveys of Cape Province, South Africa, for the life cycle of the blue orchid of Table Mountain.

Betty Smith with her Lockheed Dialog computer terminal at the British Library in Boston Spa, Yorkshire, gave us early access to key material which languishes in scientific papers in more than fifty libraries.

Alan Wesencraft, sympathetic but by no means credulous guardian of the Harry Price Library at London University, gave us a superb insight into that wonderful treasure house of evidence which is Harry Price's finest memorial.

The full story of the long-distance telepathy experiment carried out by Harold Sherman and Sir Hubert Wilkins is told in their book *Thoughts Through Space*. A new edition has recently been published by Amherst Press, Amherst, Wisconsin 54406.

The American and British Societies for Psychical Research have kept the most meticulous records – the British Society was 100 years old in 1982 – and these are an important source for any researcher. No study of Strange Powers would be possible without reference to the *Journal* of the Society for Psychical Research which, from the Society's rooms at 1 Adam and Eve Mews, London W8, vigorously maintains its tradition of publishing case histories and the results of research into all aspects of the paranormal. Miss O'Keefe was especially helpful in locating and supplying illustrations.

Though the contemporary evidence which provides the main thrust of this book requires exhaustive first-hand research, the historical background has been discussed in many books, and we are particularly grateful to Sheila Fitzhugh and Rosemary Smith of the Yorkshire Television Library and the librarians at Aberdeen University and the London Library for obtaining the rarer volumes for us.

Fiona Greig of Yorkshire Television, a diligent and perceptive researcher, tracked down many of the individuals, still alive, whose weird and disparate experiences are recounted in this book.

Adam Hart-Davis, the producer of the television series, has been an indefatigable and generous contributor and an unfailingly alert critic. Melvin Harris, always constructively sceptical, drew our attention to some of the intriguing stories and to the doubts surrounding some of the classic cases of premonitions and extra-sensory perception. Jane Taylor's researches provided valuable insights into stigmata and claims of reincarnation. Our manuscript was deciphered and typed by Elaine Hardcastle and Pat MacArthur. Hilary Powell is the owner of the eye used in the photomontage on the front cover.

The director of the television series was Charles Flynn and the cameramen wee Mostafa Hammuri, Charles B. Wilson and Mike Shrimpton.

# Photo Credits

13 Rex Features
14, 16, 30, 33, 43, 45, 84, 91, 102, 108, 119, 120, 130, 145, 181, 185, 187, 188, 191 John Beckett
15 Explorer/Regnault
17 Mrs J. Paden
18 Axel Poignant
21, 37, 213 Syndication International
22, 34, 171, 184, 194, 202, 205 Harry Price Library
25 Dr Hans Kramartz
29 Neue Revue/John Beckett
35 Sheffield Newspapers/John Beckett
36 Associated Newspapers
39 Methodist Church Archives/National Portrait Gallery
40 Mary Evans Picture Library/The Star/Harry Price Library
48 Spectrum Colour Library/John Topham Picture Library/National Army Museum/Victoria and Albert Museum
53 Syndication International/John Beckett
54 Keystone Press Agency/John Beckett
55 Dr Lucille Wood-Trost/Colorific/Time/Dale Howard
57 By courtesy of James Bryant/John Beckett
59 Press Association/John Beckett
62, 67, 83 BBC Hulton Picture Library
65 John Beckett/Colorific/Don Snyder
66 John Hillelson Agency/Sygma/John Beckett
69 Central Press/Mary Evans Picture Library
70–1 Mary Evans Picture Library/BBC Hulton Picture Library/Popperphoto
73 Fortean Picture Library/Mary Evans Picture Library
74, 138 Foundation for Research on the Nature of Man
78–9 Colorific/Ted Serios/Jule Eisenbud/Waistel Cooper
85 Colorific/John Beckett
90 M. H. Collins
92 Guy Lyon Playfair/John Beckett
93, 133 (drawings) John Cutten
95 SORRAT/John Beckett
99, 122, 168, 175, 177, 183 Mary Evans Picture Library
100 Deborah Koss Warner/Joseph Koss
105, 123 Fortean Picture Library
110 John Beckett/Georgina Feakes
111 Professor W. Jackson
115 Juliette Soester/Mary Evans Picture Library/Harry Price Library
116 Martha Hertzman
118 Jarrolds/John Beckett
121, 179, 193 John Topham Picture Library
125 United Press International/John Beckett/Royal Geographical Society
127 Joyce Acker Hurth/John Beckett
134 Society for Psychical Research
137 United Press International/Psychic News
139 Soal and Bateman, *Modern Experiments in Telepathy*
141 Harry Price Library/Soal and Bateman *ibid.*
142 Dick Jones
147 Rev Anthony Burrus
148 Neue Pinakothek, Munich/Jurgen Hinrichs
150–1 Casa Abresch/Sonia Halliday/Jane Taylor
154 Harry Price Library/BBC Hulton Picture Library
157 Mrs Moody
159 Pix Features/Stern/Archivo Iconografica, SA
162 Transworld Features Syndicate
164–5 Vision International/Brun/Explorer
166 G. F. Wheeler
167 Dr W. Larbig
180 Colonel H. Grattan
197 M. T. Geddes
199 Mary Evans Picture Library/Psychic News/John Beckett
203 Mansell Collection
204 Professor E. Dawes/Harry Price Library/Psychic News
206 Mary Evans Picture Library/Harry Price Library
209 Mary Evans Picture Library/Mrs V. Laughland
210 Mary Evans Picture Library/Psychic News
212 Musam
215 Psychic News/Mary Evans Picture Library
218 John Beckett/The Psychic Observer
220–1 Photographers International/ Scottish Portrait Gallery/Mansell Collection
222 TV-am
225 Syndication International/Associated Press
228 Dr Kampman/British Library
231 Millie Markham
235 Syndication International/John Topham Picture Library
236 Elizabeth Long

# Index